# Learning from Burnout

*Developing sustainable leaders and*
*avoiding career derailment*

# Learning from Burnout

*Developing sustainable leaders and avoiding career derailment*

Tim Casserley and David Megginson

Amsterdam • Boston • Heidelberg • London • New York • Oxford
Paris • San Diego • San Francisco • Singapore • Sydney • Tokyo
Butterworth-Heinemann is an imprint of Elsevier

Butterworth-Heinemann is an imprint of Elsevier
Linacre House, Jordan Hill, Oxford OX2 8DP, UK
30 Corporate Drive, Suite 400, Burlington, MA 01803, USA

First edition 2009

**British Library Cataloguing in Publication Data**
A catalogue record for this book is available from the British Library

**Library of Congress Cataloging-in-Publication Data**
A catalog record for this book is available from the Library of Congress

ISBN 978-0-7506-8387-6

For information on all Butterworth-Heinemann publications
visit our website at www.elsevierdirect.com

Printed and bound in Great Britain

09 10 11 12 13    10 9 8 7 6 5 4 3 2 1

To Our Mothers

*Peggy Casserley, 'the effect of her being on those around her was incalculably effusive: for the growing good of the world is partly dependent on unhistoric acts'.*

*Jean Megginson, who went on giving, until there was nothing left to give.*

# Contents

# Acknowledgements

Of all the people involved in this book, it has been the 100 high flyers we interviewed that have been the most influential and important in the writing of it. Your willingness to share your hard fought understanding of your lives made this book possible. Your generosity in talking about the inner struggle on the path to leadership was an inspiration for us. We hope you find the meaning that you are searching for. In order to preserve your anonymity we have changed your name, together with organizational and other details that might reveal your identity.

We are indebted to those who opened doors into their organizations and allowed us to interview their high flyers. In particular we'd like to thank Alex Fergus whose support at a difficult time in the research brought the project back on track.

This book would never have appeared without the talented contribution and persistence of our research team. Pauline Whiting and Mary Malecaut travelled the length and breadth of 'greater Europe' conducting interviews during the initial stages of the research, and spent many long days and nights trying to make sense of the vast amount of data we collected. Pauline's cool advice helped to steer the project away from the rocks during the early days. Robert Wylie's tireless and steadfast work on the majority of the research interviews, and his invaluable insights into some really complex issues of interpretation made the research sing.

Richard Mansfield's unswerving encouragement for the project has been a central feature throughout the research. He has been the power behind the quantitative aspects of the study, designing surveys built from our own research – including the Work Stress Survey – running analyses and helping to interpret the data we accumulated. His patience and generosity, and gentle questioning of some of the more arcane aspects of the qualitative study have been invaluable.

Dr John Briffa wrote the appendix on the physiological consequences of burnout and helped us to understand burnout from the body's perspective. We also want to thank those colleagues who have helped us to develop our ideas on leadership learning, coaching and psychology: fellow Edge Equilibrium Board members: John Leary Joyce, who helped us develop the three-phased impact of burnout on the organization in Chapter 3; Ellen Dunne, who wouldn't let us forget it had to be written; Gill Thewlis, whose idea it was to make the financial impact of burnout calculable; David Lane, who helped to start the thing; Bill Critchley, who broke the shell of our understanding; Victoria Cassells, who challenged our thinking; and Jerry Hyde, personal guru extraordinaire, whose unflagging support and wondrous knowledge of the works of Hunter S Thompson gave this book its distinctive edge. Prahbu Guptara hosted us at UBS Wolfsberg and, unbeknown to him, helped us to write the final chapter. Our many, often passionate, conversations with each of you have enhanced the value of the ideas in this book. Our much missed colleague David Casey has hugely informed our thinking and the way we approach coaching and leadership learning. Our thanks also go to Robert Bell, who helped to smooth out the vagaries of a somewhat frantic writing style at various stages in the book.

We'd also like to thank Frits and Inge Janum and Greg and Rachel Sinfield for their practical support and bountiful spirit which literally made it possible for us to finish the writing of this book.

Although this book is dedicated to our mothers, it is the other women in our lives who have provided the love, tolerance and compassion, and who have helped us overcome the many ordeals involved in the creative struggle – Charlotte Janum Casserley and Vivien Whitaker.

# Introduction

This book has a colourful history. Its early life was distinguished by a struggle to form its own distinct identity. For a while it seemed that the authors would not be the progenitors of their own book. Other people had strong opinions about the book's purpose. They wanted to bestow upon it their own meaning. They had a version of the book's identity which they held in their heads and wanted to see in the world. There was a struggle over authorship. Was it to be the authors', or was it to be those who wished to control what the authors wrote?

In a sense, this book's 'story' is similar to that it tells of young high flyers that burn out in their jobs. Like them, this book has struggled to live its own life rather than the one others wanted for it. It is also similar in as much as the writing of it was a self-defining act: it was written not because the authors harboured illusions of fame or recognition, but because its message was personally meaningful for them.

Having made a parallel between our book's journey and that of the talented burnouts we describe, it is important to say that we have been helped and challenged by a talented team at Elsevier and in particular by Ailsa Marks, who has been with us every step of the journey. We are also grateful to the reviewers, whose sometimes trenchant comments have helped us to forge our ideas more clearly.

We were inspired to write this book both for reasons of personal biography as well as professional practice. The biographical reasons concern one of us burning out in their early thirties while working as a high-flying human resources executive for an IT company. Nowadays we both consult to organizations on managing and developing their leadership talent, so the reasons of professional practice concern our work in this area, particularly among high flyers with symptoms of burnout. We noticed an increasing trend among this population towards action addicted, adrenalized working lives and what appeared to be – based on the number who were burning out – unsustainable approaches to the pursuit of career. At the same time we recognized that organizations were becoming increasingly more demanding and absorptive, and as a consequence, work and workplaces increasingly more all-consuming. Like the high-speed internet connections that serve our offices and our homes, work seemed to be always on. It had become a seven-day-a-week preoccupation which was always there, brought into every facet of human life through the wonders of the Blackberry and the mobile phone. Work, it seemed, never slept, and those enslaved to it were sleeping a great deal less than they used to.

Burnout was the inevitable consequence of this heady combination of addictive behaviour and organizational greediness, or so it seemed to us. But when we referred to the literature on burnout we discovered that the leading authorities in the field believed burnout was largely caused by organizations, rather than both the organization and those who work for them. We thought this rather odd. It did not resonate with our own experience of burnout, or with what we were seeing among high flyers with whom we were working. Nor, apparently, did it resonate with leading authorities in the field of occupational stress research. For example, Cary Cooper and his colleagues noted the absence of the individual dimension in most explanations of burnout, commenting that 'Despite the obvious relevance of personality issues, relatively little attention has been given to these variables in empirical research, and evidence for their association with burnout is inconclusive'.[1]

In addition nearly all the literature talked in fervent, almost biblical terms of banishing or preventing or otherwise casting out burnout. Burnout, it seemed, was the seed of the devil and it needed to be exorcized, preferably using as many colourful exhortations as possible. This equally did not resonate with our experience. Almost no one mentioned anything about the possibility of good coming out of bad. Our personal experience of burnout was transformational. Why did no one refer to the learning that might emerge as a result of burnout? The nearest we could find was literature on the connection between trauma and personal change. But most of this concerned the psychological trauma that ensued from serious physical events such as wars and road-traffic accidents.

It was this sense of something not being quite right about what we were being told, that sent us off on our research journey into burnout. In the intervening five years we have recorded, transcribed and analysed in-depth interviews with 100 high flyers, made up of 29 different nationalities, working in 21 different countries. We have conducted survey research with this group as well as a much larger group using our own and others' survey instruments. We have subsequently re-interviewed half of the high flyers a year after they were first interviewed, to track the incidence of burnout among them. We have led numerous focus groups and workshops with business leaders, human resource executives and coaches to explore perceptions of burnout, its causes and ways of dealing with it. We have explored our findings with the organizations that participated in our research, to both reality test our claims, and to progress our sense-making of the causes and consequences of burnout.

At this point the attentive reader will no doubt be wondering about the connection between high flyers and burnout. What makes them so special? Surely anyone can burn out? And indeed, in the popular currency of our time, anyone can. To many people burnout is little more than a colloquial term with little explicit meaning beyond having had a bad day at the office. Popular psychology and self-help books have reinforced this indiscriminate use of the term by claiming that burnout can occur to anyone, in any context, at any stage of life. As a result, burnout has become a universal, context-free phenomenon – it is not necessarily related to work but can happen anywhere. Apparently you are equally vulnerable to burnout whether you're an over-stressed baby boomer, in a bad marriage, having a mid-life crisis or a female indoor sex worker.[2] Seen through this lens, burnout is 'no longer an unusual event' but has become 'part of a normal life cycle'.[3]

And yet the overwhelming weight of 25 years of serious, scholarly research on the subject says that burnout is a work-related phenomenon that occurs largely to those at the early stages of their careers. These are people who are more likely to be in their twenties than thirties or forties, who are restlessly ambitious, career-orientated and achievement-focused. In most organizations such individuals, if they are not formally identified as high flyers, will be perceived as such.

Despite such strong evidence to the contrary, the evocative power of the term burnout leads many people to insist they are suffering from it. Often they do so in the absence of many of the symptoms of the phenomenon. Sometimes they claim burnout even when manifesting a different, often more immediately threatening condition. A parallel metaphor is with obesity and bulimia. Bulimics think that they have a weight or obesity problem, but at some level we 'know' they don't – they have a 'bulimia' condition. A 40-year-old may have stress, exhaustion, overload, chronic fatigue syndrome, depression, existential crisis, a psychotic episode or mid-life blues, but they are highly unlikely to have burnout.

This book presents the results of our five-year research journey. Our findings point to burnout being a function of the relationship between the individual high flyer and their work environment. Certainly, organizations – or rather their leadership teams – create the conditions for burnout to occur. The constant scramble after growth and shareholder return, an obsession with market share and performance metrics and the resultant year-on-year raising of the performance threshold for employees inevitably leads to a culture of burnout. Boardroom decisions to increase profit margin or market share more often than not lead to more work being done by less people. But it is the individual high flyer who, through his or her own choices, determines whether they burn out or not. It is not the work situation – however dysfunctional – that is the primary cause of burnout, but the way in which people interpret and choose to handle that situation.

Both organization leadership and high flyers are implicated in causing the phenomenon, but ultimately it is the individual that is the primary driver. We've interviewed high flyers in the same office, working for the same boss, experiencing the same highly stressful work environments, and quite simply some burn out and others don't. Denying there is individual volition involved in burnout confounds attempts to tackle it at an individual level, and is, we suggest, patronising for those involved. It paints a picture of 'willing slaves';[4] semi-sentient creatures who obediently follow an autocratic work structure, in an environment where there is no room for individual choice.

Our research indicates that more often than not, those who burn out collude with dysfunctional working environments. They choose to make work and career central to their lives. They are driven by a desire for fame and recognition, and this, together with a lack of consciousness about their lives having some theme or pattern – a story, if you will – leads them into burnout. High flyers' addiction to action and adrenalized work styles often hide an identity that is strongly externally referenced – on work and career success – rather than anything from within. There is also an element of paranoia. A belief that pushing back, asking for more time or resources or confronting unreasonable demands will adversely affect career prospects.

Some of the leading researchers in the field maintain that 'popular opinion' and 'conventional wisdom' lay the cause of burnout on the individual.[5] This has not been our experience during the five years we have been researching the subject. We agree that it is incredibly unproductive both for individuals and organizations to view burnout purely as 'a problem of the people themselves'.[6] And although our research didn't discover such a pervasive belief within the cultural context within which we conducted research, we can understand the need to push the spotlight back onto the organization given a different context. However, we believe the pendulum has now swung too far the other way. The paradigm one encounters within most European businesses nowadays is that burnout is a flaw of the organization and can only be addressed through some kind of organization change initiative focusing on delivering better work/life balance. Faced with the prospect of a big change project, amidst environments which are characterized by initiative overload, all but the most enlightened leadership teams have stopped in their tracks. In addition, it is difficult to find the business case for making the organization change required when there are so many competing change initiatives. In our experience, as soon as doing something about burnout equals changing the organization, leadership teams swiftly move onto the next agenda item. Though unmistakably well-intentioned, such an approach has effectively frozen attempts to address the burnout issue in large organizations.

What about the other reason for us writing this book – the absence of almost any references to the learning or change that might emerge from burnout? Here our research uncovered a paradox. We found that the greater the degree of suffering of those who burn out, the greater the potential learning. However, learning occurred for only a few. For most, burnout froze the development of identity and the evolutionary course of the individual concerned. For the lucky few, burnout revealed its transformational learning potential. It accelerated maturity and led to systemic growth. By virtue of being a kind of personal trauma, burnout caused high flyers to confront their own fallibilities and limitations, helped them gain a sense of perspective, humility and humanity, and be clearer about their own identity. This growth was hard won, however, and at considerable cost to the individual concerned. High flyers who came by this depth of learning suffered the modern equivalent of a 'dark night of the soul'. They were required to give up the story they had constructed about themselves – their old identity – in order to form anew. For some, giving this up was like giving up their own life.

The transformational nature of the learning also significantly benefited high flyers' organizations. Among other things, it led to the development of wisdom, a greater sense of perspective, more grounded business decision making and a sense of duty and service to others.

The reality for most of those who encountered it, however, was that burnout was a wholly destructive experience that led to the derailment of their careers. But because burnout is as much volitional as the product of the working environment, one cannot just stop it. One cannot exhort high flyers to stop burning out and expect them to do what they're told. Only the individual at risk of burnout can take responsibility for stopping it. It is in their hands. And the simple fact of the matter is that a large proportion of them won't stop it because they don't think there is anything to stop. Which leaves us with a dilemma. If we know that a large proportion of the high-flyer population is likely to burn out and we can't control it, what do we do about it? The proposition we explore in this book is how high flyers and their organizations can manage burnout so that it becomes transformationally developmental rather than destructive. We look at how the lessons of burnout can be assimilated so that the numbers of those who are transformed by the experience increase substantially.

But although this book is about burnout and the learning that may emerge from it, it is principally concerned with the significance of this learning for the development of high flyers and leaders generally. This learning emerges out of failure rather than success. It emerges from struggling with ordeal and resisting despair rather than strong and masterful accomplishment. It emerges from stumbling and going to the edge rather than being in control and walking tall. Many organizations have models of leadership that tend to lionize success and denigrate stumbling. Their picture of how leaders are developed is sanitized. Any notion of learning from adversity has been excised. The money is put on those whose careers have enjoyed an ever-upward trajectory, who have never stumbled (to anyone's knowledge) and who have always complied with the organization's tight, atavistic definitions of what good leadership should be. Those who do not comply, including the stumblers, are quietly removed from succession plans. The outcome is that such organizations end up with leaders who are hopelessly ill-prepared; who not only lack humanity but do not see themselves as entirely human, who act as if they were intergalactic time lords who transcend the earthly realm of us mere mortals.

Accepting the lessons of burnout requires an altogether more enlightened, more civilized and more developmental approach to leadership learning and what purports to be good leadership. Who – for example – is likely to be more emotionally robust and mature, more capable and more in tune with his or her fellow workers – the clean-shaven MBAer who has risen meteorically through the ranks without any trace of a stumble and no experience of real hardship, or the battle-scarred, succession plan outsider who has had their ups and downs and has learnt from them? Who would you trust to lead your organization? We have no hesitation in choosing the latter. We'd go so far as to say that we would actively de-select from top management succession those who have no real experience of hardship either in their professional or personal lives.

Whatever one's view of leadership, it is plain that good leadership and good leaders are not in abundance. This is in spite of the fact that year on year millions are spent on developing leaders. Perhaps it comes down to how one defines good leadership and good leaders. And there is the problem. Because different stakeholders appear to have different views of what makes good leadership at different times. The markets applauded the strong leadership of Kenneth Lay and Jeffrey Skilling before Enron's collapse in 2001. British voters thought Tony Blair's leadership principled and strong before he plunged the country into war in the Middle East for highly questionable foreign policy objectives. Shareholders praised Lee Iacocca's charismatic turnaround of Chrysler before his obsession with furthering his personal brand led to Chrysler's stock falling 31% below the market.[7]

Since this book concerns the development of sustainable leadership – how high flyers can develop a sustainable version of themselves – we need to be clear about what we mean when we talk about leadership. We believe the practice of good leadership is timeless. It is not something that needs to be handed down to us by some faddish guru, nor by business schools – who, despite their protestations to the contrary, did not invent leadership in the last 20 years. There have always been leaders and there has always been leadership. Some of it has been good.

Leadership is essentially what leaders practise – what they do rather than what they are, their praxis rather than their characteristics. Unfortunately we have become so obsessed with discerning the qualities that make leaders good or great, that we have forgotten to look at their practice. How is good leadership practised? What do good leaders do? These seem to us to be more important questions – particularly if you are on the receiving end of the leadership in question – than whether leaders are strong, charismatic, principled, visionary, results-orientated or any of the other endless attributes which are purported to be prerequisites of good leadership.

'A bequest of stories',[8] some contained in the rich literature of our civilization from the beginning of recorded time, some simply tales which have been repeated over the ages, point to some universal and timeless practices of good leaders. We see these to be:

- forms and sustains the enterprise they are leading so that it endures over time
- brings value (more often than not, insight or learning) not just to their followers but to the wider community of which they are a part
- holds and protects their followers, providing them with inspiration to continue on the journey
- creates a climate of balance in which the collective contribution of all is sought and creativity, learning and trade can flourish

- embodies mature, vital humanity and compassion that sustains their followers through the most challenging times
- is a great source of wisdom, sound judgement and balanced decision making.

As we will see, burnout's lessons touch every one of these practices.

The purpose of this book, then, is not so much to question prevailing paradigms of burnout – although it does – but to question prevailing paradigms of leadership development and in so doing put forward a new paradigm of leadership learning.

## The nature of our research

Passion makes some academics and academic publishers nervous. Passion together with experience of the research area can lead to alarm. It doesn't quite gel with the positivist fantasy of the rational scientist, objectively examining 'reality' in order to define absolute truths. Researchers with first-hand experience of their subject area are perceived by some as labouring under a considerable disadvantage. Their minds are assumed to be clouded with emotion. Yet in the workaday world this experience determines a person's capability to bring value. The first thing we want to know before hiring someone to help us is what experience they have of that with which we need help. They may have read about the issue, they may even have studied it for several years, but we know that without this 'experiential knowing'[9] they will struggle to understand our problem. As a result any ideas they might have regarding what to do about our issue will lack resonance.

We believe that social researchers have to experience what they are researching for their research to be valid and reliable. The majority of authors on burnout appear not to have this experience.

This book is based on scientific research and theory. The data are high flyers' lived experiences of performing demanding roles in high-pressure work environments over prolonged periods of time. Our study's use of talk as data will no doubt disturb academic researchers of a positivist persuasion. We mention this because the overwhelming majority of burnout research is of a quantitative nature. Most of it is based on people's self-reports of their burnout using the Maslach Burnout Inventory (MBI) survey tool. As a result the most widely used conceptualization of burnout is the model represented by the MBI. As Schaufeli and Enzman say, 'The MBI is the instrument of choice to measure burnout. No wonder that the definition of burnout has become equivalent to the way it is measured by the MBI!'.[10]

Many social science scholars hold the belief that only quantitative research – that which is based on numerical and statistical analysis of 'objective data' – is valid research. They distrust qualitative methodological perspectives. Wilmar Schaufelli and Dirk Enzmann, for instance, whose wonderfully robust and incisive work on burnout is referenced throughout this book, write that only 'rigorously designed and thoroughly conducted *quantitative* studies'[11] should be considered serious contributions to burnout research. Fortunately this is not a view held by every researcher in the field. Cary Cooper and his colleagues, for instance, note that 'Qualitative methods reflect a richness in their approach to data gathering and analysis and should be viewed as offering a number of insights into interpretation and understanding separate from those provided by quantitative methods. If a distinction is made between description (quantitative) and meaning (qualitative), then the convergence of both approaches offers a balance and draws on the strengths of both approaches to unravel the complexities of the stress process.'[12]

While for the lay reader this may all seem academically precious, the distinction between quantitative and qualitative research methodologies is an important one. In the case of this study, which sought to explore the learning that emerged from burnout, and focused on understanding people's internal response to the experience, a largely qualitative approach was more likely to generate valid and reliable data. This becomes more obvious when one realises that the research addressed, in large part, the level of reflexivity of the high flyers concerned.

## The structure of this book

The conception of job burnout as total, individual psychological and emotional devastation is very much in common currency, aided and abetted by many scholarly writers on the subject, from Freudenberger (1980) onwards. Thus there is a widespread belief that, by and large, people either burn out or they don't. Congruent with its largely qualitative and lightly held social constructionist nature, our research holds otherwise. We see total devastation (or *crashing and burning*) as one of several possible outcomes for those experiencing burnout, or exhibiting some of the symptoms of the condition. The others are a *chronic self-destructive pattern* which is repeated over the course of a person's career indefinitely or until they find a way of breaking it; and – for those demonstrating some but not all of the symptoms of burnout – a *joyless depletion* in which careers are lived unsustainably through addictive work styles and a failure to find sufficient nourishment and balance.

Chapter 1 presents each of these 'types' of burnout, starting with a story of crashing and burning, followed by a story of chronic self-destruction from one of our lives, and concluding with joyless depletion. We decided to let these stories stand without commentary in Chapter 1. Somehow the thought of putting a gloss on people's authentic experiences rather than letting them speak for themselves seemed dishonourable. In any case, we refer back to each of these experiences in Chapter 2 to illustrate the external, environmental and intra-psychic causes of burnout as well as its consequences.

In Chapter 2 we provide our research findings on the nature and symptomatology of burnout, touching briefly on causes and consequences. This chapter is useful for the reader who wants to understand our conceptualization of burnout, how it is manifest and the current state of play in burnout research. In Chapter 3 we explore the financial, reputational and risk management consequences of burnout for organizations. Readers who want to find a way of quantifying the organizational repercussions of burnout on their high-flyer populations will find guidance here.

Chapter 4 explores burnout from the perspective of the individual: how do individuals bring about burnout, or contribute to it, and what determines whether or not they do burn out? It lays out our main research findings in each of these areas. This chapter will be particularly useful to anyone who believes they may be going through burnout themselves.

In Chapter 5 we look at the lessons burnout teaches, and the learning process of those who both learn and don't learn. We also explore the key determinants of burnout further. Those who manage high flyers, their coaches and leadership development specialists will find this chapter useful in helping them understand the learning that emerges from the experience.

Chapter 6 sets out the business case and approach for organizations to embrace burnout as a learning process. It also details the coaching model that enables learning from burnout. This chapter provides those supporting high flyers in burnout – be they bosses, coaches or HR professionals – with practical tools to capture the learning from the experience.

In the book's final chapter we pull together those findings from our research which mark a substantial departure from prior research, outline the significance of them for high flyers, organizations and those who work for them, and set out a new paradigm of leadership learning. Those who want a sense of the main research thrust of the book and its conclusions will find them here.

We have written this book for those experiencing or at risk of burnout, those supporting them – such as bosses, coaches and mentors, human resources professionals and family members – and those for whom burn-out among high flyers represents a strategic issue, namely CEOs and Boards of Directors. We have tried to make it readable, accessible and interesting while at the same time imparting what are, admittedly, some fairly technically complex findings. We hope we have succeeded.

Finally, we need to say something about the tone of this book. It is explicitly developmental rather than deterministic. Our experience of leadership is that it is not something that is bestowed upon us by genetic coincidence, nor is it a divine right handed to us by God. Leadership is learned through experience. Leaders are principally made and not born.

## End notes

1 Cooper, C.L., Dewe, P.J. and O'Driscoll, M.P. (2001). *Organizational Stress: A Review and Critique of Theory, Research, and Applications*. London: Sage

2 Vanwesenbeeck, I. (2005). 'Burnout among female indoor sex workers (psychology of prostitutes).' *Archives of Sexual Behaviour*, vol. 34, no. 6, pp627–39

3 Glouberman, D. (2002). *The Joy of Burnout: How the End of the World can be a New Beginning*. London: Hodder and Stoughton

4 Bunting, M. (2005). *Willing Slaves: How the Overwork Culture is Ruling our Lives*. London: Harper Perennial

5 Maslach, C. and Leiter, M.P. (1997). *The Truth about Burnout: How Organizations Cause Personal Stress and What to do About It*. San Francisco: Jossey-Bass

6 Maslach, C. and Leiter, M.P. (1997). *The Truth about Burnout: How Organizations Cause Personal Stress and What to do About It*. San Francisco: Jossey-Bass

7 Macalister, T. (2007). 'Fallen titans show charisma is the most volatile stock of all.' *The Guardian*, 9 October

8 Lessing, D. (2007). 'A hunger for books'. Nobel Prize for Literature acceptance speech. Reprinted in *The Guardian*, 8 December

9 Heron, J. (1989). *The Facilitator's Handbook*. London: Kogan Page

10 Schaufeli, W. and Enzmann, D. (1998). *The Burnout Companion to Study and Practice*. London: Taylor and Francis

11 Schaufeli, W. and Enzman, D. (1998). *The Burnout Companion to Study and Practice*. London: Taylor and Francis

12 Cooper, C.L., Dewe, P.J. and O'Driscoll, M.P. (2001). *Organizational Stress: A Review and Critique of Theory, Research, and Applications*. London: Sage

# 1

## Sitting at the ashes of the fire

*It's like being lonely…like you know…sitting at the fire…sitting at the ashes.*

RESEARCH PARTICIPANT

*If you want to know me, then you must know my story, for my story defines who I am. And if I want to know myself, to gain insight into the meaning of my own life, then I, too, must come to know my own story.*

DAN MCADAMS

### Holger – a story of crashing and burning

*Holger's story is an example of a 'crash and burn' experience because he comes to a point after one series of events following close on to each other where he ends up derailing his career and spending a long time being not employed.*

Last autumn, I made the decision to go for manager. I started to make a plan to delegate more, but it wasn't easy because everybody in our group had too much to do. I didn't want to end up doing all the work myself, but I was too nice and I ended up doing most of the work myself. Maybe I should have been stronger but it didn't make me feel good thinking of one of my colleagues working from eight in the morning to three o'clock at night to finish something, when I could do it in two or three hours.

I normally go for a medical check up every two years. My last check up was the beginning of December last year. The doctor asked me some questions about my working hours and I said, 'Yes, I work a lot, I know I do'. Suddenly he said 'Stop! You need to take it easy because what you're telling me now is crazy!'. I had told him that in two weeks I was working about 250 hours. He said, 'Even if you go on holiday, forget it, because the holiday won't be long enough. You need to stress down. This is not good'.

It's easy when you have no girlfriend living here. It's easy to say 'Hey I can work until 8' and when it's 8 o'clock 'Oh I can work until 12 because nothing's happening tonight – I'm not going training, not until tomorrow', and then suddenly you'll be sitting in the office until two o'clock at night and then you're back again at seven the next morning.

After seeing the doctor I took a long Christmas holiday and went to see my family. I started to think maybe the Doc was crazy! I'm a healthy 33-year-old, so what's the problem? But then I talked to a good friend, who said maybe he was right. He's a very clever guy, this friend of mine, I always go to him when I have problems. I think this was the first time I ever thought I might be working too much.

I didn't learn anything because I got back to work in January and started working a lot again. The first two weeks I said 'No, I don't want to work too much', but after that I forgot what I was thinking about at Christmas. I was working on a client's financial statements, nothing new, but I was working a hundred hours a week, maybe more. Some weekends too. Sometimes I would take work home with me and watch a little bit of sport on TV and work at the same time.

Everything was fine and then after two or three months I started to get a lot of headaches. At first I thought it was because I was only sleeping a couple of hours every night. I thought it would be OK if I could get enough sleep at the weekend. But these headaches got stronger and stronger and stronger and by the end of March it was impossible to work.

One day just before Easter I was playing bridge with a friend of mine and I found I couldn't remember the cards anymore. It was such a shock not remembering something so basic.

I went to see the doctor again, and he told me that I needed to take a rest. I took a long Easter holiday for two weeks. I wasn't sleeping a lot and I was very tired all the time so he gave me some tablets.

After that I wanted to get back to work because I knew my colleague had a lot of things to do and the office was very busy. I asked my doctor and he told me I could go back to work but I must not work overtime. The quality of the work I was turning out was really bad because I kept forgetting things from the headaches. It was crazy for me to go back to work after being sick like that. I feel my boss should have told me to go home but instead he gave me more and more and more work. He knew I was doing really poor work because he was reviewing it and the client was calling him to complain.

When I got back to the office from my Easter vacation I met with my boss and told him about what the doctor had said about no overtime and that I could only work eight hours a day. I started work at eight and needed to go home at four. At three-thirty my boss sends me an email giving me a new piece of work and tells me the deadline is tomorrow morning. It was about three or four hours' work. I was angry but I thought, OK I'll do it. It was very, very important for the client because they were going to raise their stock portfolio, and it was a lot of money for them. I guess I didn't do it for my boss but for the client. But I should never have done it.

I don't think my boss cared, it's that simple, he just didn't care. There's always someone else who can do your work. If you quit, there isn't a problem, they'll just find a new one. Somebody should have told me to go home, because the work I was doing was so bad. They knew about my situation and they should have seen that.

I don't remember much of the weeks after that. I was doing stuff but I was doing it badly. Clients would call to say I had to fix something, so I'd fix it. Then they called back and told me I had forgotten a whole load of stuff. I was physically at work but I wasn't really there at all. Then one day I thought, no, this is no good! Even for me it's no good! It's no good for my boss because it's a client and I'm not doing my work properly. So I got up from my desk and said 'Sorry, you have to do this. I have to go. I can't be here anymore'. I called my doctor. He said to me, 'OK if you feel like this, quit today, stop working right now' and I did stop. I stopped working two or three days before a lot of deadlines. I had to apologise to colleagues, 'Sorry it's too much, I'm not here anyway really....'.

I went for a lot of tests and the doctor told me not to go back to work for six weeks. I started to feel really good again and by the beginning of September I had a lot of new energy. I met up with my boss in the office who asked how I was. I said I hoped to be starting work again after this break. He said, 'Maybe it's better for you and for us, when you're healthy again, that you quit'. At the time I thought it was OK for him to say that, but later I realised it was about them protecting their reputation by making sure I was healthy before I found a new employer. So first they wanted to build me up and then they wanted to break me down.

But I did go back to work, and everything was OK for two or three weeks. I wasn't working much overtime, but during the third week the headaches came back. I started to feel frightened again that I wasn't going to be able to deliver my work. Anyway, the doctor put me on cortisone and I've been off work ever since.

I've tried to analyse what went wrong. Was it the kind of work I was doing or was it that things were wrong in my work? I'm starting to think maybe I burnt out or maybe I was just very, very tired of the work and I needed to change it. I just couldn't go back to working for those guys anymore because they didn't support me when I needed them.

Sometimes I feel as if I'm not here anymore. It's really hard for me to get out of this downward spiral. I really want to find a new job as soon as possible because I'm thinking the longer I stay here, the more difficult it's going to become.

I've learnt that work is not everything, and that I'm never going to work a hundred and twenty hours a week again. I'd rather have less salary and a good life. I think money is not everything and work is not everything. The most important thing is feeling good about yourself. Maybe the thing I've learnt most this last year is that friends mean more than anything else….

## Tim – a story of chronic self-destruction

*Tim's story is a case of chronic self-destruction in that it takes place over a 10 year period and has episodes of extreme symptoms interspersed with times when he was able to cope with, at least, the work aspects of his life.*

If only I had burnt out. I mean really burnt out. Maybe I would have become a goat herder or the owner of a beach bar or, even, a psychotherapist. Maybe I would have found the real, integrated me a lot quicker. Maybe my life would have been a lot happier and freer. Maybe. I'll never know. I crashed but I didn't burn. I crashed without realising it, destined to walk through life for the next 10 years repeating the same self-destructive pattern, time after time. Until finally I did burn. And then things changed forever….

We spill out of the basement restaurant in Mala Strana and weave our way down the precipitous cobbled streets towards the Charles Bridge and our hotel in Wenceslas Square. I savour the feeling of exhilaration as the wintery Eastern European air mixes with the alcohol in my bloodstream and works its magic. I feel like there's never been a more beautiful night than the one I am experiencing right now. Although barely known to me, my companions now seem like old friends who I should gift with my insights about the beauty of this night. I do so and they laugh like drains. I feel like I'm floating over the cobblestones, like I could leap into the night sky and – like Neo from the Matrix – fly up amongst the stars. Maybe my personal life is in ruins, but here, at work, I am someone. I have more than 30 people reporting to me in 15 different countries, I have a multi-million dollar budget and I'm a respected member of the leadership team. I've earned that respect by working 70-hour weeks and delivering on 10 different projects at any one time. And I've done all that with inadequate resources and against a background of constant back-stabbing and dirty politics. I'm a one hundred per cent, genuine corporate hero and they ought to give me a bloody medal!

We enter Town Square. In the corner is a bar playing loud dance music, young people spilling out onto the street. I immediately make towards it, urging my friends to join me. They hesitate then politely demur, using the excuse of needing to be on the ball for tomorrow's conference. I try to persuade them but they refuse. Finally, I shrug, bid my goodnights and make my way into the melee.

I wake the next morning to discover myself fully clothed and booted, lying face down on my hotel bed. I have no recollection of how I got there. I have only very vague and shadowy recollections of the moments immediately after I walked into the bar the previous night. I move my head and realise to my surprise I do not have the usual symptoms of headache and nausea that I associate with a bad hangover. A series of confused and disconnected thoughts pass through my mind. Maybe this has something to do with being on antidepressants? What happened last night anyway? Think I made a pass at some girl. Can't remember. Did she hit me? How did I get here? I look at my watch. I am over an hour late for the conference which I should be facilitating. I undress and walk into the shower feeling like the world is made of cotton wool.

I arrive at the conference room. My colleague, Sue, has started proceedings and now the delegates are working in small teams on separate projects. I apologize to her profusely. She asks me what happened and I explain, as best I can. She fixes me with a steely glare. I apologize again. She says something about looking so unprofessional. I agree. I realize I am still drunk. I also realize I am feeling very attracted to Sue. I make a mental note to act on this at a suitable moment.

We reach the point in the conference when the teams report back their findings. One or two of the senior players have decided to take over the orchestration of proceedings, reducing Sue and my role to that of mere spectators. They choose to ignore both the process and the outcomes we have mapped out for them. I sit writing notes, unable to disguise my utter contempt for the way in which the event has been sabotaged by the incompetence of these over-paid buffoons. I begin to realise how much I hate these people. They're emotional eunuchs that are incapable of self-examination. And they obviously dislike me. More than that, they're ridiculing me by screwing up this process by reducing it to an intellectually moribund debate. I realize I have to leave before I explode. I stand up, walk over to Sue and explain – in less than sotto voce – that I have to go and walk out of the room.

'What have you done?' These words, spoken by my boss, echo the voice inside my head. He appears more despairing than angry. Close to tears, I pour out the events of the last year, grinding to a halt every now and then to control the spasms of emotion running through me. I tell him about the job, being consumed with the work and what that's meant for my personal life. I tell him about my girlfriend leaving me and how the only place I find peace right now is at the bottom of a bottle. I tell him about the antidepressants. I don't tell him about the talking therapy or the promiscuity or the drugs. Kind and fair man that he is, he tells me my reputation may never survive this, that I am going to have to start over, that things will never be the same again. But he doesn't fire me. He wants me to see a psychiatrist.

I see the shrink; am terrified by the experience. The assessment of my mental health becomes the responsibility of another person. I no longer have influence on what is judged to be normal, sane behaviour. I lie in bed that night and every night for the next six months, repeating the Lord's Prayer over and over again, pleading with God to save me, the tears rolling down my cheeks as I realize what I have become. The lowest point comes one quiet Sunday afternoon when I come close to suicide, but after several hours realise I do not have the courage to end my life.

### Twelve months later...

- 'I feel like I'm in uncharted territory at the moment...'
- 'Yes, I think that's a good description of where you are right now...'
- 'Everything is so uncertain for me. I really have no idea, not the slightest, what the future will bring. I'm fumbling my way along in the dark here. I am filled with the sadness of the life I have been living. I haven't had the warm glow of someone who is happy to be himself for so long. I've had more a sense of identity and purpose in my professional life than anywhere else. I've bottled up my true feelings and my needs. I lost a sense of joy in my life; lost a sense of my heart's desires. Until now. 10 years later, I wake up... All this time. Working like a dog to cover up my real needs, masking my feelings, using it as an addiction. I've got to the point where I can spend a whole year, where only 15% of my working life gives me an experience of being alive.'

### Ten years earlier...

Midnight on a damp Sunday night in the middle of spring. I am cocooned in intense silence, interrupted only by the muffled footsteps of passers-by on the pavement outside our North London flat. On the dining room table in front of me reams of notes written in my own hand to prepare me for tomorrow's workshop. The words swim in front of my eyes as I attempt to learn my opening lines for the next day. My head feels as if it has been put in a vice which is steadily being tightened. I have never in my life felt under so much pressure as at this precise moment. I keep telling myself this is an easy thing to do and yet somehow the words don't penetrate. I am left with feelings of panic and loneliness. I feel abandoned. Abandoned by a bullying, mean-spirited boss whose idea of supporting me is making me feel I am not up to the job. Abandoned by my girlfriend, who now, when I most need her, is cold and distant. And in the midst of this turmoil, this sense of being utterly and completely out of my depth in a way I can't even try to explain, I wearily turn off the lights and make my way to bed, dreading another sleepless night and what the next day will bring.

My career had been slow to take off. I had hardly ever been given the space to demonstrate my true capabilities and on the few occasions when I did my efforts were flattened by jealous and unsupportive superiors. But the last two years had been good to me. My boss was very much 'old school'– a socially gifted gentleman whose laid back style allowed his subordinates a considerable amount of autonomy. Under his arm's length but nurturing tutelage I had proven myself a hard working and talented HR professional. I was promoted not once but twice, first to a larger generalist role, then to a divisional specialist role and developed a reputation for innovation in the field. And my personal life also blossomed as I successfully transitioned out of an unhappy marriage into a feisty, fun relationship with lots of potential.

But then my old boss retired and I started to work for a younger, much more driven and ambitious man. I was glad when Brian set the performance bar several metres skyward. I'd always thought the atmosphere in the department was too easy going. I responded to his demands for us to raise our game by working harder than I had ever done before. I had a long commute but made sure I was in the office for 7:30 and worked 10–12-hour days. Of course I didn't have as much time for my friends anymore and it put a bit of a strain on the relationship with my girlfriend but she was very career orientated as well, so she understood.

One of my biggest challenges was rolling out a new set of management processes developed at group level. We were actually the last division to implement them so there was a lot of pressure for us to conform. It involved me designing and running tens of workshops for our managers to introduce them to the new concepts. I had never done this kind of work before so I found it really tough. The managers were sceptical of anything that came down from group headquarters so it was an uphill struggle trying to get them to take it seriously. And to make matters worse, I didn't feel like I had much credibility with them because I was so much younger and inexperienced.

In one of the early workshops one of the managers challenged me about my experience of man management in front of the whole group. When I said I had no direct experience because of the nature of my role, several of them walked out and the whole event descended into chaos. My boss got to hear about it but wasn't very supportive. He said he had never been convinced I was up to the role but had gone along with it because of others' recommendations. This confirmed he was right to have doubts about my competence. I was going to have to prove myself and the only way to do that was to master the workshops. I was upset. I'd expected some kind of support or advice but instead I got a slap in the face. I decided to work even harder. I was going to crack this even if it killed me.

The environment at work got steadily worse. Every time Brian became frustrated with the slow progress we were making in improving standards he flew into a rage. He began to scare the living daylights out of everyone in the team. On one memorable occasion he made the former head of training, a very experienced, middle-aged man, cry in one of our staff meetings. All this created a poisonous atmosphere and led to a lot of very unpleasant rivalry and bitchiness.

I found it increasingly difficult to hold myself together. I thought I was pretty balanced and self-aware but I kept on losing control of my emotions. I found myself crying in the office for no reason at all. That was so unlike me. I had to lock myself in the loo until I had calmed down. I had no idea what set that off.

I hardly seemed to see anything of my girlfriend anymore – she started to go out a lot and our sex life became a distant memory. We argued a lot and she became very distant, even accusing me of having an affair. That was a joke. Where was I supposed to find the energy to do that? I think she started to regret moving in with me. Our social life began to resemble that of a middle-aged couple as we attended one classical music concert after another, enthusiastically organized by my mother.

The thing that really bugged me was the amount of uncertainty I had to put up with at work. In one instance I was introduced to some guy Brian had brought in for a meeting only to discover he was being considered for my job. I felt angry and undermined but I knew I had no alternative but to try harder to prove myself.

While I wasn't going to give up just yet, I was getting very worn down and confused. I lost my diary – at least I couldn't find it anywhere – and was having difficulty remembering commitments. I wasn't sleeping well. It took me a long time to fall asleep and when I did I would wake up in a cold sweat in the middle of the night. There were upsides too. I didn't have to worry about dieting anymore; the weight was dropping off me.

Meanwhile they – the company – kept on reorganizing us. In one year it happened three times. We were making a lot of people redundant as well. People who had been working for the organization for most of their lifetime. And yet despite all of this – and a boss who made Genghis Khan look like a pushover – they expected me to perform my role, in their words, to the best of my abilities. And there would be hell to pay otherwise. I became bitter and angry and disillusioned. My boss was a bullying pig, my clients hopeless ingrates and the organization a fascist regime. They used to think I was a high flyer and how do they treat me? They break me, rip me up, burn me.

I struggled on and in the process of struggling became a very different person – cynical, disengaged, withdrawn, distant, lifeless. It dawned on me that there might be ways in which I was creating problems for myself. I concluded this was due to poor influencing skills and booked myself on a course. I was lucky. I chose the right course. It was designed by a genius,[1] confronting me with self-defeating behaviour and surfacing unspoken needs. At the end of the week, on a hot Friday afternoon, I had a conversation with one of the trainers which changed the future course of my life (or so I thought):

*'I feel like a failure. I feel like a failure and I feel like I'm being punished for being one.' I stop to wipe away a tear. My voice is breaking with emotion but I go on. 'I feel isolated and alone, like nobody cares for me anymore. I don't know what to do. I've worked so hard. I've really tried. But everything has conspired against me. My boss, the organization, the people working with me, my girlfriend. They've all let me down. I feel broken. I don't know who I am anymore. I'm in pieces.'*

*'Do you realize how close to the edge you are right now?' he says. I gasp for breath, it catches in the back of my throat and I start sobbing, 'No, please, please, don't say that…please….'*

*'You need help, more help than I can give you. I have some names I can give you. People who can help you. It's OK, it happens. You've just had a really rough time. You'll be OK, you'll see….'*

## Jarvid – story of joyless depletion

*Jarvid's account is one of joyless depletion in that he continues over an extended period but without the extremes of emotion that characterize Tim's story.*

I got into the marketing assignment some time in September '96 and for the first three or four months spent time understanding the business and trying to formulate what needs to be delivered. It was quite early in my career so I probably wasn't wise enough to understand the resource requirement in terms of time and people to deliver. So I put together a plan and I was responsible for two big vehicle categories, which is motorcycles and cars, and just to give a context, today in the Indian organization the role that I was doing is actually done by about five people, so it was quite stressful. I'm sorry there is a call that I might have to take, sorry. [Takes call] OK, yes, so it also was a fact that at that point in time both cars and motorcycles were poised for big growth as a business for us. The environment was also quite favourable because motorcycle manufacturers and car manufacturers were just about setting up shop in the country, so we needed to be there first, we needed to be active in a number of channels, we needed to be aware of the technology changes so it was actually quite complex and it involved constant work, about 14 to 15 hours a day, and it used to be on an average six days a week, sometimes seven days. This was actually over a sustained period of time [*Author's note*: This was over a three-year period].

People did realize that I was a bit too stressed and I did get some assistance in terms of having some management trainees and people like that coming in. But since there was no continuity in the person it created quite a bit of stress. This was also combined with the fact that we had a number of brand launches, about seven new brands that we launched during a three-year period, which kept putting a lot of stress on me.

There was a 72-hour stretch where I had a total of about four or five hours of sleep. That came about because we had a number of things happening together, so we had a product launch happening, plus there were some communications that we were developing, a programme that we were putting together for the sales team and so on. It sort of all happened at the same time. And that meant that apart from meeting or working with people during normal working hours, I had to find a lot of time to do other work which didn't involve other people, and the only time I had to do that was either very, very early in the morning or very late at night. I just had to work like that at that point of time.

I got married in November '98 and I was working till the day before my marriage, I mean before the wedding ceremony. That was quite tense because I had to finish work and then rush and get married and then in the midst of my honeymoon I had to actually take off a couple of days because there was something quite critical.

It's funny because often during that period, I felt quite energized actually. In the sense that it was quite exciting because lots of things were happening, so it's not something that I look back and say 'Oh shit why did I do that?'. But apart from the physical tiredness I found myself to be quite energized by those challenges. And, I mean to be fair, I also seemed to be doing quite well from a career point of view. So at that point in time it seemed a fair sacrifice to make. I mean a lot of people would sort of remember me as a manager taking a lot of stress who delivered, and that's something I think was quite OK from my point of view at that stage.

A lot of times I felt that I'd bitten off more than I could chew. Sometimes I sort of felt, why did I do it? But by then I was committed and I didn't want to go back and lose face or things like that, so I had to find a way to deliver it.

People said I was quite snappy at times, rude, arrogant, those sort of things. My focus was quite heavily on ensuring that I delivered, so to be honest with you I don't think I cared much at that stage. It would be very, very different now, but at that stage I was actually obsessed with ensuring that the delivery happened. There were opportunities there for the business to grow and also there were the commitments I'd made to myself and the organization. So I wanted to deliver on those.

The experience had positive as well as negative impacts on me. I think the positive impact is that I knew that I could actually take a fair amount of stress and work through it for quite a period of time without suffering some sort of breakdown or mental fatigue. The other positive one, of course, was that friends, especially colleagues at work, saw that I could be trusted to deliver if I committed to something. The negative areas were that I completely missed the chance to learn how to get things done through people, how to prioritize. I think in the process that I might have made a lot of enemies. Sorry there's another call. [Takes call] Yes I missed an opportunity to make a lot of friends at that time. I think that was to do with my obsession with seeing that stuff gets done, irrespective of how people are feeling.

## End note

1 Roger Harrison, one of the most influential organization consultants in the history of management consulting and the creator of the 'Positive Power and Influence' programme.

**2**

# The edge and how to explain it

*The edge...there is no honest way to explain it because the only people who really
know where it is are the ones who have gone over.*

HUNTER S. THOMPSON

## What is job burnout?

The term 'burnout' or 'staff burnout' came to light as a psychological
phenomenon during the 1970s, most notably through the writings of
American psychiatrist Herbert Freudenberger.[1] Freudenberger's 1980
landmark book, *Burnout: The High Cost of Success and How to Cope with
It,* based on his observations of severe psychological strain among human
service workers, posited burnout as a chronic affliction of the over-
achiever. For a long time the phenomenon was dismissed as 'pop psychology', largely because of its origins as a description of people's workplace
experiences rather than as a scholarly notion. Indeed, there are still those
in the fields of psychology and stress research who deny its existence (for
more on this see below).

Over the intervening two-and-a-half decades, 'burnout' has entered
the popular lexicon in just about every world culture to the extent that
it has become a colloquial term to describe a condition of having nothing more to give; a place of total and utter exhaustion. Although an over-
simplification, this is not a million miles away from the research-based
construct. However, the popularity of the term as a 'language of the people'[2]
has meant that it is often used indiscriminately, both by the public and by
authors who are little concerned by the rigour or accuracy of their data,
to the extent that, 'the concept can easily be expanded to mean anything,
so that there is the danger that in the end it does not mean anything at
all'.[3] Indeed, it has become quite fashionable to refer to oneself as 'burnt
out'. The term has been so misused it has become virtually meaningless.

Why should this be a concern, you may ask? Well, for two very good reasons. First and foremost because the confusion about what burnout is and who it affects effectively sabotages attempts to do anything about it. And, secondly, because it has little or no connection with what existing research says about the correlates of burnout – in particular the individual characteristics of those who burn out. Writing at the end of the 90s, Schaufeli and Enzman warned against the dangers '…of the "popularity trap". That is, the popularity of burnout stimulates the articulation of quick and simple solutions, dubious assessment methods, and inferior interventions by those who want to make fast money in the booming burnout business. Inevitably, the commercialization of the popular burnout concept takes its toll – it remains associated with myths, fairy tales, and unverified "facts".'[4]

Unless we are clear about the precise nature of burnout, how can we ever do anything to seriously address it? And unless we do something about it, what is the point of understanding its true nature? Equally, those who are mistakenly labelled as experiencing burnout would be better served by an accurate diagnosis.

## Towards a common definition of burnout

Since the 1980s there has been a massive explosion in social scientific research on the subject. Schaufeli and Enzman estimated that over 50 research dissertations had appeared each year since the mid-80s and over 300 studies per year with the word 'burnout' in the title since the end of that decade.[5] This enormous amount of research has resulted in some common ground about the conceptualization of burnout. The following generally agreed:

- Burnout is a negative 'psychological condition' that develops over a long period of time among individuals who do not manifest behaviours indicative of mental illness.
- It is often 'unnoticed for a long time by the individual involved'.[6]
- It is primarily a work-related phenomenon.[7] This is a very important distinction without which it would be impossible to differentiate burnout from other psychological constructs such as stress, chronic fatigue syndrome and depression.[8] As stated previously, this distinction is essential for the treatment of burnout, as opposed to these different but related constructs. Hence burnout is often referred to as job burnout or employee burnout.

- Burnout occurs more often among younger employees during the earlier stages of their careers than older employees. Although this continues to be a contentious point among some researchers and those who feel they have burnt out later in life, there is no denying that the vast majority of prior research has consistently correlated age with job burnout.[9] A recent meta-analysis of the relationship between burnout, age and years of experience confirmed these findings.[10] Schaufeli and Enzman write that, 'Among younger employees, burnout is observed more often than among those aged over 30 or 40 years'.[11] As will be seen later, our research generally concurs with these views but expands the age range when employees are most vulnerable to burnout from their twenties to their early thirties.

- Burnout occurs among those that have a very high level of motivation to succeed in their careers and high expectations and goals about their own accomplishments; they 'restlessly pursue success in their jobs'.[12] Freudenberger described burnout as an 'over-achiever syndrome', a premise later supported by one of the foremost contributors to the study of burnout.[13] Another leading author in the field says that, 'In order to burn out, one has first to be "on fire". A person with no such initial motivation can experience stress, alienation, depression, an existential crisis, or fatigue, but not burnout'.[14] An integration of previous approaches to burnout identified a strong initial motivation among those who burn out as one of the common themes, the authors noting that, 'A paradox exists: the most valuable and successful professionals are those who, for that very reason, run the largest risk of burning out'.[15]

- Burnout is a 'multi-dimensional syndrome'. It is manifested by symptoms of severe exhaustion and distress at being overwhelmed and over-extended, feelings of ineffectiveness and inadequacy, reduced motivation and commitment, and 'dysfunctional attitudes and behaviours at work'.[16]

- Burnout appears to be a universal and pervasive phenomenon which is not strongly culturally dependent and whose form is similar across national, cultural and occupational boundaries. The majority of the research literature has found there to be more similarities than differences in terms of the symptoms of burnout, although some symptoms appear more pronounced than others in different countries.[17] This includes developing countries as well as the West. There is a need to explore this further by looking at specifically how burnout is manifest in different national contexts.

In summary then, we define burnout as

*a state of extreme exhaustion that occurs, regardless of culture, in highly demanding work environments among career-driven younger employees who become overwhelmed by prolonged work pressure and are no longer able to cope. It is likely that those who are most at risk of burnout will be seen as high flyers by their organizations.*

Being young and highly achievement orientated is of course neither a precise nor a comprehensive definition of a high flyer. On the other hand, our experience tells us that organizations are often far from precise in how they identify high flyers, particularly among younger employees. Those who make it onto the high potential list are often simply well-motivated, energetic, high performers. There is, as yet, not a lot of science behind being perceived as a 'rising young star'.

## Does burnout exist?

There remains the question of whether burnout is a phenomenon distinct from other related conditions. Is it, as some clinicians and social scientists would have us believe, simply a colloquial term for work stress, depression or chronic fatigue syndrome? We asked our research participants to identify the difference between burnout and work stress. Of the 100 people we talked to from 29 different national cultures, virtually all defined stress as an everyday occurrence; an inherent part of the job which, when experienced to a certain degree, can be motivating, healthy and make one more productive. It was seen as a state in which control of the boundaries between work and non-work was temporarily threatened. Most, however, believed their resources were sufficient to wrest control back again. Burnout on the other hand was seen as an end point, a condition in which one stopped functioning, could no longer cope with the work demands made of them, was paralyzed and gave up. It was stress taken to the extreme over the long term resulting from being overwhelmed and exhausted by the pressure and volume of work. A few also talked about burnout as a search for meaning and purpose – a point in life when you stop believing in what you are doing. It seems, then, that employees have little problem distinguishing between work stress and burnout. This is, of itself, sufficient grounds to justify the existence of burnout as a distinct condition. Even 'burnout deniers' – those who refuse to accept the very existence of burnout – must accept that if large numbers of people share a definition of the condition that distinguishes it from other conditions, then to all intents and purposes it exists, whatever their protestations to the contrary.

Most people understand burnout to be a special type of extreme occupational strain that develops over a prolonged period of time and from which it is difficult to recover. This is in line with what existing research has to say on the subject. Most authors consider burnout 'a particular kind of prolonged job stress'[18] or 'an intense form of job-related strain'.[19] Stress is viewed as a temporary adaptation to environmental stressors that brings with it psychological and physical symptoms while burnout indicates a failure to adapt resulting in 'chronic malfunctioning'. In addition, burnout occurs over a longer timeframe than stress among younger employees who are highly motivated and career driven. It also involves symptoms such as the manifestation of negative attitudes and behaviours at work which are not traditionally considered a stress variable. This distinction also applies to depression and chronic fatigue syndrome. Both of these latter conditions can be experienced in non-work as well as work settings and thus, unlike burnout, are not necessarily job related. Some researchers have suggested that burnout can lead to depression, 'Depression should be differentiated from burnout, in that the former refers to a particular psychological condition that should be regarded as a potential outcome of burnout rather than as part of the burnout syndrome itself.'[20]

## Our research

Our research follows the findings of prior studies which show burnout to be more prevalent among younger employees who are highly motivated and career driven. We therefore chose to examine burnout specifically among high flyers and to explore all other aspects of the above conceptualization in our research. Since our research sample was a distinctly multinational one, we also decided to examine the degree to which burnout can be truly described as a cross-cultural phenomenon.

We initially invited over 40 multinational and public sector organizations to be involved in the research by allowing us to interview and survey a representative sample of their top talent pool. Of these, three multinationals representing the energy, professional services and security systems industries took up our offer together with one of the UK police forces. The energy and security systems companies were headquartered in Europe while the professional services organization was an Anglo-American enterprise. One hundred interviews were conducted, with these four organizations providing 95% of the research participants.

Participants were chosen on the basis of their membership of the high potential talent pool and were not pre-selected for manifesting signs of burnout. Twenty-nine different nationalities were represented among these participants, who were domiciled in 21 different countries.

The remaining five research interviews were conducted with high flyers believed to be at risk of burning out or to have previously experienced burnout, and who came from a variety of different companies. These interviews were used as a control group and were excluded from analyses regarding the prevalence of burnout and its stability across organizations and national cultures.

Research participants were asked to complete the Maslach Burnout Inventory[21] as well as our own Work Stress Survey measuring their use of specific coping behaviours to deal with severe work stress. The Work Stress Survey is a self-assessment questionnaire developed from the data emerging from our initial qualitative research and subsequently refined. It measures the frequency with which individuals demonstrate various ways of dealing with work pressure, grouped under seven 'coping dimensions' (see Figure 2.1).

| Coping dimensions | Definition |
| --- | --- |
| Working hard | Working long hours and sacrificing personal and social activities |
| Working smart | Organizing and prioritizing for greater efficiency |
| Negotiating | Asking for more time or assistance |
| Setting boundaries | Saying 'no' to work demands from management or clients |
| Renewing | Making time for satisfying personal activities |
| Relating | Seeking social contact and support outside of work |
| Reflecting | Thinking about one's own work-related behaviour to gain understanding and insight |

**Figure 2.1**  Coping dimensions on the Work Stress Survey

The data from these survey tools was analysed and subsequently debriefed during a three-hour interview with the participant, who was asked for their response to the results. Participants were also asked for their perceptions of their work environment – for instance, the degree to which they experienced it as stressful, what made it so, the organisation's approach to the issue of stress and burnout, their overall assessment of the seriousness of the issue of stress and burnout for the organization, and so on.

Most of each interview was dedicated to participants talking about their experience of severe work stress over the course of their working lives. They were asked to recount the story of the most severe periods of prolonged work stress during their careers. Participants largely focused on the recent past. All recounted two or more stories. Most concerned the participant's experience with their current employer. None ignored their current employer by talking about their experience with a previous employer. Stories were audio recorded and subsequently transcribed for analysis. Our role as researchers was to encourage high flyers to narrate their experiences and to elicit as much specific detail as possible. We also asked participants to review their experiences retrospectively – even if they were in the middle of it – and to tell us what sense they were currently making of it. Nearly all participants found this a highly insightful and therapeutic event in its own right. Few had ever told the story of these often traumatic experiences in their entirety, and they found themselves able to find new meaning in the telling of them.

Researchers recorded their reflections on the interview once the participant had left. This was in the form of a directed and undirected awareness review capturing the researcher's reflections on the meeting and what was evoked in them by the conversation with the research participant.

We conducted follow-up interviews with around half of the participants one year after the initial discussion.

A drawback of basing our research on high flyers was that, typically, organizations do not identify potential until several years into someone's career. Consequently our research may be affected by what social scientists call 'survivor bias'. We may have interviewed the survivors who exhibited lower levels of burnout, whereas those who had burned out early in their careers had already left the organization. In addition, in common with other burnout studies, our research was based on those who were still at work and, we can surmise, were more or less healthy. There is therefore a possibility that our research may underestimate the extent of burnout among the high-flyer population.

The remainder of this chapter provides a high-level overview of our findings in terms of the prevalence and nature of burnout (including the degree to which burnout is experienced across organizational and national cultures), those most at risk and what happens when you burn out. We go on to look at the causes of burnout as well as the consequences. Chapter 3 looks in detail at the consequences of burnout for the organization while Chapter 4 provides considerably more detail on the causes and consequences for the individual.

## The prevalence of burnout among high flyers

More than 20% of our total research sample, excluding the five research participants used as a control group, exhibited symptoms of burnout at the time they were interviewed. This group also demonstrated a high fit to a profile of burnout on the Maslach Burnout Inventory: an 83% fit compared to 33% for those who were not demonstrating symptoms.[22]

A further 7% described previous experiences of burnout while working for their current organization. Overall professional services had the greatest number of high flyers demonstrating burnout symptoms, closely followed by the police service. Although high flyers were not pre-selected for burnout in our research, sample sizes were much larger for professional services than other industries. This may account for the higher percentage of those exhibiting burnout symptoms among professional services' employees. The 'Control Group' was composed of high flyers previously identified as possible burnout candidates, hence the very high percentage figure of those exhibiting burnout symptoms. See Figure 2.2.

The majority of research participants, 83%, were European nationals, and 38% of these held Eastern European or Commonwealth of Independent States (the former Soviet Union) nationality. The remainder came from the Middle East and Africa, Asia and the Americas. There was a more pronounced incidence of burnout among British, Irish, CIS

| Industry | Percentage of total research sample | Percentage exhibiting symptoms of burnout |
|---|---|---|
| Professional services | 64 | 23 |
| Energy | 10 | 20 |
| Security solutions | 12 | 17 |
| Police service | 9 | 22 |
| Control group* | 5 | 60 |

**Figure 2.2**    High flyer profile by industry. * Excluded from analyses of prevalence and stability of burnout

and Eastern European high flyers than other nationalities. There was no apparent correlation between industry and the high incidence of burnout among British and Irish nationals as the research participants were spread across the different industry groups. However, the Eastern Europeans and CIS participants all worked within professional services so there is a strong likelihood of correlation with industry among this group. See Figure 2.3.

High flyers living in the CIS countries and the UK experienced the highest incidence of burnout, despite a higher proportion of participants living in Eastern Europe and the rest of the world. We conjecture that the substantially higher risk of burnout experienced from living in the UK and the CIS countries may result from the cultural work ethic of these countries. However, most of those living in the CIS were local nationals and were entirely drawn from the professional services sector so the higher risk may well have as much to do with the industry and nationality as with the country of residence. See Figure 2.4.

| Nationality | Percentage of total research sample | Percentage exhibiting symptoms of burnout |
|---|---|---|
| CIS countries | 17 | 25 |
| Eastern European | 19 | 22 |
| British/Irish | 20 | 27 |
| Norwegian | 10 | 10 |
| Greek/Greek Cypriot | 12 | 18 |
| Other | 22 | 20 |

**Figure 2.3**  High flyer profile by nationality. **Note:** Control group has been excluded from this analysis

| Country in which research participants were domiciled | Percentage of total research sample | Percentage exhibiting symptoms of burnout |
|---|---|---|
| CIS countries | 17 | 31 |
| Eastern Europe | 23 | 24 |
| UK | 14 | 29 |
| Norway | 11 | 10 |
| Greece | 12 | 18 |
| Rest of the world | 18 | 11 |

**Figure 2.4**  High flyer profile by country of domicile. **Note:** Control group has been excluded from this analysis

| Occupational group of research participants | Percentage of total research sample | Percentage exhibiting symptoms of burnout |
|---|---|---|
| Accountants | 56 | 19 |
| Consultants | 10 | 33 |
| Policemen | 10 | 22 |
| Executive management | 17 | 13 |
| Human resource professionals | 4 | 75 |
| Marketeers | 3 | 25 |

**Figure 2.5**  High flyer profile by occupational group. **Note**: Control group has been excluded from this analysis

More than half of the high flyers interviewed were accountants and the remainder were largely composed of those in executive management, consultancy and policing. Although only representing 4% of the total research sample, three-quarters of HR professionals were suffering from burnout. Given the small numbers involved it is impossible to draw reliable conclusions from these figures as they may simply be attributable to chance. However, consultants, marketers and policemen also demonstrated a higher incidence of burnout than the relative size of these occupational groups would suggest. These findings lend weight to the hypothesis suggested by earlier studies that those in 'high touch', interpersonally demanding roles may be more prone to burnout symptoms. See Figure 2.5.

Follow-up discussions were conducted with around half of those exhibiting burnout symptoms one year after the initial interview in order to assess their current state. More than 50% described their condition as having deteriorated over the year. Several had left their organizations stating burnout as the primary cause. Less than a third described signs of improvement such as being proactively able to manage themselves more effectively.

All of those re-interviewed one year on thought the risk of burnout in their current organizations was very high. However, many believed that the upsurge in the local economy would make it easier for them to find alternative (and less stressful) employment.

## Is burnout a culturally distinct phenomenon?

We looked at the data for those currently suffering from burnout in terms of the degree to which the condition was affected by the national culture of the research participant, the national culture in which they were domiciled and the national culture of the organization for which they worked.

We also looked at the similarity and differences between the incidences of burnout in the different organizations in our study. We found remarkable stability in terms of the nature and basic symptomalogical pattern of burnout across all burnout candidates.

However, the national cultural context within which high flyers worked had an important bearing on the way in which burnout symptoms were manifest. We can illustrate this by using the way in which dysfunctional attitudes and behaviours were demonstrated across different cultures. British, Russians and North Europeans tended to be more sceptical about their employers and more ambivalent generally about work than North Americans. It was more acceptable for high flyers' clients to become very aggressive in Greece and Russia, much less acceptable in the UK, and totally unacceptable in Scandinavia. Equally, it was slightly more acceptable for employees to voice their anger to one another in Greek and Russian cultures, though not to clients. In Greek culture public displays of anger were used as a way of making colleagues understand the passion with which one held particular views or needs. In the UK and Scandinavia such behaviour was generally frowned upon. It is therefore important to distinguish between the functional use of anger, which usefully establishes boundaries and makes the seriousness of one's purpose and position clear to others, and the dysfunctional use of anger. In the latter, one loses any sense of intent or purpose about expressing anger, as well as any subsidiary awareness of those around one and as a result runs the risk of damaging relationships.

Without this important cultural calibration one would unwittingly exaggerate the presence of this particular burnout symptom. As Philippe Rosinski puts it, 'Our behaviours depend in part on the particular cultural context'.[23]

## The nature of burnout

Our research shows burnout to be a state of mind with clear psychological and physiological symptoms. Fiona, a senior manager in the energy sector, described how burnout affected her:

*It literally felt like I was carrying the weight of this whole department on my own shoulders and that's the point where it started to go wrong and what I felt was a huge physical tiredness. Emotionally I struggled to cope with stuff – managed not to show it at work, but lots of tears and emotion at home, that kind of thing. My confidence took an absolute dive so whilst I was doing all of this work, and continued to deliver to an extent, I felt like a failure for quite a long period of time, and that mindset kind of grew and grew and grew, and I didn't know how to shift it.*

All of the high flyers currently experiencing burnout or who had experienced burnout previously, attributed their symptoms to work, rather than home life. While for some there were other factors, such as the recent break-up of a relationship, this was not viewed as a prime cause of burnout or indeed even a contributing factor to it. As Scott, a police officer on the British police forces' fast track scheme, put it:

*The daily journey was about an hour and a half each way to work on top of 8 to 11 hour working patterns. After what happened in February I was physically exhausted all the time, emotionally exhausted and withdrawn. I'm quite introverted anyway but this was withdrawal to a new definition of withdrawn.*

Interestingly, many of those not exhibiting psychological symptoms of burnout were displaying some physiological symptoms such as constant tiredness, severe headaches, gastrointestinal problems, skin conditions, weight loss (or gain), disturbed sleep patterns, increased use of alcohol, and so on.

Burnout appeared to emerge out of the kind of relationship that developed between high flyers and their work environment. This relationship constantly changed but like any relationship could get stuck in habitual, rigid patterns that failed to serve the individual. One of our researchers asked Fatima, a high-flying HR manager, about her level of commitment to the job,

*Researcher*: You say you were giving up your sleep and you didn't take time off?

*Fatima*: No, I couldn't, I couldn't because I was worried all the time – will this be OK, will it be on time? I had lots of things to do, you can imagine of course with these big numbers, and there is nobody to help. I believe I couldn't have any rest or sleep just then.

Clearly, organizations and their leaders play their part in creating burnout by making unrealistic or excessive demands of their high flyers, but equally there is an element of volition and choice in high flyers acquiescing to these demands. However, few entertained the idea of pushing back or negotiating for longer timescales or more resources.

Burnout is a long-term process. All of those experiencing burnout talked about events that occurred over a period of several months or more. We also found many examples of those who did not notice they were burning out or, if they did notice, they discerned only individual symptoms and didn't see how this fitted into an overall pattern. Our own experience of burnout supports these observations. We had a feeling that something was not right – a pervasive feeling of malaise – but not a clear understanding of what was happening to us. It was only much later, after we had recovered from burnout, that we could piece together and make sense of our experience. As Søren Kierkegaard put it, 'Life can only be understood backwards; but it must be lived forwards.'[24]

## Those most at risk from burnout

As would be expected from high flyers, most of our research participants described themselves as being strongly motivated to achieve success in their careers and holding high goals and expectations for their work (an average of an 80% fit against a self-descriptiveness rating across the entire research sample). Those currently exhibiting signs of burnout were within the first nine years of their career with an average age of 32, although in most cases their experience of burnout had begun up to twelve months previously.

Wilmar Schaufeli and Dirk Enzman refer to burnout being applicable to 'normal populations' who do not suffer from 'psychopathology'. In other words, they are individuals who do not manifest behaviours indicative of mental illness. There is nothing we have seen from our research population, from our non-clinical but psychologically informed view, that would appear to contradict that.

## How do you know when you're burning out?

### Exhaustion and distress

Probably the most obvious and pervasive symptom of burnout is extreme exhaustion. This can manifest itself initially in a number of different ways, dependent on the degree to which the individual is in touch with their own needs. For some, exhaustion appears as a physical lethargy – an inability to get out of bed to go to work the next day or, having returned from work, to do anything but sit on the sofa and stare at the TV. For others, it manifests as emotional weariness. People find themselves involuntarily breaking down as a result of the smallest of triggers. There is a strong desire to avoid facing the world and any form of interpersonal contact. Scott described his experience:

*I had very little social life, very little social contact. Spent an awful lot of time in the house – apathetic, lethargic, lying around watching meaningless television, not engaging with a social life, wasn't going to the gym. I wasn't eating. I lost about a stone and a half in about three months which for me it was very noticeable 'cos I've always been sort of fairly stocky build so at a stone and half I was looking pale and gaunt. Wasn't sleeping, wasn't eating. As I say apathy and lethargy, no energy to do anything, no desire to engage in the relationship that I was in or engage in relationships with family and friends. I just felt ill.*

Others simply do not notice their level of exhaustion until their bodies tell them. In the last chapter, Holger described consistently working 120 hours a week and not being able to understand why he was getting severe headaches. When his body failed to cooperate his response was to say, 'I'm a healthy 33-year-old, so what's the problem?'. Another of our high flyers, Keith, talked about a time when he was on an overseas posting working crazy hours because there was nothing else to do,

*It was the summer of '98 in Vietnam. I found myself basically lying on the floor at home. I just couldn't move. I was all cramped up and I was shaking and crouched. I just felt absolutely helpless. I eventually managed to get to phone and so then the ambulance comes and people were trying to calm me down. I was just like fighting, and I felt what is happening to my body? This is not me being in control, and I do like being in control. I was in hospital for a couple of days on a sedative and a drip because I basically got dehydrated and had a virus. Part of how I react to stress is my body reacts to it, particularly my digestive system.*

Some of those who burnt out pushed themselves to extreme limits and almost killed themselves in the process. Piotr described a point in his career when he was consistently working on projects with impossible deadlines over a three-year period,

*I remember, for example, I was sitting 36 hours non-stop in the office. And what stopped me working was that I had to go to my mother-in-law to do something. It was in the middle of the night and I took the car and I fell asleep over the wheel. And I woke up in the middle of a crossroad. I didn't have an accident because it was night but the light was red. And I said come on, it's enough! I have to take a break and in fact I was too exhausted to go home because I was living 20 kilometres outside town. So I took a hotel close to the office and I slept, showered and then came back for another 24 hours.*

Exhaustion is often accompanied by either physiological or emotional signs of distress. All of the high flyers exhibiting symptoms of burnout suffered from various physical ailments, including disturbed sleep patterns, digestive problems, weight loss, severe headaches and skeletomuscular disorders. Some talked about resorting to substance abuse or risk-taking behaviours to alleviate their feelings of anguish. Vladimir told us about a time when he was under intense pressure:

*I bought a new car at that time and I started driving really fast. I was coping with my stress on the road, so I was just speeding and all kinds of things. I kind of tried to find excitement in small things and live between those moments. And thinking that it's gonna change over time.*

Tim's story of disintegration in Chapter 1 details the emotional distress that those who burn out often feel but rarely articulate to anyone.

For others, distress can be less colourful but just as painful. Many of the high flyers we interviewed talked about the bright ideals they once held about about their careers fading in front of their eyes:

*There were times when I woke up in the morning and said 'Oh no, it's another day, I've got to go back to office' which was the first time that something like that had happened to me in my work career.*

## *Reduction in performance and productivity*

The most widely accepted model of burnout contends that, in addition to exhaustion, the condition is manifest by a sense of reduced personal accomplishment as well as a distant attitude to work and people encountered on the job.[25] Our findings broadly support the last of these dimensions, but not the first.

We found little evidence of our participants having a sense of reduced personal effectiveness during their burnout episode. Of the 100 high flyers we interviewed, 30 either exhibited symptoms of burnout or described having experienced burnout in the past. Of these, seven (23%) reported some awareness of a reduced sense of accomplishment. The remaining 77% did not. These findings were supported by the results of the Maslach Burnout Inventory (MBI). The majority rated themselves as being very satisfied with their work accomplishments and effectiveness. Could these data be explained by feelings of anxiety about disclosing potentially career-damaging information? We think it unlikely, given our experience of participants during the interviews. However, it was evident from people's stories of burnout that their performance *did* suffer. For example, one high flyer told us that 'My work performance I thought was improving and was going from strength to strength, despite the very negative appraisal'. Another disclosed his boss had told him to change his behaviour because it was disempowering those who worked for him. In other cases we heard from the high flyers' bosses or their colleagues that things were not going well. Our own experience of burnout would support the notion that performance does tail off. Tim's description of facilitating the conference in the last chapter is one such example.

We conclude, therefore, that participants did not have much of a sense of a drop off in performance because they did not notice it.

How can high flyers, supposedly the 'brightest and best' in the organization, manage not to notice their performance is suffering? We suspect that poor performance is such a taboo for high flyers and so disconfirming for their professional identity that it is the last thing they are willing to look at.

High flyers' identities are closely tied up in success on the job. To admit a tail off in performance would be like saying they are not who they thought they were. Burnout is a form of deep personal crisis. In the midst of crisis, the last thing most of us are likely to do is to seek out or give credence to disconfirming data about our identity. It is entirely natural to want to reduce your vulnerability in such circumstances and to find ways of protecting yourself.

In addition, high flyers have, as Chris Argyris says, 'rarely experienced the embarrassment that comes with failure'.[26] Their lives have been hitherto primarily characterized by success. They simply have not experienced failure to any great degree and as a consequence do not know how to deal with failure when it comes their way. When it does, their response is to '...put the blame on others. Their ability to learn shuts down precisely at the moment they need it most'.[27] One of our participants talked about the challenges of starting up a new business for a large energy multinational:

> *It's just that we hadn't anticipated the number of problems we were facing up front. Because the feedback when it came was very, very stressful to handle – to go back and sort of be questioned about my ability. That was very stressful. And while I can't speak about other people, what I can say about myself is that in the rest of my working experience I've never heard someone telling me that they don't have faith in me delivering something.*

The grandiosity of this last statement also illustrates another dynamic that is often at play among high flyers – arrogance. In his book *High Flyers* Morgan McCall refers to a process in which

> *success after success leads to arrogance. Each successive success, whether a technical accomplishment or a business result, adds to the opportunity to believe one's own press clippings or to admire the trophy case. Whether they were military aviators, physician managers, or executives, none were above interpreting accomplishments as further proof that there was something special about them (as indeed there was). For some, that specialness translated into egotism...*[28]

As a consequence, high flyers develop a blind spot about their failure to meet their own high standards. As Karen Blakely puts it, 'Blind spots emerge when, for a variety of reasons, we do not want to listen or to learn. The reason for this is that learning can be both painful and time-consuming; as a result, we often avoid it'.[29] This blind spot serves to insulate the high flyer from what is happening to them. It may also explain the prolonged nature of burnout and the reason why it often goes unnoticed by high flyers for a long time.

## Disillusion and reduced commitment

A sense of disillusion with the work and the organization was evident among almost 70% of those we interviewed who were currently demonstrating symptoms of burnout. In addition, five of the six high flyers who described previous experiences of burnout also spoke of how their experience had made them disenchanted with their work. Holger voices a strong sense of anger in Chapter 1 with the way he feels he has been used by the organization. Some high flyers talked about getting to a point where they just didn't care anymore, 'It's bad because I hate coming in to the office…[I am] demotivated. I feel I don't care…(sighing) I don't feel like I have any creativeness or anything…', said Csilla, a high-flying HR professional. These feelings are often accompanied by a sense of outrage and anger. In the previous chapter, Tim talks about becoming bitter and angry and disillusioned, feelings which he projects onto the organization. Inevitably, this leads to an erosion of commitment and engagement to the job and the organization. Our research found those exhibiting burnout symptoms were less committed to the job and the organization than those not experiencing burnout. The average rating of the level of commitment of the former was 4 on a 1 to 10 point scale of commitment. This was a 3 point difference with those not experiencing burnout. As Piotr puts it:

> A few years ago I was emotionally connected to the firm. I was trying to do a lot of things for the firm. Not anymore. I just use it as a place to work and earn my money. I don't have an emotional connection with the firm anymore. I feel treated unfairly and I do my best to be professional but without any emotional connection to it. But on the other hand I'm a very ambitious person and it's really painful when your effort is not recognized and you have the feeling that the firm doesn't give a shit about what you are doing…I treat it just as a contract. They're paying me so I am doing this but that's it.

Piotr adopted an instrumental approach to the organization for which he worked. He was not willing to sacrifice his sense of professionalism by doing shoddy work, but the emotional connection with the organization has been severed. Inevitably, this often translates into high flyers leaving the organization. But worse – they leave it angry.

We know that high flyers tend to be strongly motivated to achieve success (earlier we referred to an 80% fit against a self-descriptiveness rating in this regard for the entire research sample). Could it be that those who burn out tend to set unrealistically high expectations for themselves and others and that this puts them at risk of becoming disillusioned? It would not be a surprise were this the case.

## Dysfunctional attitudes

All but one of the high flyers experiencing burnout were demonstrating feelings of detachment from the work or a distant and sometimes cynical attitude towards colleagues or clients. In making these observations we were mindful that the relationship between high flyers and interpersonal sensitivity is often fraught. McCall reminds us that insensitivity is, 'the most commonly reported flaw among derailed executives.'[30] Other studies cite feedback from the direct reports of high potential employees about their bosses' thoughtlessness and failure to empower their subordinates because they are too focused on competing with other colleagues.[31] Given that insensitivity is inherently part of the package for some high flyers, we were keen to ensure we made a distinction between whether high flyers experiencing burnout were more dysfunctional than those who were not. Those experiencing burnout rated themselves as between high and medium on the cynicism dimension of the MBI. In addition, most described their dysfunctional behaviour as something which was not normally part of how they approached their work or interacted with others – it emerged during the course of their burnout experience. Larissa, a high-flying accountant, told us about the management issues she faced on a large multi-site audit:

*I kind of expected that of her so I wasn't really angry. I just over-ruled her, because it was too late to do it through conversation and I just told her to do it this way. And I went to the client and pushed them really hard, so they began to know what we needed. And then it started to get moving. But everybody on the team was always standing up when I was coming into the room. I wasn't yelling, I was just making them do what I wanted them to do without asking them what they thought about it, because it was too late to do that.... I started to notice I didn't feel myself, you know, when it's me and it's not me, and I kind of saw myself from – I'm somewhere there, and my other part is somewhere there! It wasn't pleasant for me, of pushing people, and making them do what I want, especially on this first project.*

Dysfunctional behaviour arose out of exhaustion from trying to do the impossible – either in terms of workload or trying to change a situation or other people. In Chapter 1, Jarvid gives an example of being put under extreme pressure early in his career and becoming snappy, rude and arrogant and making a lot of enemies. Tim describes several examples of depersonalizing others over a longer timeframe in a work environment characterized by excessive work pressure. Kirill, another high-flying professional services employee, described his distress at seeing his behaviour change as a result of trying to achieve the impossible and becoming utterly exhausted:

> *Kirill:* It's become very easy to make me…shout at people or not be very loyal to the client, not trying to save them things. In the past I was a very kind of soft guy. It was very difficult to make me wild about something. Now, I start to worry about myself and what's going on.
>
> *Researcher:* You mentioned your wife earlier, has she noticed some changes about you over the last year or so?
>
> *Kirill:* Yeah, she noticed.
>
> *Researcher:* What did she notice?
>
> *Kirill:* I tend to be very sceptical and sarcastic.

### Addictive behaviour

The link between burnout and work addiction is a contentious area as most of the burnout literature believes it to be weak. In addition, what some authors call 'expansiveness' among high potentials can 'lead to compulsive, addictive behaviour' and 'a loss of choice and perspective'.[32] Once again, then, research in this area needs to be wary of being confounded by the inherent predilections among some high flyers – this time for addictive behaviour.

Goodman's definition of addiction was used to guide our research into the degree to which high flyers at risk of burnout are displaying addictive behaviour over and above that demonstrated by those who are not. This definition, which is widely used in addiction literature, states that addiction is 'a process whereby a behaviour, that can function both to produce pleasure and to provide escape from internal discomfort, is employed in a pattern characterized by (1) recurrent failure to control the behaviour (powerlessness) and (2) continuation of the behaviour despite significant negative consequences (unmanageability)'.[33]

We found numerous examples of both powerlessness and unmanageability which were different in nature from those who were not experiencing burnout. Fatima described how she could lose her temper quickly and become very nervous under pressure, a pattern which she identified over the past six months. She didn't like it, wanted to change it, but didn't see how. There was no stigma attached to having a coach or a mentor in her organization, yet she was unwilling to find one. She felt no one would be willing to talk to her from within the organization because most people would normally be asking her for help. She therefore felt powerless and was resigned to repeating the same pattern of behaviour.

Holger, in Chapter 1, provides a graphic illustration of addictiveness. He talks about saying yes to a lot of work projects even though he knew he didn't have time for them (recurrent inability to control behaviour) and continues to work 120-hour weeks despite suffering increasingly painful and debilitating headaches (unmanageability) to the point where he has to be given medical leave.

Jarvid's willingness to sacrifice his personal life is another such example. Later in the interview he talked about the pressures he was under when heading up a large restructuring project,

*My son was born in July 2004 and I remember carrying my laptop to the room in which my wife was staying. This was just after her surgery. I was still on my laptop, sitting in her room. That's actually one memory that sticks! Not the best but it's something that my wife keeps reminding me about! It was just that there were things to be done and things that hadn't happened and a new team was coming in place and it was quite important that they see that their leader is somebody that they can look up to in terms of saying, 'OK, the situation is difficult but he's willing to sacrifice that, so we should be willing to give that bit extra'.*

The addictive behaviour that is a part of burnout turns high flyers into automatons. It flattens their senses and they lose their humanity. They become work junkies. Larissa described this process,

*I didn't really feel myself, I was just working, travelling around all these projects. Sometimes my fiancé was bringing my clothes and stuff to the airport or the train station and I was changing and going to the next project, I didn't even go home! But I didn't really feel – didn't really feel as if I was alive, I just did the work, didn't really think about my health or my emotional state or anything like that. Sometimes I couldn't sleep at night because I was thinking 'Oh my God! What's happening on this project? Are these guys doing fine or doing badly?' and so on. And it goes on in your head and it drives you – I wasn't mad actually, for me I was normal, I was just doing my job, but for outside people it was evident that something was really – that it was becoming very difficult for me…*

As with other addictions, it is easy for those closest to the burnout sufferer to enter into a co-dependent relationship with them. They do not dare to challenge the person's addiction for fear of losing their love. And, again, like other addictions it is normally these people who become collateral damage. Larissa continues her story,

*For some time in April I couldn't sleep for almost three weeks, I just couldn't sleep – and I didn't want to, I just didn't want to sleep, I was working, I was completing all this stuff, and it's – of course it's not normal, and it's not the way it should be. Also I realized I was growing apart from my fiancé, I was just growing apart from him. I wasn't at home, I just didn't see him. And when I realized that I'm kind of growing apart from him – that was a disaster.*

The insidious thing about the addictive behaviour that is a part of the burnout condition is that it is officially sanctioned by the organization. Organizations expect very high workloads and performance outcomes from their high flyers, and thus provide positive reinforcement to those prone to workaholic tendencies. Unlike other addictive behaviours, there is no social stigma to working excessively. At least not until burnout occurs. In fact the closest analogy is the way the drinks industry and society handles the issue of under-age binge drinking. The drinks industry sanctions the act by aggressively marketing alco-pops, retailers encourage excessive consumption through massively discounting the product, and society colludes with the process until it witnesses throngs of brawling teenagers vomiting on its streets.

Our conceptualization of burnout based on our findings on its nature, biographical characteristics and manifestation is summarized in the Figure 2.6 below.

### A typology of burnout states

At the beginning of this book we introduced the notion of three possible 'burnout states' which were then illustrated in the vignettes in Chapter 1. These states emerged out of our conversations with those who were currently or who had formerly experienced burnout. Total, individual psychological and emotional devastation was characterized as the conception of burnout most in common currency. Those who 'crash and burn' (the term we chose for this burnout state) are the most unaware of their condition. As we saw with Holger, burnout comes as a surprise to them. They are young and seemingly indestructible. Why should they slow down?

The chronic self-destructive pattern illustrated by Tim's story describes a state which is repeated over the course of a person's career indefinitely

| Nature of burnout | |
|---|---|
| 1 | A negative psychological condition which is closely linked to negative physiological effects |
| 2 | Primarily work related |
| 3 | Develops gradually and is a long-term process – occurs over a timeframe of several months or even years |
| 4 | May remain unnoticed for a long time by the individual involved |
| 5 | Is a function of the relationship between the individual and their work environment |
| 6 | Is a pervasive phenomenon, not strongly dependent upon national culture. However, symptoms may be manifest somewhat differently dependent upon national culture |
| **Those most at risk** | |
| 1 | High flyers – high potential or top talent employees<br>Those who have high goals and expectations for their work and who are strongly motivated to achieve success |
| 2 | Largely experienced by those in their 20s and early 30s; within the first 10 years of a career |
| 3 | Occurs in 'normal' individuals who do not suffer from psychopathology |
| **How burnout is manifest (symptomatology)** | |
| 1 | Overwhelming exhaustion – emotional, cognitive and physical |
| 2 | Distress – affective, cognitive and physiological<br><br>Affective/cognitive symptoms include: anxiety, feelings of powerlessness and hopelessness<br>Physiological symptoms include disturbed sleep patterns, insomnia, gastrointestinal problems, weight loss or gain, severe headaches, skeleto-muscular disorder, chronic fatigue, increased use of alcohol or drugs, injuries from risk-taking behaviour |
| 3 | A reduction in performance and productivity<br><br>This goes unnoticed by the majority of those experiencing burnout, who are not aware of a reduced sense of effectiveness or accomplishment |
| 4 | A sense of disillusion leading to decreased motivation and job satisfaction<br><br>This leads to reduced commitment and engagement with the job and organization, sometimes resulting in intention to leave the job and actual job turnover |
| 5 | Dysfunctional attitudes and behaviours at work<br><br>Feelings of detachment from the work and often the adoption of a cold, distant and cynical attitude towards others |
| 6 | Addictive behaviour<br><br>A recurrent failure to control work addiction and continuation of this behaviour despite negative consequences |

**Figure 2.6**  Definition of burnout (with acknowledgements to the work of Wilmar Schaufeli and Dirk Enzman (1998) *The Burnout Companion to Study and Practice: A Critical Analysis*)

or until they find a way of breaking it. Although they may be aware of their pattern, these individuals appear unable to disorganise it and so are fated to repeat it over and over again. It seems to be rigidly organized within them and highly resistant to change.

Finally there are those, like Jarvid, who are not burning out but who manifest many of the symptoms of burnout. These are individuals for whom work holds the joy of the short-term fix but nearly always at the sacrifice of their home lives. As a consequence their lives permanently lack equilibrium. Their careers are lived unsustainably through addictive work styles and a failure to find sufficient nourishment and balance. They are always teetering on the edge of burnout and at risk of tipping over.

## What causes burnout?

Over the past five years we have interviewed 100 high flyers and had numerous tangential conversations with bosses, coaches and human resources executives involved in their management and development. In a few cases we have even been able to interview the high flyer's family members. Just about everyone was unequivocal about attributing burnout to the environment in which the person burning out worked. Even some of those in the most senior positions in the organization lamented the unrelenting pace of business, 'Of course, we have to deliver against target, but do we really need to do it with this unremitting sense of urgency and speed?'. And yet, no one knew what to do about it. Not even those at the top of the organization. Rather like the war on terror, the inhuman pressure of work was blamed on abstract nouns. It was the system, the way society was structured, the way global business was operating these days. There was a sense of powerlessness and resignation about what simply 'is'.

There is no doubt in our minds that organizations, partly driven by a variety of external macro- and socio-economic pressures and partly by a fantasy of their own making, create the conditions that nurture burnout. These workplace factors – primarily workload and time pressure, but also such things as leadership style and the culture of the organization – are the pre-determinants of burnout. But to attribute the cause of burnout purely to the social environment at work is what Paul Watzlawick and his colleagues refer to as a 'terrible simplification'.[34] It colludes with the human tendency to refuse to accept responsibility for our behaviour. It is a refusal to see the complexities inherent in the interactions between individual employees and their work environments. Denying there is any problem at the individual employee level is a gross simplification. It is irresponsible. It allows people to avoid owning the often painful consequences of their actions.

Moreover, the proponents of this stance pretty much adhere to the formula outlined by Watzlawick et al. That is, they deny there is a problem at the individual employee level – or at worst, it's merely a difficulty of poor fit – and then go on to attack anyone who points out that there might be a problem as either 'mad or bad'. In *The Road Less Travelled*, M Scott Peck explains the inevitable consequence of such an approach:

> *Whenever we seek to avoid the responsibility for our own behaviour, we do so by attempting to give that responsibility to some other individual or organizational entity. But this means we then give away our power to that entity, be it 'fate' or 'society' or the government or the corporation or our boss. It is for this reason that Erich Fromm so aptly titled his study of Nazism and authoritarianism Escape from Freedom. In attempting to avoid the pain of responsibility, millions and even billions daily attempt to escape from freedom.*[35]

Those of us who have actually experienced burnout are likely to have a slightly different take on the whole issue of causality. The latitude for individual choice was far greater. Indeed in retrospect, some of us might think it was almost unlimited, albeit many of the choices we could have taken would have been very painful. We could have chosen not to be high flyers as well as to be high flyers. We could have chosen to walk away from the work situation; in a near-to-full employment economy we could have chosen to walk away from the job. In a large organization, we could have chosen to find a job in another part of our employer. We could also have chosen to either curtail or temporarily downplay our career aspirations. Burnout occurs in the crucible of a relationship, and that relationship exists between the individual and their work environment. While researchers have spent considerable time focusing on the organizational part of that equation, little has been invested in understanding the individual's contribution to their own burnout. To paraphrase Cary Cooper et al,[36] burnout occurs in the individual's transaction with their work environment. In the encounter with their social environment, the individual interprets what confronts them, gives meaning to this interpretation and organizes their action on the basis of this meaning. In this way, burnout results from the way in which people organize themselves to deal with the dysfunctional features of the social environment in which they work. It is not the situation that is the primary cause of burnout, but the way in which people interpret and handle that situation. Thus, it is our belief that while the organization creates the conditions for burnout to occur, it is the individual – through his or her own choices – who determines whether they burn out or not.

In our research we discovered that some high flyers burn out and others don't, even when they are working in the same environment, doing the same job with the same boss. Some researchers explain this as a result of a lack of fit between the individual burning out and their work situation. The implication is that in a different work environment there would be a better fit. Our experience is that those high flyers that burn out make choices that cause them to burn out across different work environments, a conclusion that is supported by recent longitudinal research among UK doctors.[37] Because high flyers choose to be high flyers, these environments are always characterized by high workload and high pressure but not always by other stressors.

Proponents of the job/person fit approach argue that the workplace needs to be changed to address the lack of fit. As a result, employers are left in the invidious position of having to change the workplace because some of their people are suffering from poor fit and are burning out whereas others are not. Where, then, is the incentive for organizations to make massive changes to the structure and functioning of the workplace?

The remainder of this section contains our findings on the workplace stressors which create the conditions for burnout. We also provide an outline of our conclusions about the individual component to burnout – the characteristics of those more at risk of burnout. The data supporting these findings can be found in Chapter 4, together with a more in-depth description of them.

### *Workplace stressors*

In line with previous research the most frequently cited sources of workplace stress by high flyers were workload and time pressure.[38] An almost permanent state of inadequate staffing often contributed to the high volume and intensity of work. Many felt that additional discretionary effort was a requirement in order to continue to be regarded as high potential. This meant that they had to take on additional roles such as being the chairperson of the HR committee as well as their day jobs. Exceptionally long working hours and impossibly short deadlines was another much quoted issue.

The other two most often reported stressors were organizational climate and the leadership style of superiors. Nearly all of our research participants commented that saying no – for instance, to additional work or unreasonable client or management demands – was regarded as unacceptable in their organizations. We suspect this was as much about high flyers' perceptions of their boundaries as it was the organization's norm for high flyers. Nevertheless, high flyers felt it was impossible and indeed pointless to set clear boundaries with the organization. This was confirmed by high flyers' scores on the dimensions of negotiating and setting boundaries on the Work Stress Survey. These dimensions were scored lowest overall of all seven coping dimensions across the entire research sample, indicating they were seldom used by high flyers.

Pushing back was not an option, but nor was negotiating with power holders in the organization to obtain more resources or longer timescales. Related to this was a lack of trust in colleagues and a climate that was characterized by competitive politics and potentially damaging gossip. Many commented on stress and burnout being taboo and perceived as an admission of failure in their organizations – of not being able to take the heat. Several high flyers identified a key stressor as being management's requirement that they toe the party line and do things by the book, as opposed to responding to the local situation and context on the ground. High flyers found following procedures when they might not be the best solution for a specific situation as inherently stressful, probably because it cut across closely-held values around high-quality professionalism. This last concern was particularly prevalent among police officers and those in professional services.

Not surprisingly, leadership teams who consistently shifted corporate direction, made strategy 'U' turns and continually moved the goal posts, were perceived as a major cause of stress for our high flyers. Equally, superiors who failed to sufficiently engage with their subordinates caused anxiety. Some superiors appeared to become invisible at peak moments of stress during our high flyers' careers, thus effectively withdrawing an important source of social support when it was most needed, and inevitably intensifying the stress. High flyers in professional services firms suffered particularly from highly competitive, macho management teams who were more concerned with fighting internal political battles than providing support to those beneath them. Finally, many commented on the degree to which superiors appeared to act out of expediency and in the process lost any sense of compassion for their people as a cause of stress.

A perceived inability to control the work situation and having to deal with ambiguity was seen as a stressor by police officers and those in the energy industry. High-flyer programmes which involved moving people frequently into new roles where they had little competence was cited as a particular cause of stress in this regard. Another was the inherent stress that comes from being in a leadership role – being responsible for the delivery of results but dependent on others to achieve this.

Lack of recognition and feedback was a stressor for professional services employees and police officers.

Finally, professional services employees referred to difficult interpersonal relationships with clients as an important stressor in their roles. This was often caused by the gap between clients' expectations of the service they would receive compared to what the firm was willing to offer. Other sources of conflict included clients supplying low-quality information and – particularly in developing countries – clients' perceptions of auditors and accountants as agents of the state who were there to penalise them.

Our findings broadly support previous studies which have shown that workload and time pressure explain about 25–50% of the variance of burnout, particularly in terms of emotional exhaustion. High flyers across all the organizations involved in our research reported this as a key stressor. Only professional services employees referenced emotionally-charged interactions with clients as a source of stress.

## Individual characteristics

Our research revealed two individual characteristics which are, by far, the most important driving factors for the vast majority of burnout cases. We provide brief outlines of these characteristics here and discuss them in more detail together with the data behind our assertions in Chapter 4.

Firstly, those high flyers at risk of burnout tend to derive their identity largely from their jobs and their career. They over-identify with work. They tend to blur boundaries between their working lives and their lives outside of work to the extent that the personal self and the professional role become indistinguishable. The lack of boundary between themselves and their job means they lose a sense of their inner identity and their own needs. This 'dysfunctional closeness'[39] requires that they agree not to disagree with the sometimes unreasonable demands made of them by bosses and colleagues. If they do push back on these demands they feel obliged to apologize for doing so. Because they cannot tolerate boundaries they tend to end up in repeated patterns of psychically and interpersonally difficult situations. They demonstrate a willingness to sacrifice what might be personally important for them, by, for instance, taking on work they know is beyond their capacity to deliver. And they often lack a connection with their feelings and their bodies. This may become evident through a cavalier attitude towards their health or physical needs.

Identity is closely tied up in what provides meaning and purpose in our lives. Coupled with an externally referenced identity, high flyers who burn out also have a tendency to centre the purpose of their lives on the acquisition of fame and recognition. Meaning is chiefly derived from winning the respect of others or the achievement of personally important goals that confer such respect.

Secondly, the ability to self-interact – to have conversations with ourselves and evaluate and interpret what comes towards us and act upon this interpretation – is either poorly developed or interrupted. Reflexivity has been described as humankind's distinctive attribute. It allows us to take control of our lives and not simply respond to external stimuli. We are constantly engaged in conversations with ourselves, making sense of what we confront in our lives and finding ways of dealing with the meaning that emerges out of this sense-making process. This ability is either less well formed among high flyers more prone to burnout, or it has become disrupted by the high flyer cutting themselves off from data about their feelings, sensations and needs. As a consequence they become less able to process the complexity of their experience.

## What are the consequences of burnout for the individual?

There were four major consequences for high flyers who burnt out in our study. These were psychosomatic issues, reduced engagement, development versus career derailment and a change in the sense of one's self-identity. The first two are discussed in this chapter. The remainder are dealt with only briefly in this chapter. The impact of reduced engagement *on the organization* is discussed in more detail in Chapter 3. Development versus career derailment is a major feature of Chapters 4 and 5 and change in identity is dealt with in Chapter 4.

### Psychosomatic issues

Earlier in this chapter we referred to all of the high flyers who experienced burnout in our study as suffering from some kind of physiological disorder. The most common of these were disturbed sleep patterns, gastrointestinal problems, weight loss, severe headaches and skeletomuscular disorders. However, the full list of physical symptoms was endless and included amnesia, insomnia, weight gain, chronic fatigue, skin conditions, increased use of alcohol or drugs, and injuries from risk-taking behaviour. Prior research has proven burnout to lead to an elevated level of cholesterol, and a risk factor in coronary heart disease.[40] A 2008 longitudinal study of 10,308 British civil servants over 12 years found that stress can lead to coronary heart disease either directly, by activating stress pathways controlled by the interaction between the nervous system, the endocrine glands and their hormones, or indirectly via its association with unhealthy lifestyles.[41] Evidently, burnout can lead to some very serious health problems. However, it is difficult to assess whether psychosomatic issues are a consequence of burnout and we therefore agree with the views of other authors that they are best seen as concomitants.[42]

Appendix 1 provides a summary of the physiological consequences or concomitants of burnout.

## Reduced engagement

We have previously referred to the reduced level of commitment among those experiencing burnout. Overall, high flyers appeared to be highly committed to their jobs and their careers, but much less committed to and engaged with the organization for which they worked. We specifically asked high flyers about their organization's approach to the issue of stress and burnout. We used this as a way of eliciting data about their perceptions of organizational motives and the degree to which they felt cared for. They were largely ambivalent about the degree to which their employer cared about them. Most believed that their organization made the right noises about ensuring people didn't burn out, but in practice tended to take a passive, reactive stance on work/life balance; they acted in a crisis or when asked to do so. Some mentioned their employer had set up systems to try and prevent burnout but few would be willing to use them because of an endemic lack of trust in the organization's motives. Indeed in some organizations there was a stigma attached to seeking the support that was available. Overall, most felt that their organization saw burnout as a sign of weakness and failure. The degree to which individuals would be willing to be open about burnout was thus severely qualified, as was their trust and emotional engagement in the organization.

## Career derailment or development

Burnout was an entirely destructive experience for most. It normally led to the early derailment of a career from which it took considerable time and resources to recover. For those stuck in a chronic, self-destructive cycle, derailment often occurred much later. Holger's story from Chapter 1 illustrates the first and Tim's the second. Derailment in this context can range from being removed from the high potential talent pool, being passed over for promotion, leaving the organization, or needing to take medical leave of absence. Whatever the cause, derailment involved the 'non-voluntary cessation of career progress in that organization'.[43] For a very few, burnout was catalytic and led to a transformation of the way in which they made sense of and behaved in the world.

## Change in identity

Put in simple terms we define identity as answering two questions:

- Who am I? My current sense of self, both my inner life – the quality of interaction I have with myself – and my outer life – the quality of interaction I have with others.
- What am I here for? Those aspects of my life that provide me with meaning and purpose.

Those who burnt out experienced either an irreversible change in their sense of identity or their identity became stuck and stopped evolving. Burnout rocked high flyers' worlds – either in a positive direction, by spurring them to review the core constructs making up their identity, or in a negative one, by making them more externally referenced and less able to see the individual choices open to them.

## The stigma of burnout

'We have a lot of young people between 25 and 35 and it's not really accepted to be stressed out, like, it's seen as a weakness. There was one girl who burnt out and was away from work for half a year. When I heard people talk about her, it was more like, "Oh, what is she doing…?"' The high flyer paused and then continued despondently, 'Round here there is a mentality that taking time off for stress is a sign of failure, of not being up to the job…'. We were conducting research interviews in the Scandinavian office of a prestigious professional services firm. The high flyer's lament was a familiar one for us by now, particularly among Northern Europeans and Anglo Saxons. The majority of those we interviewed felt their employers had a low tolerance for their high flyers admitting to burnout or showing symptoms that resulted in a decline in performance due to work pressure. For many, disclosing that they were experiencing burnout symptoms amounted to an admission of failure. They felt it would give their organizations sufficient cause to remove them from the high flyer talent pool. They would no longer be seen as having high potential. Such a prospect was seen as tantamount to career suicide. As a consequence, a strong subculture of fear and lack of openness had developed among high flyers within some of the organizations we visited. It was not seen as safe to disclose how they felt to those inside the organization because of the potential impact on their careers. It was regarded as decidedly risky to seek support or counselling. And for some – those working under the most incredible pressure, in workplaces where the atmosphere was described as intense and unbearable – it was even perceived to be dangerous to go on holiday. We heard stories of high flyers who called into the office once or twice a day during a vacation because they feared colleagues would blame them if something went wrong.

Burnout stigmatizes those who experience it. It is understood by high flyers to be materially different and more destructive than stress and it is feared. It is feared because it is perceived to be on the cusp of that other last great workplace taboo, poor mental health.

But burnout also stigmatizes organizations. In today's market, employer brand is a key attractor for the many talented professionals they need to recruit. Employers invest considerable time and money in developing their 'employee value proposition', the organization's unique offer that defines what employees will get from working for it. So being labelled as little more than a 21st century sweat shop is like raising a white flag in the war for talent.

As a consequence, burnout has become the elephant in the room. Everyone knows that high flyers run the risk of flying too close to the sun and, like Icarus, crashing and burning, yet no one wants to talk about it. We have a conspiracy of silence in which organizations and their high flyers are so concerned about the consequences of 'coming out', they prefer to remain mute but bleeding.

## Conclusions

In this chapter we have made the case that burnout is not merely attributable to the social environment at work, but is in part the result of individual volition. It is our firm belief that while the organization creates the conditions for burnout to occur, it is the individual – through his or her own choices – who determines whether they burn out or not.

We needed first to examine the term 'burnout', which – with its beginnings as a social construct rather than as a clearly defined academic one, and its somewhat 'zeitgeisty' air – has been used indiscriminately to cover pretty much anything from anxiety to total collapse. We characterized burnout by reference to its key components, principally: high motivation, relative youth, a demanding work situation over a prolonged time period, extreme exhaustion, distress, disillusion, dysfunctional behaviour, an inability to cope and – ultimately – paralysis. Our research showed burnout to emerge from the individual's relationship with their work, and to manifest both psychological and physiological symptoms. We found that burnout brought about a reduction in the high flyer's performance but that, contrary to the prevailing orthodoxy in burnout research, this often went unnoticed by the individual. We also found evidence of addictive behaviour (often insidiously sanctioned by organizations' overly-high expectations).

The fact of burnout emerging from the individual's relationship with their work we found highly significant. We agreed with Cooper et al that burnout was transactional: 'neither in the person nor in the environment but in the relationship between the two'.

We distinguished burnout from stress, chronic fatigue syndrome and depression in two key aspects: the negative attitudes and behaviours to which it gives rise, and an inherent failure to adapt, resulting in chronic malfunctioning. We observed that some people insist they are suffering from burnout despite the absence of symptoms, or the manifestation of a different, often more immediately threatening, condition. To claim one is burning out is, after all, considerably more sexy than discovering one has chronic fatigue syndrome or clinical depression. Such is the evocative power of the term that some people claim ownership of it even when presented with evidence to the contrary. We also noted that the national cultural context had an important bearing on the way in which symptoms were manifest.

The consequences of burnout for the individual were also distinct: psychosomatic issues, reduced engagement, development versus career derailment and a change in sense of self-identity. For most, the latter had a negative effect, rendering them less able to make personal choices. For a few, it spurred them on to review their notion of their identity. We will discuss these more fully in Chapter 4.

Workload and time pressure was clearly the most significant of the workplace stressors that create the conditions for burnout, followed by leadership style (over-demanding, unsupportive, inconsistent) and a workplace characterized by competitive politics and gossip. In this context we considered the important role of stigma in burnout, concluding that it is stigma, both to individuals and to organizations, that has given rise to the damaging conspiracy of silence that surrounds the phenomenon.

Thus we arrived at our observation regarding the part played by the individual in their own burning out: that it is not the situation that is the primary cause of burnout, but the way in which people interpret and handle it. We outlined the three most important driving factors for the vast majority of burnouts: over-identification with work (Clarkson's 'dysfunctional closeness'), a sense of purpose built on fame and recognition and a failure to self-interact (reflexivity), which we will discuss in more detail in Chapter 4, together with the data behind our assertions.

In the next chapter we consider the many financial and other consequences for organizations of ignoring burnout, and look at why they should remove their heads from the sand on this issue.

## End notes

1  Freudenberger, H.J. and Richelson, G. (1980). *Burn Out: The High Cost of Success and How to Cope with It*. London: Arrow Books
However, this book was preceded by Freudenberger's 1974 paper entitled, 'Staff Burnout'.
2  Maslach, C. (2001). 'Job burnout.' *Annual Review of Psychology*, vol. 52, pp397–422
3  Schaufeli, W. and Enzman, D. (1998). *The Burnout Companion to Study and Practice*. London: Taylor and Francis
4  Schaufeli, W. and Enzman, D. (1998). *The Burnout Companion to Study and Practice*. London: Taylor and Francis
5  Schaufelli, W. and Enzman, D. (1998). *The Burnout Companion to Study and Practice*. London: Taylor and Francis
6  Schaufeli, W. and Enzman, D. (1998). *The Burnout Companion to Study and Practice*. London: Taylor and Francis
7  Cooper, C.L., Dewe, P.J. and O'Driscoll, M.P. (2001). *Organizational Stress: A Review and Critique of Theory, Research, and Applications*. London: Sage; Maslach, C. (2006). 'Understanding job burnout', in A.M. Rossi, P.L. Perrewe and S.L. Sauter, *Stress and Quality of Working Life: Current Perspectives in Occupational Health* (pp37–53). International Stress Management Association, Information Age Publishing
8  Schaufeli, W. and Enzmann, D. (1998). *The Burnout Companion to Study and Practice*. London: Taylor and Francis
9  Schaufeli, W. and Enzman, D. (1998) quote the following studies: Mor and Laliberte (1984), Birch et al (1986), Poulin and Walter (1993a); Cordes, C.L. and Dougherty, T.W. (1993) in 'A review and an integration of research on job burnout', *Academy of Management Review*, vol. 18, no. 4, pp621–56, cite links between age and emotional exhaustion in the following literature: Anderson and Iwanicki (1984) Gold (1985), Russell et al (1987), Zabel and Zabel (1982). Cooper et al (2001) claim few studies have found a consistent correlation between age and burnout. However, this assertion is based solely on a 1996 review by Leiter and Harvey into research among mental health workers.
10  Brewer, E.W. and Shapard, L. (2004). 'Employee burnout: a meta analysis of the relationship between age and years of experience.' *Human Resource Development Review*, vol. 3, no. 2, pp102–23
11  Schaufeli, W. and Enzman, D. (1998). *The Burnout Companion to Study and Practice*. London: Taylor and Francis

12  Schaufeli, W. and Enzman, D. (1998). *The Burnout Companion to Study and Practice.* London: Taylor and Francis
13  Maslach, C. (1982). *Burnout: The Cost of Caring.* Englewood Cliffs, NJ: Prentice Hall
14  Pines, A.M. (1993). 'Burnout: An existential perspective,' in W. B. Schaufelli, C. Maslach and T. Marek (eds), *Professional Burnout: Recent Developments in Theory and Research.* London: Taylor and Francis
15  Schaufeli, W. and Enzman, D. (1998). *The Burnout Companion to Study and Practice.* London: Taylor and Francis
16  Schaufeli, W. and Enzman, D. (1998). *The Burnout Companion to Study and Practice.* London: Taylor and Francis
17  Jamal, M. (2005). 'Burnout among Canadian and Chinese employees: A cross-cultural study.' *European Management Review,* vol. 2, pp224–30; Schaufeli, W. and Enzman, D. (1998). *The Burnout Companion to Study and Practice.* London: Taylor and Francis; Cooper, C.L., Dewe, P.J. and O'Driscoll, M.P. (2001). *Organizational Stress: A Review and Critique of Theory, Research, and Applications.* London: Sage
18  Schaufeli, W. and Enzman, D. (1998). *The Burnout Companion to Study and Practice.* London: Taylor and Francis
19  Cooper, C.L., Dewe, P.J. and O'Driscoll, M.P. (2001). *Organizational Stress: A Review and Critique of Theory, Research, and Applications.* London: Sage
20  Cooper, C.L., Dewe, P.J. and O'Driscoll, M.P. (2001). *Organizational Stress: A Review and Critique of Theory, Research, and Applications.* London: Sage
21  The Maslach Burnout Inventory or MBI is the most widely used psychometric research tool to identify job burnout.
22  The MBI version used in this study was the GS. Because percentage scores are easier to understand than other scores we decided to convert the 1 to 6 fit to a burnout profile on the MBI GS to a percentage fit, as follows:

- MBI-GS scores were calculated for each survey respondent for EX, PE and CY.
- Each score was categorized as Low, Medium or High based on the ranges suggested for categorization in the MBI Manual.
- The total number of steps by which each categorization differed from the high burnout profile was calculated for each scale. For example, the high burnout profile includes a High score on Exhaustion. If a participant's score was also High on Exhaustion, the number of steps was 0; if the participant's score was Medium, the number of steps was 1; if the participant's score was Low, the number of steps was 2.
- The total number of steps by which the participant's profile differed from the high burnout profile was calculated by summing across dimensions. For example, if the participant's profile was the same as the high burnout profile (High on Exhaustion and Cynicism, Low on Professional Efficacy), the total number of steps was 0. If the participant's profile was the opposite of the high burnout profile (Low on Exhaustion and Cynicism, High on Professional Efficacy), the total number of steps was 6. The total number of steps could range from 0 to 6.
- The total number of steps was subtracted from the maximum (6) to obtain a Burnout Profile Fit Score for each participant. These scores could range from 0 to 6, with high scores indicating greater fit with the high burnout profile.

- The Burnout Profile Fit Score (BPFS) was then converted to a Percentage Fit with Burnout Profile Score (PFWBPS) by using this formula: PFWBPS = 100 X BPFS/6. The PFWBPS scores have a possible range of 0 to 100.

23  Rosinski, P. (2003). *Coaching Across Cultures: New Tools for Leveraging National, Corporate and Professional Differences.* London: Brealey

24  Hong, H.V. and Hong, E.H. (eds) (2000) *The Essential Kierkegaard.* Princeton: Princeton University Press

25  Maslach, C., Jackson, S. and Leiter, M. (1996). *Maslach Burnout Inventory Manual* (3rd edn). California: Consulting Psychologists Press

26  Argyris, C. (1991) 'Teaching smart people how to learn.' *Harvard Business Review,* vol. 69, no. 3, pp99–109

27  Argyris, C. (1991) 'Teaching smart people how to learn.' *Harvard Business Review,* vol. 69, no. 3, pp99–109

28  McCall, M. (1998). *High Flyers: Developing the Next Generation of Leaders.* Boston: Harvard Business School Press

29  Blakeley, K. (2007). *Leadership Blind Spots and What to do About Them.* San Francisco: Jossey-Bass

30  McCall, M. (1998). *High Flyers: Developing the Next Generation of Leaders.* Boston: Harvard Business School Press

31  Grattan, L. and Pearson, J. (1994). 'Empowering leaders: are they being developed?', in C. Mabey and P.A. Iles (eds), *Managing Learning.* London: Thomson Learning

32  Iles, P. (1997). 'Sustainable high-potential career development: A resource-based view.' *Career Development International,* vol. 2, no. 7, pp347–53, quoting Kaplan, R.M. (1990). 'The expansive executive.' *Human Resource Management,* vol. 29, no. 3, pp307–26.

33  Goodman, A. (1990). 'Addiction: Definition and implications.' *Addiction,* vol. 85, no. 11, pp1403–408

34  Watzlawick, P., Weakland, J. and Fisch, R. (1974). *Change: Principles of Problem Formation and Problem Resolution.* New York: Norton

35  Scott Peck, M. (1978). *The Road Less Travelled.* London: Arrow Books

36  Cooper, C.L., Dewe, P.J. and O'Driscoll, M.P. (2001). *Organizational Stress: A Review and Critique of Theory, Research, and Applications.* London: Sage

37  McManus, I.C., Keeling, A. and Paice, E. (2004). 'Stress, burnout and doctor's attitudes to work are determined by personality and learning style: A twelve-year longitudinal study of UK medical graduates.' *BMC Medicine,* vol. 2, no. 29. The authors say that 'High perceived workload and poor support are therefore determined as much by doctors themselves as by specific working conditions.' That view was expressed in another article in the special edition of *BMJ Careers*: 'A critical element contributing to the stress that many conscientious doctors experience is internal ...'. A similar conclusion was reached in a previous study of ours when these doctors were PRHOs, and multi-level modelling showed that stress is not a characteristic of jobs but of doctors, different doctors working in the same job being no more similar in their stress and burnout than different doctors in different jobs.

38  Schaufeli, W. and Enzman, D. (1998). *The Burnout Companion to Study and Practice.* London: Taylor and Francis

39  Clarkson, P. (1989). *Gestalt Counselling in Action*. London: Sage

40  Shirom, A. et al (1997). 'Effects of work overload and burnout on cholesterol and triglycerides levels: The moderating effect of emotional reactivity among male and female
employees.' *Journal of Occupational Health Psychology*, vol. 2, no. 4, pp275–88.
This study of healthy employees in Israel focused on chronic stress and used a construct validated definition of burnout that did not confound it with depression or
other affective states. The authors found that burnout elevated the level of cholesterol.
This corroborated earlier research (Appels and Schouten, 1991) implicating burnout
as an independent risk factor for coronary heart disease.

41  Chandola, T. et al (2008). 'Work stress and coronary heart disease: What are the mechanisms?' *European Heart Journal*, vol. 29, pp640–48

42  Schaufeli, W. and Enzman, D. (1998). *The Burnout Companion to Study and Practice*.
London: Taylor and Francis

43  McCall, M. (1998). *High Flyers: Developing the Next Generation of Leaders*. Boston:
Harvard Business School Press

# 3

# On committing corporate suicide

*Call on God, but row away from the rocks.*

HUNTER S. THOMPSON

In the last chapter we outlined the results of our research into the nature and prevalence of burnout. We also detailed some of the causes and consequences. The implications for the organization are profound. Burnout affects around 20% of the emerging high potential talent pool, regardless of the nationality of high flyers or the culture of the country in which they are working. Derailment is the inevitable consequence for most of these individuals. This is preceded by a drop in performance and productivity together with commitment to the job and the organization. Most become disengaged from the job and difficult to work with. They develop a range of psychosomatic conditions which can lead to medicalization and prolonged absence. Attempts to get them to change self-damaging behaviour will be frustrated by a lack of awareness of their condition or the consequent decline in their performance. If they leave the organization – and many will – they are likely to project their anger onto their former employer, causing reputational damage to the brand. As former high potential 'stars' their opinions are likely to carry more weight, and they are likely to be more resourceful in how they transmit these views. Over time this will negatively impact on the image of the organization among would-be new hires. It will also affect the emotional engagement of those high flyers left in the firm. Given enough time it will dilute bench strength and adversely impact succession plans. Job burnout can thus effectively jeopardize talent management strategy and succession planning and threaten the retention, commitment and productivity of high flyers.

The burning platform is obvious. Burnout represents a serious threat to the retention, growth and productivity of your top talent. Ergo, bang goes your leadership pipeline and your succession plan. One would assume that having invested considerable sums of time and money in selecting these people, companies would assiduously protect this valuable resource for the future. And yet it appears that often this couldn't be further from the truth. We explore the reasons why this happens at the end of this chapter. But first we take a look at the rationale for identifying flyers in the first place. We then go on to outline some current, global employment trends that provide a backdrop to help us better understand the threat to high flyers from burnout. Finally we explore the corporate consequences of burnout in more detail.

## Why have high flyers?

For most multinationals and national flagship companies this might appear a somewhat inane question. How else, after all, can you ensure a reliable supply of talent for senior leadership positions? However, there is a body of opinion that holds otherwise. The proponents of this stance maintain that investment in leadership development should be applied to the 'many' rather than 'the few'. Bill Drath at the Centre for Creative Leadership, for instance, believes that leadership is 'a communal capacity' for 'communal achievement'. It is 'located in the processes through which people relate to each other, rather than the characteristics of the individual'.[1] In Drath's view, leadership is a property of the social processes of the organization and thus distributed at all levels.[2]

Others come from a more ideological and less informed perspective. For them, high flyers are wrong because the concept is elitist and offends their deeply held personal values about parity and fairness. Ideology often lends itself to simplistic solutions. We imagine that the existence of burnout among high flyers could easily be used as an argument for not having high flyers in the first place. No high flyers, no burnout. As practitioners in the field of leadership development for many years, we believe the debate about whether an organization should invest in the few or the many is largely an academic one. In practice, it's not a case of either/or, but both/and. We applaud the work of Drath and others in challenging the prevailing business paradigm and its over-proscriptive focus on ensuring a succession pipeline and leadership capability at the top. At the same time, the identification and nurturing of the leaders of tomorrow makes absolute business sense. To fail to do so, an organization would have to believe that its future senior leaders would somehow magically emerge. In other words, we are back to that old corporate myth that the cream always rises to the top. Patently it doesn't. The organizations who act on the misguided belief that it does, usually become the victims of their own folly in the long run. We present some examples of where this has happened later in this chapter. By far the best and most powerful explanation of the foolishness of what Morgan McCall calls 'right stuff thinking' – the idea that developing leaders in a process of selecting those with the 'right stuff' and then finessing these pre-existing qualities through trial by fire – is given in his book, *High Flyers*.

The rationale for identifying high flyers is to create and sustain business competitive advantage by:

■ creating a pipeline of leadership talent to supply senior leadership positions over time, ensuring it is sufficient to fund both leakage and business growth
■ providing the developmental experiences required to prepare people for the challenges they will face at the top of the organization.

We believe the last point to be pivotal. Since the cream doesn't just rise to the top, the organization needs to focus developmental effort on those most able to learn from the experiences provided and who aspire to the risks and pressures that high office will bring (surprisingly, not everyone does). The kind of developmental experiences required to grow a future CEO are materially different in nature from those required at other levels. In summary, the point of having high flyers is so that the organization can target its efforts on growing the next generation of senior leaders on people who are open to learning what needs to be learnt and whose values and aspirations are in line with the requirements of executive leadership.

What are the business benefits of high flyers? Over the last decade there has been considerable research into the relationship between talent management and corporate performance, culminating in a body of evidence proving the link between investment in high potential leaders and the delivery of strong results for shareholders. The now-famous 1998 study by Sibson and Company and McKinsey showed a direct link between the quality of succession management and shareholder return.[3] A 2003 Hewitt Associates survey[4] of 100 large US companies found that those companies performing in the 75th percentile or higher of total shareholder return (TSR) consistently used a formal approach to identify high potential leaders. A subsequent McKinsey study demonstrated that total returns to sale of companies best at talent management were 22.4% higher than industry averages.[5] Hewitt's 'Top Companies for Leaders' research consistently demonstrates a linkage between what it calls a 'fanatical focus on developing top talent' and better financial performance. All of the top performing companies in the 2005 study – identified by their strong leadership practices as well as a combination of financial measures including three- and five-year return on equity, revenue growth and total shareholder return – emphasized the identification and development of high-potential leaders. Sixty two per cent of top quartile performing companies identify high potentials early in their careers, compared to only 35% of other companies.

However, companies do not generally seem very smart at identifying leadership talent. A 2002 Conference Board report showed that only 34% of companies are effective at identifying capable leaders early in their career.[6] Inevitably this leads to problems with the leadership pipeline. A Corporate Leadership Council survey of 4,000 hiring managers in more than 30 companies found that approximately three-quarters of companies worldwide are not confident in their ability to effectively staff strategic leadership positions over the next five years.[7] To make matters worse, organizations do not seem to know how many of their high flyers are actually leaving.[8]

## Global employment trends

In the popular parlance of our times, organizations are suffering from a crisis of public trust. The well-publicized financial scandals of recent years, coupled with repeated examples of declining business ethical standards and outrage at 'fat cats' salaries, have taken their toll on the public's perception of big business. Hollywood has mirrored this zeitgeist by depicting business leaders as self-seeking and avaricious in films like *Wall Street, The Insider, Erin Brokovitch* and many more. In the psyche of those who have lived through the corporate re-engineering, downsizing and delayering of the past few decades, organizations are soulless wastelands whose leaders are hell bent on maximizing shareholder value and personal wealth at any cost. As an example, one of us worked for a well-known IT company in the early 1990s who actively pursued a strategy of firing employees in their 40s and 50s and replacing them with young graduates, referring to this process as 'ventilation'. As a result many employees, including high potentials, have adopted a guarded and instrumental relationship in their dealings with employers. The expectation of the post-modern organization that people should bring the whole of themselves to work, that they should emotionally and psychically invest in the job, is often a forlorn one. Indeed, some commentators believe that the breakdown of the old psychological contract between organizations and their employees has created a new class of 'corporate avengers' with no loyalty to their company, displaying cynicism, selfishness and self-interest alone. High potentials in particular may use their new found marketability as "me plc" to leverage their position and rewards'.[9]

In his book *Meaning Inc*, Gurnek Bains tell us that large sections of the working population lack genuine engagement and commitment and that business leaders are becoming increasingly frustrated because the old ways of gaining the cooperation of the workforce just don't seem to be working anymore. This is hardly a surprising outcome given the employment experience of so many during the eighties and the nineties. What is surprising is that this should come as a shock to some employers when many either neglected their duty of care for their people or simply never felt they had such a duty. We suspect these were the same organizations who, like the IT company we referred to above, were making a big noise about their people being their greatest assets while simultaneously 'ventilating' them.

Unsurprisingly, opinion polls repeatedly report low levels of trust in business leaders,[10] along with declining levels of job satisfaction and employee engagement. A 2007 Conference Board report[11] described the continuing fall in job satisfaction levels among the US workforce over the previous two decades to a point today where less than half of all Americans are saying they are satisfied with their jobs.

At the same time, we are told that the 'war for talent' is intensifying. A McKinsey Quarterly Survey of 9,300 global business executives[12] rated 'finding talent' as the biggest challenge facing managers. Additionally, 73% cited cost and availability of talent as a significant constraint on growth. In addition, when the Corporate Executive Board conducted an international poll of senior human resources managers, 75% of them believed that attracting and retaining talent was their company's number one priority.[13]

The survey also spoke to 4,000 hiring managers in more than thirty countries and was told that the average quality of external candidates had declined by 10% since 2004. More than a third of these managers said they had hired below-average candidates merely to fill a position quickly. And this situation is set to get worse as the population gets older. By 2025 the number of people aged 15 to 64 is projected to fall by 7% in Germany, 9% in Italy and 14% in Japan. Companies in the USA are expected to lose more than 50% of senior managers in the next five years due to the retirement of ageing 'baby boomers'.

Meanwhile those coming onto the labour market have very different expectations of work. As Madeleine Bunting puts it, 'They view the working culture of their parents with horror'.[14] Most feel little connection with 'the work hard, play later' attitude of earlier generations and what they see as an obsession with work to the detriment of every other aspect of life. Social networking sites and blogs are the preferred medium through which these views are expressed. The following examples of views expressed about one prestigious professional services firm are taken from the website Urban Dictionary (www.urbandictionary.com):

*A ... firm which hires bright young college graduates and converts them into arrogant, stuck up, lifeless souls who are proud of the fact that they are working 80-hour weeks, despite being paid at an hourly rate lower than the average McDonald's toilet cleaner.*

*From many accounts [firm's name] is the last form of slavery in the US. This is where many young people begin careers and work 115 hours a week until they either quit or die from exhaustion. Former [firm's name] employees often have scarred backs from the whip marks.*

Clearly, such robust opinions are likely to tarnish an organization's brand and its image in the marketplace, making its employee value proposition less than credible.

This generation of employees seeks meaning beyond the corporate mantra of career advancement and a slow rise up the greasy pole. To attract them and keep them engaged, some companies are beginning to offer a very different employee value proposition – one that provides more meaningful work that is linked in some way towards the achievement of a purpose other than purely maximizing shareholder return; a more balanced perspective on the place of work in one's overall life; and power and authority structures that genuinely engage them.

The trends outlined above present organizations with considerable challenges to how they relate to their workforce. The diminution of trust over a prolonged period, together with changing expectations of the 'psychological contract' has led to more savvy, less forgiving and more demanding employees for whom companies must demonstrate they have a 'licence to operate' as an employer and who must earn the right to win their people's engagement and commitment.

If companies get this right they will distinguish themselves from competitors and extend their competitive advantage in the market. Only on this basis can they focus on identifying and developing their top talent employees; those with the greatest potential to grow into strategic leadership roles. Unfortunately many companies do not know how to define 'talent'. Some use the term to mean high flyers while others, 'employ it as a synonym for the entire workforce, a definition so broad as to be meaningless'.[15]

# Consequences of burnout for organizations

## The financial and productivity impact of burnout

Burnout is a pervasive phenomenon that conservatively affects 20% of the top talent pool. The empirical data presented on the prevalence of burnout among high flyers presented in Chapter 2 is supported by our consulting experience. More often than not, our coaching of high flyers revolves around how people organize themselves to manage the pressures they are experiencing. The annual staff surveys of those organizations to which we have consulted regularly identify work/life balance as a very significant issue. Sixty per cent of respondents in one professional services firm reported that their work schedule did not allow them sufficient flexibility to meet their personal or family needs.

Burnout adversely impacts the financial performance of organizations by:

- reducing the engagement, commitment and retention of high flyers. Ultimately this can lead to the loss of high flyers from the organization either through resignation, medicalization or termination of employment
- reducing the productivity, health and wellbeing of high flyers
- presenting substantial risk management issues for the brand, market image and public reputation of the organization
- jeopardizing the talent pipeline and succession management.

The financial impact of burnout can be considerable. A 2005 UK study revealed that burnout is having a direct impact on the bottom line and the corporate reputation of 15% of UK businesses,[16] with more than a third of employers reporting a decline in productivity and the majority seeing an increase in the number of sick days being taken. There is considerable, indirect experience of burnout among UK employers with more than a third claiming they witnessed colleagues experiencing burnout. The study goes on to say that UK businesses increasingly feel burnout is affecting their bottom line by contributing to a loss of talent and damage to corporate reputation and profitability.

## Calculating the financial impact of burnout

As we have previously mentioned, burnout can be viewed as a form of early career derailment. Prior research has estimated the cost of derailment on a range between high and very high. A study by the Corporate Leadership Council calculated the cost to be $275,000 (as of the year 2000) in terms of search firm fees, severance, wasted salary and so on, without including indirect costs such as lost productivity and the impact on morale both in the employee's own team and other parts of the organization.

However, a more precise calculation of the actual costs of burnout to the organization is achievable. This calculation is made possible by, firstly, our ability to define the difference in value between the performance of high flyers and others, and, secondly, our ability to discern different phases in the progression of burnout affecting high flyers.

## Defining the difference in value

Most organizations define high flyers as those who have the potential to rise to the highest levels of the organization. Invariably, such people are required to be performing at a consistently high level and to be rated as superior performers – the top 10%. We know from the work of Hunter, Schmidt et al[17] that the difference between average and superior performers is one standard deviation in performance. Dependent on the complexity of the job, one standard deviation is worth between 19% and 48% of output for non-sales jobs, and 48% to 120% for sales (see Figure 3.1).

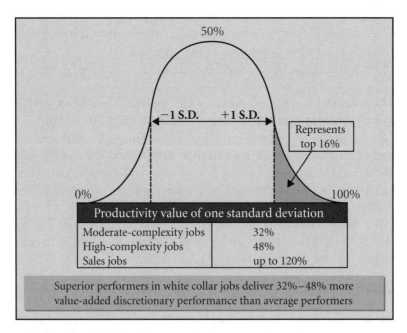

**Figure 3.1**   What superior performance is worth. *Source*: J.E. Hunter, F.L. Schmidt, and M.K. Judiesch, 'Individual differences in output variability as a function of job complexity'. *Journal of Applied Psychology*, 75 (1990) pp 28–42. Reprinted with permission of John Wiley & sons, Inc.

---

**Partial withdrawal**

Between 48% and 120% reduction in performance output (i.e. operating at the equivalent output of an average performer), lacks engagement and commitment to the job and the work/mission of the organization.

**Full withdrawal**

100% reduction in performance output, plus health insurance costs from long-term sickness absence. Remains employed and may return to work.

**Total loss**

Exits the organization, no possibility of return, severance costs, rehire costs at circa five times total cash compensation for the job plus opportunity costs, costs of lost productivity and impact on productivity of own team and morale of wider organization.

---

**Figure 3.2**   Three-phased impact of burnout on the organization

Since high flyers are likely to be in high complexity and sometimes sales roles, it is safe to assume that they produce between 48% and 120% more value-added discretionary performance than average performers. So, for example, a professional services employee who is professionally qualified, has three to four years' experience, and is performing at an average level might be billing client fees of £500,000 per year. An outstanding performer in the same job (someone who is likely to be seen as a high flyer), might be billing between £750,000 and £1.1 million.

## Different phases in the progression of burnout

We have identified three phases in the progression of burnout affecting high flyers which will be discernable to the organization (see Figure 3.2). Partial withdrawal is the stage when high flyers first show signs of burnout. Full withdrawal represents a later stage of collapse in the job. And total loss is a final stage (at least as far as the organization is concerned) in which the high flyer exits the organization.

Using our understanding of what superior performance is worth and the progressive phases of burnout, we can calculate the financial impact of the condition based on the following data:

- the average salary of the high potential cohort in question
- the average productivity output of an average performer in the jobs held by high flyers, expressed in financial terms (this is invariably

easier to calculate for client facing roles; however, it is possible to calculate for internal/non-client roles using a little imagination)

■ the average total cash compensation for the high potential cohort in question

■ the average value of the base investment or sunk costs for the high flyer cohort in question (e.g. costs of hiring, induction and integration, training, professional qualifications etc.).

## A worked example

We can show how this calculation is made using the example of the professional services employee we mentioned above. We said that this high flyer is professionally qualified and has three to four years' experience.

*Average salary: £45,000*
*Average productivity output of average performer in role: £500,000*
*Average total cash compensation: £55,000*
*Average value of base investment: £88,000*

*Organizational cost of burnout:*

1  *Phase one – partial withdrawal: £305–£655,000*
   *This is composed of:*
   ■ *Deterioration of performance to that of an average performer, so a 48–120% drop in productivity output or £250–£600,000 per annum.*
   ■ *The cost of other people having to do the work that is not being done – around a year's work, £55,000.*
2  *Phase two – full withdrawal: £332,500–£682,500*
   *This is composed of:*
   ■ *The cost of partial withdrawal above plus the cost of up to six months' leave on full pay, or £27,500.*
3  *Phase three – total loss: £607,500–£957,500*
   *This is composed of:*
   ■ *The cost of 1 and 2 above plus rehire costs of around five times total cash compensation,[18] or £275,000.*

In addition to these costs one would normally factor in sunk or base investment costs. This would produce the following *total costs of burnout to the organization* across the three phases:

1  £393,000–£743,000
2  £420,500–£770,500
3  £695,500–£1,045 million.

Note that none of this takes into account either the damage done to the organization's reputation and its image in the labour market, residual damage such as potential litigation costs arising from the mistakes made by the high flyer that is burning out or the impact on morale both in the employee's own team and other parts of the organization.

## *Other indicators of the financial impact of burnout*

Outside of our research, there are far more reports of the financial impact of occupational stress than there are of job burnout. According to a survey by the European Foundation for the Improvement of Living and Working Conditions, stress is the second most common health symptom reported by European workers.[19] Prior to the accession of the new Eastern European states, the European Union estimated that work-related stress affected at least 40 million workers in its (then) 15 member states at a cost of 20 billion euros a year.[20] Workplace stress is a huge problem for British workers. In 2007 the British Health and Safety Executive (HSE) estimated that the British economy lost 13.8 million working days as a result of work-related stress, anxiety and depression, with losses in terms of productivity levels of up to £3.7 billion annually.[21] A 2007 HSE survey of working conditions indicated that around 13.6% of all working individuals thought their job very or extremely stressful. In 2004/2005 the HSE estimated that around half a million people in Britain believed that they were experiencing work-related stress at a level that was making them ill.

Occupational stress is estimated to cost the USA more than $300 billion each year in absenteeism, accidents, employee turnover, reduced productivity, health care and workers' compensation, according to the American Institute of Stress in New York.[21] The US National Institute for Occupational Safety and Health has calculated that workers who report that they are stressed incur health care costs that are 46% higher than other employees.[22] In a national survey conducted by the Northwestern Life Insurance Company, 25% of employees viewed their jobs as the number one stressor in their lives and seven in ten indicated that job stress was causing frequent health problems and decreasing their productivity. The American Academy of Family Physicians found work-related stress to be the greatest cause of poor health and they estimated that 50 to 80% of serious illnesses (heart disease, strokes, ulcers, cancer, chronic headaches, diabetes and depression) have stress-related origins. According to a survey of 800,000 workers in over 300 companies, the number of employees calling in sick because of stress tripled from 1996 to 2000. An estimated 1 million workers are absent every day due to stress.[23]

A study by global recruitment and HR consultancy Hudson in 2005 revealed a widespread acceptance among employers and employees that the phenomenon of burnout is real and present in the current UK working environment.[24] More than 96% of employees believed burnout to be an issue for the UK workplace (compared to 92% of employers) and half of these had noticed an increase in extreme workplace stress and fatigue over the last five years. One in seven of the HR managers interviewed had lost one or more members of staff due to burnout and over a third of employers had witnessed a decline in productivity. Employees engaged in accountancy, technology, media and telecommunications and financial services were more likely to believe burnout existed within their sector whereas those working in manufacturing and engineering and marketing, advertising and sales were less likely to believe this.

## The reputational and risk management impact of burnout

In many ways the financial impact of burnout is the least of employers' worries. Much more serious is the risk to the brand and the organization's image in the marketplace resulting from negative publicity from former and existing employees as well as the possibility of litigation. The rise of the internet and the speed with which reputation-bruising news stories can bring global organizations to their knees (or at the very least force them to make a humiliating U-turn, witness the recent Facebook campaign run by UK university students against HSBC, should not be underestimated).

The danger to organizations from litigation due to burnout is very real and recent court rulings in Europe have reinforced this. In February 2007 computer-chip maker Intel lost an appeal against a UK court ruling that found the company had been negligent in allowing an employee to suffer debilitating work-related stress. Although Intel provided a counselling service, the court held that this did not absolve it from liability, as the counselling service could not reduce the employee's workload. Effectively this means that the provision of an employee assistance programme is not a panacea and does not eliminate the employer's duty of care for its employees. In an earlier ground-breaking UK court case[25] the High Court ordered the employer to pay damages to an ex-employee on the grounds that they had a duty not to cause their employee psychiatric damage by giving him too much work and/or insufficient back-up support. The former employee's solicitor estimated that the cost of the employer's management failure was over £400,000, made up of damages, trial costs, sick pay and medical retirement. These and other similar cases have largely produced out-of-court settlements of between £25,000 and £203,000.

In Italy, judgements by the Corte di Cassazione (the third most important court in the Italian legal system) have dealt with stress. The court determined that an incident in which a worker was run over by a car when he was going to catch the bus home at the end of his working day was a work-related accident. It was found that the worker was suffering from stress and crossed the road without looking because he had done a long working day. In another case the court found that the employer should compensate a worker for a heart attack caused by an excessive workload resulting from staffing cuts, which forced the worker to work excessively long hours.[26]

## The succession management impact of burnout

Burnout's negative impact on high flyer engagement, sometimes leading to departure from the firm, has long-term consequences for leadership bench strength. High flyers in burnout are likely to become 'unengaged stars'.[27] These are employees with a lot of aspiration, ability and potential but who – as a result of burnout – no longer feel an emotional connection with their work or the organization and feel suspicion for organizational motives. As a result they have considerably less likelihood of being successful at the next level of the organization – some estimates put it as little as 13%.[28]

As we saw in Chapter 2, organizational attitudes towards burnout affect the levels of trust and emotional commitment high flyers have in their firms. Because of this, high flyers working for organizations with little perceived tolerance for burnout (our research suggests this is most organizations) tend to be highly committed to their jobs and their careers, but much less committed to the organization for which they work. Prior research has shown that 'the extent to which employees value, enjoy, and believe in their job, organization, team, and manager' is the most effective way of motivating employees towards higher performance. Indeed, it has been found to be four times more effective than building people's rational commitment – the degree to which they believe it serves their best interests to continue working for the organization through such things as pay and promotion prospects.[29]

However, because of its long-term nature and the fact that it occurs in early career it is difficult to directly attribute burnout as a cause of later problems in succession management in the higher reaches of the organization. Nevertheless, it is highly likely that burnout's depletion of high flyers in early career will adversely impact succession planning; particularly as we know from the research on talent management that organizations are notoriously bad at providing enough suitable successors for each critical role. Indeed expert experience says that the same three to five names often tend to get recycled for multiple positions in the succession plan.[30] What is burnout's contribution, we wonder, to the succession management crises witnessed over recent years at the likes of Merrill Lynch, Barclays and the UK's Network Rail?

---

**Head of leadership development at Network Rail reveals lack of succession planning after Hatfield disaster**

HR at Network Rail was so bad in 2004 that there were no plans in place to replace the executives facing corporate manslaughter trials over the Hatfield disaster, it has been revealed.

Marc Auckland, head of leadership development at the privatised track maintenance firm, spoke last week of his shock at the lack of people management when he joined three years ago.

He told delegates at a talent management conference run by Symposium Events that Network Rail received the world's lowest ever score on the Q12 employee engagement questionnaire – the benchmark standard developed by business information firm Gallup. 'There was total disengagement and morale was very low,' said Auckland. 'Performance management was sporadic there was no consistent approach.'

In 2005, three Network Rail employees faced corporate manslaughter charges over the October 2000 train crash in Hatfield that killed four people and injured 70.

'That shows the responsibilities that go with leadership,' said Auckland. 'I asked at a governors' meeting about successors to the people in court and got blank looks all round.'

Auckland was stunned by the lack of logic to the ensuing argument over succession planning and drew up a three-year leadership development plan to change the company's culture.

Employees are now analyzed, tracked and put through an in-house training centre. 'We now have a world-class training set-up,' he said. 'Morale has improved and there is an internal talent pool that gives managers more choice when they interview for roles.'

Source: Greg Pitcher, Personnel Today, 9 May 2007

## Ignorance is bliss?

'You've probably guessed that burnout is a big issue for us...we'll defi-nitely come back to you on this.' The female HR manager from the big American investment bank had spent the last hour taking copious notes as she quizzed me for information about our research. But her assurances were unconvincing, as were her motives for asking for the meeting. By this point we assigned companies to one of three categories. There were those who would simply not respond, or for whom our research never managed to become a priority. These companies accounted for the major-ity. Then, there were those who, like the investment bank, would pump us for information under the guise of an interest in the research. And finally, there were those who were genuinely interested and took part – in all, 5 of the 40 companies we contacted.

So why did so few companies participate in the research? At first we thought it was due to our inability to present a believable business case. But when we presented at business conferences we drew big audiences who overwhelmingly understood and supported the case we were mak-ing. We believe there are several reasons for companies ignoring the impact of burnout on their high flyers, and in the process committing the equivalent of corporate suicide.

- Existing research literature makes two fallacious assumptions about burnout that get in the way of organizations doing anything about it. The first is that job burnout is primarily caused by characteristics of the work as well as the organization; it is 'the social environment in which people work'[31] that is the problem. These characteristics include work overload and time pressure, insufficient resources or authority, leaders who fail to support, recognize, provide feedback or include their people in decision making and a perceived lack of fairness in the way in which people are managed. It is also caused by a lack of 'fit' between the values and aspirations of the individual employee, their jobs and the organization for which they work.[32] The second is that burnout is a negative experience with negative outcomes that needs to be prevented. This is best accomplished by building employee engagement with both the work and the organi-zations that employ them.

  Consequently, tackling burnout means changing the way organi-zations are structured and led. Implicitly it means reducing work-loads and helping employees find greater work/life balance. For most organizations – particularly those with an aggressive growth strategy – such ideas may appear naive and counter-intuitive. They are likely to be dismissed out of hand. Since organizations are the primary culprits, individuals are not implicated. In fact, according to the prevailing research paradigm, there is very little individual responsibility for the burnout experience. Burnout is something that happens to people. There is no room for individual volition.

Our experience of burnout – as well as that of our research participants – was markedly different from this. To a greater or lesser extent, we contributed to what befell us. How therefore does one account for the current nostrum that burnout is largely a function of the work environment, rather than of the individual? The notion was developed by researchers with a strong social psychological perspective and this may have overly influenced their research findings.

- We recently came upon a review of a book about a fashionable new office disease that claimed that burnout had become socially acceptable.[33] The authors of the book[34] believe that stress (and one assumes by implication burnout, since they reference the two terms interchangeably several times) is 'socially desirable' because it makes someone important and 'it is funny to talk about stress'. Presumably the authors' eagerness to embrace popularity and attention-grabbing headlines had encouraged them to present a simplistic portrait of burnout. Unfortunately this portrayal of burnout as a faddish affliction has gained popular currency and is in danger of trivializing the condition (and persuading companies they need do nothing about it). If burnout is little more than a catch-all term that can be used by people of all ages, across all work environments to mean they are more than a little bit stressed, it has lost any connection with the scholarly research that has proven it a distinct condition. This reduces the potency to influence businesses that it needs to be managed. Those who, like the authors of the fashionable new book, claim that burnout is socially desirable have no experience of burnout and equally are strangers to robust research. In simple layman terms that would presumably appeal to them and their reviewers, they need their heads examining!

- In his book, *High Flyers*, Morgan McCall refers to organizations holding the 'misleading assumption...that people with the right stuff will, through the process of survival of the fittest, eventually rise to the top.' He goes on to say,

*assumptions like this encourage organizations and their leaders to neglect without guilt their investment in executive development...believing that the fittest will survive without much nurturing, organizations not only overlook people with the potential to develop but also frequently and unintentionally derail the talented people they have identified as high flyers by rewarding them for their flaws, teaching them to behave in ineffective ways, reinforcing narrow perspectives and skills and inflating their egos.*

Our experience in designing and leading high-flyer programmes for multinational corporations leads us to conclude that this is indeed the prevailing paradigm guiding the way in which organizations think about the development of their leaders. The unspoken belief is that leadership is a genetic trait that can be identified and used to select the leaders of the future. Thus, you don't so much develop leaders, as put them through a series of trials by fire to work out whether they've really got what it takes. As a consequence, the pressure on the individual high flyer to measure up to exacting performance standards and the organization's cultural norms about leadership is immense. Inevitably then, high-flyer programmes create conditions which cannot help but have negative consequences for the development and wellbeing of high flyers; and in which job burnout is an inevitable consequence for some.[35]

Faced by such a range of reasons for organizations not to take burnout seriously it is tempting to adopt a dogmatic mindset. Organizations really should accept their responsibilities for the health and wellbeing – mental as well as physical – of their people. They should stop being distracted by the faddish pseudo-science that populates the shelves of airport book stores. They should embrace a more developmental, mature and strategic approach to building leadership capability. But in our experience this kind of sanctimonious hectoring alienates senior managers and fails to bring about the change it desires. The model of change we advocate in this book is to accept how things are and attempt to work inside them (in the knowledge that time and opportunity will eventually bring about more fundamental change). Thus, we encourage the reader to notice that at this present moment in organizational history there are a constellation of beliefs in common currency that have destructive consequences for some high flyers. The point is not how do we stop organizations from believing such things, but how do we manage the development of high flyers within this existing paradigm? And how do we help organizations develop their capability to retain and manage the careers of high flyers?

## Conclusions

We gave this chapter its title because we believe that 'corporate suicide' is no less than an accurate description of what is going on. By neglecting to attend to the phenomenon of burnout, organizations around the world are damaging, even destroying, themselves, while simultaneously ignoring a body of evidence clearly proving the link between investment in high-potential leaders and share performance.

Before making the business case for organizations to take notice of burnout, we considered the fundamental question of whether they should actually bother focusing on high flyers at all. Although respectful of the view which holds that investment in leadership development should be applied equally to all, we took the position that identifying and nurturing the leaders of tomorrow makes absolute business sense. Doing so sustains competitive advantage, both by creating a leadership pipeline and by preparing individuals for the challenges they will face as part of that pipeline.

We then contended that brutal business practices in the past few decades have resulted in a breakdown of the psychological contract between organizations and their employees. We also found that the bulk of newcomers to the labour market have rejected the values of their parents, and seek meaning and purpose in their work beyond merely maximizing return for shareholders.

The chapter went on to consider the financial consequences of burnout for organizations: reduced engagement and ultimate loss of high flyers, reduced productivity, risk management issues for brand and reputation, and jeopardized succession management. We showed how the impact of job burnout on high flyers can be estimated at three distinct stages in the process: first signs, collapse in the job and leaving the organization. And we looked at studies that have put a cash figure on the cost of this form of early career derailment.

Quite apart from the direct financial consequences of burnout, however, we noted the much more serious risk posed by negative publicity and possible litigation. We also concluded that long-term consequences to leadership bench strength were very considerable, albeit that, because of its tendency to happen early in careers, burnout is difficult to attribute as a direct cause of later problems.

This brought us to the mistaken assumptions behind why organizations are so prone to ignoring burnout. The first was that burnout happens to people simply as a function of the work environment – whereas our own experience and research shows that people actually contribute to their burnout. The second was the belief that leadership is simply a genetic trait, which we also reject. We also noted a regrettable fashion for blurring burnout with stress and labelling both as socially acceptable – we hope this book may help stop that one in its tracks!

Unfortunately, the financial and other impacts on businesses of burnout, unlike those of occupational stress, have hitherto been under-researched. In this chapter we attempted to redress that imbalance by making it clear why organizations should remove their heads from the sand and pay close attention to burnout. In the next chapter we present the findings from our research into the individual's contribution to their burnout – how they organize themselves in ways that put them at risk of the condition – and the consequences of them doing so.

## End notes

1 Burgoyne, J., Boydell, T. and Pedler, M. (2005). *Leadership Development: Current Practice, Future Perspectives.* Corporate Research Forum
2 Drath, W. (2001). *The Deep Blue Sea: Rethinking the Source of Leadership.* San Francisco: Jossey-Bass
3 Chambers, E.G. et al (1998). 'The war for talent.' *McKinsey Quarterly,* vol. 35, no. 3, pp44–57
4 Hewitt Associates (2003). 'Building high potential leaders.' Lincolnshire, Illinois: Hewitt Associates
5 Axelrod, E., Handfield-Jones, H. and Welsh, T. (2001). 'War for talent (Part 2).' *McKinsey Quarterly,* no. 2
6 Barrett, A. and Beeson, J. (2002). *Developing Business Leaders for 2010.* New York: The Conference Board
7 Corporate Leadership Council (2000). *Challenges in Managing High Potential Employees: Results of the Council's Membership Survey.* New York: The Conference Board
8 'Talent management strategies are stuck in the past.' www.management-issues.com 7 November, 2003.
    'Fully half of the organizations surveyed did not know the current staff attrition rates amongst their defined top talent, while there is also little external benchmarking of standards against the very best in any chosen industry, sector or discipline.'
9 Iles, P. (1997). 'Sustainable high potential career development: A resource-based view.' *Career Development International,* vol. 2, pp347–53
10 An Ipsos Mori poll in 2006 asked 2,074 members of the British public which profession they trust to tell the truth. The survey found that 31% trusted business leaders, above politicians and journalists (at 20 and 19% respectively) but below policeman at 61%
11 Conference Board Report (2007). *US Job Satisfaction Declines.* New York: The Conference Board
12 *McKinsey Quarterly Survey* March 2005
13 Corporate Executive Board Report in A. Woolridge, 'The battle for brainpower: A survey of talent.' *The Economist,* October 2006
14 Bunting, M. (2005). *Willing Slaves: How the Overwork Culture is Ruling our Lives.* London: Harper Perennial
15 Woolridge, A. (2006). 'The battle for brainpower: A survey of talent.' *The Economist,* October

16 Hudson (2005). *Burnout Britain: Raising the Alarm for Employers.* www.hudson.com

17 Hunter, J.E., Schmidt, F.L. and Judiesch, M.K. (1990). 'Individual differences in output variability as a function of job complexity.' *Journal of Applied Psychology,* vol. 75, pp28–42

18 Research has estimated that replacing an executive costs conservatively five times the previous incumbent's total cash compensation. See for example: Smart, B. (2005). *Topgrading: How Leading Companies Win by Hiring, Coaching and Keeping the Best People.* New York: Portfolio

19 Paoli, P. and Merllié, D. (2000). *3rd European Survey of Working Conditions.* European Foundation for the Improvement of Living and Working Conditions

20 Koukoulaki, T. (2002). 'Stress prevention in Europe: Review of trade union activities – obstacles and future strategies.' *TUTB Newsletter,* no. 19–20

21 Health and Safety Executive (2007). 'Stress related and psychological disorders.' www.hse.gov.uk/statistics/causdis/stress

22 Schwartz, J. (2004). 'Always on the job: Employees pay with health.' *The New York Times,* 5 September

23 American Institute of Stress. 'Job stress.' See website www.stress.org

24 Hudson (2005). *Burnout Britain: Raising the Alarm for Employers.* See website www.hudson.com

25 Walker versus Northumberland County Council (1995)

26 Llorens, C. (2001). 'Work-related stress and industrial relations.' *European Industrial Relations Observatory Online.* www.eurofound.europa.eu/eiro/index.htm

27 This term was coined in a 2005 report by the Corporate Leadership Council. Corporate Leadership Council (2005). 'Unlocking the full value of rising talent: Capturing returns on the identification and development of high-potential employees.'

28 Corporate Leadership Council (2005). *Unlocking the Full Value of Rising Talent: Capturing Returns on the Identification and Development of High-Potential Employees.* New York: Corporate Leadership Council

29 Corporate Executive Board (2007). 'Improving talent management outcomes.'

30 McCall, M. (2005). 'Identifying and developing leadership talent globally'. ICEDR HRD Leadership Programme

31 Maslach, C. and Leiter, M.P. (1997). *The Truth about Burnout: How Organizations Cause Personal Stress and What to do About It.* San Francisco: Jossey-Bass.

32 Maslach, C. and Leiter, M.P. (1997). *The Truth about Burnout: How Organizations Cause Personal Stress and What to do About It.* San Francisco: Jossey-Bass.

33 Boyes, R. (2007). 'Forget burnout, boreout is the new office disease.' *The Times,* 15 September

34 Rothlin, P. and Werder, P.R. (2007). *Boreout!: Overcoming Workplace Demotivation.* London: Kogan Page

35 Snipes, G. (2005). 'Identifying and cultivating high-potential employees.' *Chief Learning Officer.* www.clomedia.com
'There are concerns regarding the pressure organizations put on high potentials. If the process is not monitored carefully, high potentials can burn out.'

# 4

# How to burn out

*A man's got to know his limitations.*

Clint Eastwood, *Magnum Force*

## Introduction

In this chapter we explore burnout from the perspective of the individual:
how do individuals bring about burnout, or contribute to it, and what
determines whether or not they do burn out? This chapter will be particularly useful to anyone who believes they may be going through the process of burnout themselves.

We'll look first at the particular characteristics that make some high
flyers more prone to burnout than others, specifically the nature of their
identity, their sense of purpose, and their reflexive ability. We'll then focus
on the individual consequences of burnout – in particular the possibility of derailment on the one hand as against personal development on
the other, and the change in identity that occurs as a result of burnout.
The chapter will go on to examine the characteristics of those high flyers
who don't burn out – how they organize themselves differently compared
with those who do – before we ask what significance and purpose burnout represents in an individual's life and what to do, and not to do, if you
think you are burning out.

## Is there evidence for personality
## as a cause of burnout?

What does the literature say about personality as a cause of burnout?

Of the more than 5,500 studies conducted on burnout, just over 100
include personality characteristics. Most adopt a psychodynamic or Five-
Factor Model of personality.[1] Hence the concern of these studies is with
genetically inherited and enduring traits of personality which cause people

69

to burn out, rather than with a more developmental, humanistic-focused model of burnout in which people make choices that lead them to burn out. Taylor and Cooper, for example, identified a 'stress-prone personality' as one which experiences low levels of hardiness, an external locus of control and an avoidant coping style.[2] Schaufeli and Enzman posit that neuroticism – which comprises anxiety, depression, hostility, self-consciousness and vulnerability – predisposes employees to experience burnout.[3]

In addition, several theoretical psychological approaches, some of which explain burnout in terms of people's intra-personal processes, have been put forward to explain the phenomenon. According to Freudenberger, burnout occurs when 'super-achievers' fail to retain their idealized self-image.[4] Similarly, Fischer felt that the basic sense of self-esteem of those who experience burnout is based in the narcissistic illusion that they are special and superior.[5] Expanding this theory, Glickauf and Mehlman argued that those who experience burnout suffer from low esteem and are emotionally dependent on others, due to the inadequacy of early childhood experiences.[6]

For Pines, people's career choices are influenced by unconscious forces that propel them to re-enact and overcome difficult childhood experiences. The goals and expectations they have when they enter their career are related to these unconscious forces and are expected to provide them with existential significance for their lives. When people fail to achieve these goals, they burn out.[7]

However, few of these theoretical approaches are supported by empirical evidence. In addition, they all come from a psychodynamic or adapted psychodynamic orientation.

## How people determine whether or not they burn out

We concluded in Chapter 2 that although it is organizations that create the conditions for burnout, it is the individual who, through his or her own choices, determines whether they burn out or not. It is not the situation that is the primary cause of burnout, but how people handle it; or as the Greek philosopher Epictetus put it in the 1st century AD, 'It is not the things themselves which trouble us, but the opinions that we have about these things'.

### Two characteristics driving burnout

In Chapter 2 we briefly outlined the two individual characteristics which are the most important driving factors in the vast majority of burnout cases: a sense of identity largely derived from work and career (coupled with a tendency to centre the purpose of life on the acquisition of fame and recognition), and a poorly developed or interrupted reflexive ability.

Before we look in detail at our research findings and their implications for the individual high flyer, we need to look first at the notions of identity and reflexivity that informed them.

## Our approach to identity

The notion of identity we used incorporates a narrative approach to the creation of the self as well as weaving in perspectives from Symbolic Interactionism, a sociological perspective that holds that our identities are socially formed. We also used elements of a Gestalt and a Formative psychological perspective, as well as the ideas of sociologist Norbert Elias. That approach can be described as follows.

Identity does not come to us ready-made. It is not inherited from our parents, from God or from anyone else. Identity has to be proactively formed; the individual has to actively create it. This act of creation is done through story – the narrative we create about ourselves. As Keleman puts it, 'Formed or personal self is not a given, it needs to be encouraged…in organizing a self, one acquires an identity, a somatic image going by a name'.[8] So effectively, we come to know who we are through the stories we tell others and ourselves about ourselves, and how we embody this in our somatic form.

We construct our stories or personal myths 'to bring together the different parts of ourselves and our lives into a purposeful and convincing whole'.[9] In other words, these stories perform the task of giving our lives 'meaning, unity and purpose'.[10] They emerge out of our growing awareness about our patterns, our way of making contact with the world and ourselves and the boundaries we establish with our environment. They answer the questions 'Who am I?', 'Why am I here?' and 'What is my purpose in life?'.

The stories are constructed within a social context. They are based on our experiences in the social world in which we live – how we handle social interactions with others, how we perform and act in this world in relation to others. This sense of who we are shifts over the course of life as our stories evolve. Our identities are thus socially created. It is the social context – our interactions with others – that provides us with the material on which our stories are based.

## Our approach to reflexivity

Reflexivity is the process through which we create those stories. It is us having conversations with ourselves. It is a process of 'self-interaction', allowing us to take control of our lives – to make choices – and not simply to respond to external stimuli. We discuss, evaluate and interpret what comes towards us and act upon this interpretation. Reflexivity helps us avoid simply ingesting other people's ideas, beliefs, values and personalities. It helps us to ensure that the material we use to compose our stories is also based on our interaction with others – particularly those we regard as significant – rather than solely and solipsistically on what sits between their ears.

Reflexivity is the defining human quality that separates us from the rest of the animal kingdom. Reflexivity 'alone can yield and constitute a self...With the mechanism of self-interaction the human being ceases to be a responding organism whose behaviour is a product of what plays upon him from outside, the inside, or both. Instead he acts towards his world, interpreting what confronts him and organizing his action on the basis of interpretation.'[11] Reflexivity is the chewing over of our reflections of experience: 'We do not simply respond to stimuli but act back on ourselves – discussing, evaluating, holding back...'.[12]

Reflexivity is not the same as reflecting. Reflecting is only getting to first base. Reflection is done in the head. Reflexivity is done in the head, the heart and the gut. It involves making sense of things at an emotional and an intuitive level as well as an intellectual one. As a result we produce a visceral interpretation of what is coming towards us that moves us to do something about it. It is a three-step process. It involves us creating meaning of the conversation we are having with ourselves about our experience; listening to ourselves making this meaning; and finding the will to act on the meaning we have created. Sometimes we don't listen, and we fail to realize or understand the meaning we have made. It is only when we share our inner dialogue with others who notice the meaning that has bubbled up for us, that we are able to absorb our own sense-making. Figure 4.1 illustrates the process.

There is some physiological evidence that this sense-making process genuinely occurs in the heart and the gut as well as the brain – it is not just a metaphorical figure of speech. Research at the Institute of HeartMath and elsewhere has identified three major neural networks in the body – in the brain, in the cardial sack and in the intestinal track.[13]

Reflexivity is, then, the process through which we construct our identities. Reflection produces the raw material for reflexivity to work on. Someone who is very reflective – but not reflexive – may think a great deal, but their thinking will have little impact on their story, which fails to evolve, as do they.

The process of composing our story is not constant. We are constantly talking to ourselves, but we do not constantly redefine ourselves. We

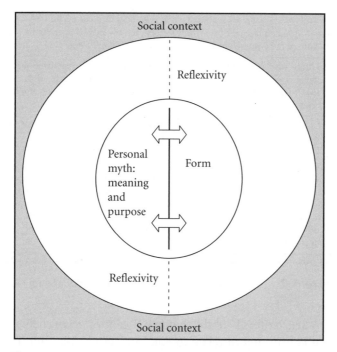

**Figure 4.1**  The relationship between identity and reflexivity

experience ourselves differently at times depending on the quality of our connection with ourselves, our environment and how we are relating to others, but unless this experience of 'differentness' is prolonged then we go back to our story. Over time our interactions with significant others and reference groups create material for our story that reconfirms it over and over again. We incorporate material from our reflexive process that supports the story we have already created about ourselves.

Our story is not immutable. We revise it as we move through the different stages of adult maturation and development. Different stages in life create a need for our stories to have a different focus. As young adults our stories are more likely to be concerned with defining an ideology or belief system by which we might live – what is true and good. In our twilight years we are likely to be more concerned with how we can pass on the torch to others. Of course, maturation is a choice like everything else in our lives. It is not a given either. Thus our stories may still be those of young adults even though we are in our 50s.

Our story also changes when we experience prolonged changes in the nature and patterning of our relations and interactions with others. We require certain kinds of responses from significant others and reference groups in order to sustain our story, our identity. When these responses

> Identity is not a given; it has to be proactively formed, actively created by the individual. It requires courage to be your own person and not simply a layer of bricks.
>
> We come to know who we are through the stories we tell others and ourselves about ourselves, and how we embody this in our somatic form. These stories perform the task of giving our lives 'meaning, unity and purpose'. They answer the questions: Who am I? Why am I here? and What is my purpose in life?
>
> Our stories and thus our identities are constructed within a social context; our sense of self is socially created.
>
> Reflexivity is the process through which we construct our stories, our identities.
>
> We revise our storied identity as we move through to a new stage of adult maturation and as the nature and patterning of our relations and interactions change over time. On a day-to-day level we experience ourselves differently at different times depending on the quality of connection with have with ourselves, our environment and how we are relating to others. This will not affect our storied identity unless this experience of differentness is prolonged.

**Figure 4.2**    The approach we have taken to identity and reflexivity

change, our sense of self subtly changes: 'I cannot go on being the same me without continuing to relate to you in a certain way, and if that way shifts we are both a little different'.[14]

Maybe we associate ourselves with new reference groups or significant others. Perhaps our external environment brings about a general change in the way in which people relate to one another. Or perhaps we experience transition or crisis and are forced to confront aspects of our identity that have outlived their usefulness. At this point we allow our inner dialogue to throw up dissonant material that causes our story to change.

It must be stressed that identity changes *over time*. We are not amorphous, diaphanous amoebas whose identities are in a constant state of flux, dependent upon the nature and quality of our relating. Our stories become embedded. They are us. We revise them as the context of our lives change, as we mature and as our social context changes. But it takes considerable energy and determination to reformulate them to a significant degree outside of this process.

The approach we have taken to identity and reflexivity is summarized in Figure 4.2.

## The findings of our interview research

Our interviews and the other data we collected on those burning out highlighted two principal findings – that they over-identified with work and that they lacked a well-formed sense of purpose. These two main themes are explored at length with verbatim quotes from our interviews to provide a sense of what it is about those who burn out which leads them to do so.

## Over-identifying with work

The first finding is that over-identifying with a rather narrowly defined attachment to work is exacerbated by a lack of well-developed boundaries, a cavalier attitude to bodily and emotional wellbeing, and an addiction to action.

Ninety-four per cent of the participants who experienced burnout, or who showed symptoms of incipient burnout, over-identified with their work or career to the extent that they forgot about – and often sacrificed – their emotional, physical or spiritual needs.

Csilla, a high-flying human resources manager, felt she had no identity and had no sense of herself without her job, which made her feel very alone: 'My confidence levels at work and as a woman are opposites. That level at work is very high, but...It's like hiding behind a mask, a good excuse. I feel comfortable working hard, even if it's stressful, because it hides the fact that...I'm on my own'.

This over-identification means that identity is largely derived from work and career. As a consequence, participants had a fragile sense of identity. Or to put it another way, they had little inner sense of the self, since identity was largely externally-referenced.

This over-identification was manifest in a number of ways.

First, there were *few or no boundaries*. Individuals were willing to make sacrifices for the sake of the job and career advancement, even though this often involved personal hardship. One participant put it succinctly: 'Even though you're working crazy hours, you keep going because of the interest you have in the work – the challenge and adrenalin'.

Lack of boundaries was also manifest by an inability to say no or to push back, often resulting in taking on work beyond the capacity to deliver. Csilla described this process:

*I felt that if I said no to opportunities, which were quite few, then I wouldn't get another. So I took them, and that was great development for me...but I pushed my boundaries so much that I physically hurt. I pushed my personal life into minus. My friends were telling me for the last six or eight months, 'Csilla you have to take care...don't do that Csilla,' but I just didn't hear the warnings, and I carried on.*

Jack explained how he found himself in a situation to which he had agreed but which left him vulnerable because of his lack of experience:

*I would come in maybe at seven o'clock, and then have half an hour – if I was lucky – to familiarize myself with any issues before being questioned quite aggressively, and then questioned again just before I went home. This happened every day, and it became harder and harder to keep on top of things. I found myself going into the boss's office not knowing enough to be able to talk confidently. I was winging it.*

Second, there was a *cavalier attitude towards bodily or emotional needs*. Keith said: 'I don't eat properly, I don't do enough exercise. I have to drive a lot for work, so that's not easy. But if I didn't do it I'd be letting people down, never mind myself….'.

These high flyers were usually driven by a need to prove themselves to others at work. It was as if their best was never good enough, particularly for themselves. They therefore behaved as if forever on the brink of losing an important career opportunity, or their status as high flyers, or even their actual job.

Fiona described how she stepped in to do her boss's job on an interim basis but kept on doing it even after her new boss arrived:

*It felt manageable because it was for a finite period. I felt a sense of pride, and I didn't really want to let it go. I genuinely thought I was doing the right thing – giving her some space to come in, but also wanting to take some of the space myself. It was very definitely driven by ambition: I wanted to prove myself.*

Jack's ambition led him to make himself vulnerable at times. He hid his inexperience from others in the hope that it would get him ahead in his career:

*I'd never done a construction project before and I actually didn't know what I should be doing. But I pretended that I did. There was a lot of expectation on me. I'd got a good reputation from what I'd done on the project so far and I was worried about losing it.*

It will come as no surprise that many of our participants were self-confessed perfectionists, who strove for standards that even they admitted were sometimes too high.

Third, there was an *addiction to action* – an urge to breathe urgency into almost every working situation, no matter what its real importance. Multiple tasks were undertaken with little or no thought of longer-term consequences for the individual or others. Decisions were made impulsively, often to avoid deep reflection. There was a strong sense of immediate goals, and lots of drive and energy to achieve them, but little underlying understanding of why all this activity was taking place.

The response of Fatima to a situation in which she felt unable to delegate work to her subordinates is illustrative:

*They were not doing things properly. I was all on my own. I was really under pressure, but I coped. All I did was to work for about two months without any days off, with maybe three or four hours sleep a day – I solved the situation by putting in extra effort. I felt upset at the beginning, but after my boss talked to me I felt happy and relieved. I told myself I needed to do more and more to prove to him that I would not let him down, that he had put his trust in the right person.*

## Loss of self

Participants tended to blur boundaries between their personal and professional lives to the extent that the personal and the professional became indistinguishable. They therefore lost a sense of their own identity and needs, creating a co-dependent relationship with the job (see Figure 4.3). This 'dysfunctional closeness'[15] meant they agreed not to disagree with the sometimes unreasonable demands made of them by bosses, colleagues or clients.

Angus, a British policeman on an accelerated development programme, told us how he went along with advice that involved him being bullied by a superior. 'I was told: "Don't worry, it's all a game. You're about to get another kicking but it's just a game, to satisfy him." So I went to see him and I got a right good verbal kicking, and I just had to sit there and take it, because they don't encourage you to stand up for yourself.'

Vadimir described the expected response to work demands: 'We were expected to say yes to everything. Obviously you could try to refuse, but you'd lose credibility. I think it was the level of demand that was significant.'

Fiona spoke of her difficulty in talking to her boss about her increasing level of distress. 'For whatever reason, I didn't go and speak to her early enough. I guess I had permission, but I wanted to show her that I

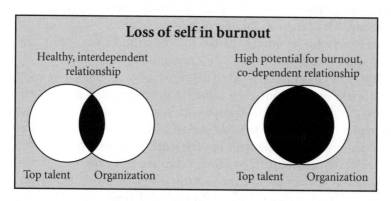

**Figure 4.3**   Loss of self in burnout

was capable so I continued to take work on and I felt I didn't have anyone to talk to about it anymore…'

If individuals did push back, they often felt obliged to apologize for it. Ingeborg told of her difficulty when leaving one project to spend time on another: 'Sometimes I just had to leave. I would go at around six and say: "I have to go now, I'm sorry…" and this happened several times over a few days when we were working on two projects at once. I just had to say: "I have to leave, its really important, sorry".'

### Some of those who didn't burn out also over-identified with work

A small proportion of research participants manifested some symptoms of burnout and appeared to derive their identity primarily from work and over-identified with it – 5% of the total research sample. They appeared to derive their identity primarily from work and yet never got to the tipping point where they actually burnt out. Sigrid put it thus: 'You don't know if the bosses expect you to work these kind of hours, and you're not sure they even see it if you do. You do it of your own free will. But at the same time, I think girls in this company and in this country are too kind: we never say no. And that's a problem'.

That said, these individuals did tend to repeat patterns of behaviour that were psychically and interpersonally difficult. Kylie ended up working for a boss with a reputation as a bully. 'I was warned that she was a nutter. People said everyone worked 20 hours a day and hated each other, and it was all because of her. But for me the pros were getting into head office and networking. It was obviously going to be hugely broadening for me.' Holger told us: 'I needed to delegate more, but it wasn't easy, as every one already had too much to do. So I often ended up doing it myself. Maybe delegating was too difficult, or maybe I wasn't strong enough. I would say, "OK, I'll do it". I'm too nice'.

We believe these individuals fall into our third category of burnout: joyless depletion. But why don't they actually burn out?

Our research doesn't provide a definitive answer. Their response to the Work Stress Survey (our own self-assessment questionnaire measuring the ways in which individuals cope with severe stress which we described in Chapter 2) indicated that they each claimed to possess some well-developed ways of coping with intense work pressure. For most, this was not noticeably different from others who had not experienced burnout, and who did not appear to over-identify with their work. However, some had several (two or more) such well-developed dimensions. We wondered if the reason they had not burned out was because of the absence of other causes of burnout. But each described their work environment as intensely pressurized and challenging. Equally, they seemed to have a sense of purpose that – like those who did burn out – was based on a need for recognition and fame.

In the end we concluded that it was a matter of degree. Some appeared to have a slightly more developed sense of self – either in terms of boundary setting or what they stood for. Others had several more well-developed coping behaviours that saw them through chronic periods of severe stress.

## The organization's contribution to over-identification

We also explored the organization's contribution to the development of over-identification by high flyers in their work. During the eighties and nineties we saw the increasing encroachment of organizations into what was previously deemed to be people's private lives – 'In the post-modern organization, individuals bring more of themselves (their ideas, their feelings) to their work. In Hirschorn's terms, "they are more psychologically present" '[16] – culminating in the rise of the 'absorptive corporation', which attempts to take over people's hearts and minds and even their souls, their innermost identities.

A great deal has been written about this phenomenon in recent years. The seminal 1998 research of Covaleski et al[17] into identity in the (then) big six accounting firms used the insights of an earlier paper by Foucault to explore how these firms used mentoring and performance management programmes to ensure that employees conformed to corporate values and culture: 'Mentoring is a technique by which junior members [of the organization] absorb, imbibe and interiorize the more subtle, tacit and non-codifiable aspects of the organization's goals' through the person of the mentor, who is normally a senior member of the organization. Mentoring 'infuses the protégé with the norms and values of the organization. Absorbing these values leads to the development of the protégé's identity'.

According to Covaleski, making individuals responsible for valued organizational goals – management by objectives – is an example of the application of a 'disciplinary technique aimed at the fabrication of a corporate clone', which effectively maps the goals of the organization into the individual. Most organizations have become knowledge-based companies over the last couple of decades, and professional services firms are considered emblematic of the knowledge-creating organization, so Covaleski's findings seemed relevant to our research.

Madeleine Bunting writes of a new psychological contract – organizations capturing people's discretionary effort by offering to provide purpose and meaning to their lives – and quotes a working paper from the Hay Group that sums this up:

> Getting engaged performance is not just about investing financially in employees through pay and benefit increases. It is about striking a new contract in which the organization invests emotionally in its workforce. In exchange, employees make a similar emotional investment, pouring their 'discretionary effort' into their work and delivering superior performance. The new contract says, 'We'll make your job (and life) more meaningful. You give us your hearts and minds'.[18]

Roger Harrison, the elder statesman of organization development and self-directed learning, presaged most of this thinking in an earlier paper based on Anne Wilson Schaef's book, *The Addictive Organization*. Harrison talked about addictive organizations using participation and employee involvement 'manipulatively and calculatingly' to win the hearts and minds of employees, and creating 'workaholic norms, such as not taking lunch breaks or vacations, or doing training and team development events on weekends'. As a result employees 'become addicted to the process of work, using it as a fix to get ahead, be successful, avoid feeling, and ultimately to avoid living'.[19]

In our research we found that over-identification was, *to some extent*, fostered by organizations – sometimes deliberately in order to form the identities of high flyers so that they personify the values of the brand, at other times unwittingly through the celebration and valuing of work addiction as part of organization norms and culture. We stress 'to some extent' because even when the organization was deliberately following a path of actively trying to form high flyers' identities, its attempts were sometimes let down by poor implementation.

Although many of the high flyers in our study were provided with a coach or mentor, only a few of these relationships appeared to inculcate the espoused values of the organization and form the employee's identity as a duplicate of the organization's. For instance, one high flyer talked about her mentor dissuading her from taking up a case of harassment because the offending behaviour was just part of the way things were done.

> My mentor's attitude was disappointing. She just said, 'Well, you know he's old school and a lot of men are like that. Sometimes you just have to take it on the chin'. She said I should go and see him, even though I didn't want to. I plucked up the courage, and told him I wasn't happy. He seemed OK about it.

However, many high flyers struggled even to meet with their mentor, either because of their own state of constant over-commitment or the mentor's.

There was strong evidence of organizations' attempts to create 'corporate clones'. Highly-performance-driven cultures evidently drove compliance with challenging performance standards. Some companies prescribed sets of competencies to identify high flyers, and then put training programmes in place for them to demonstrate these competencies in the same way and to the same level as the organization's leaders. One of the authors recalls a time when he was consulting to a major UK pharmaceutical company that had produced a list of leadership competencies which seemed to him unsustainable – all about pushing the boundary, driving exceptional performance and demonstrating extraordinary discretionary effort. The Organization Development Director confided to him that the competencies were a fantasy of the top team about how they would like to be seen themselves.

Some other companies used powerful brand cultures that attempted to inculcate organizational values into the heads of employees, thereby harnessing their emotional commitment.

And yet in all of these situations employees colluded with what was handed down to them. There was a sense of pride, of heroism, not just in working impossible hours but in belonging to a community of people who were all somehow living the same way, for the same rewards and with the same values. As Piotr put it, 'At that time that was the style of life and that was the style of work. We were pretty proud that we were part of this kind of organization. We enjoyed being professionals who worked so hard and who were so committed. It was part of the culture. There was a lot of stress, but we liked the stress'.

This phenomenon, in which organizations create highly-driven cultures that seek to provide a sense of identity and purpose and satisfy high flyers' dependency needs, in which high flyers willingly collude, is eloquently described by a Microsoft interviewee in Bunting's *Willing Slaves*:

*There's a lot of people here who get into trouble. They are addicted to Microsoft. They're in denial, but they live, eat and breathe Microsoft. It's their world. The thing is, they chose to throw themselves into something. They need to be addicted. If it wasn't Microsoft, it would be something else: they need to prove themselves. They are so absorbed by what they're doing – like Rembrandt – there's no start, no end to what they're doing. Is that Microsoft's fault? Sometimes Microsoft could be more responsible and help that person to understand they are addicted. I make my team take lunch, but a lot of people here work and work. It's a bit lame when Microsoft says it's their choice. If you have an alcoholic in the house, you don't put a bottle of gin by the bed.*

## A sense of purpose

Earlier in this chapter we described an individual's sense of purpose as being the same as their identity. We construct stories in order to give our lives 'meaning, unity and purpose'.[20] These stories form our identity, and provide answers to such questions as, 'Who am I?', 'What on earth am I here for?' 'What do I stand for?' 'To what am I really committed?'. By answering these questions, our stories give our lives a sense of purpose.

When we talk of high flyers' sense of purpose we are talking about what has been called 'the deep pulse within, the internal compass'.[21] We are talking about a profound sense of their fundamental reason for existence.

It appears to us that a clear sense of this kind of purpose is particularly important for high flyers – the future senior leaders of organizations. We agree with Pedler, Burgoyne and Boydell, that:

> *Being clear about purpose lies at the heart of leadership. This is not merely about identifying a set of specific goals or aims – it is about a deeper and more enduring sense of purpose. This more profound sense of direction is rooted in what we value, and it is what makes the risks of leadership possible and worthwhile.*[22]

### Desire for recognition and fame

High flyers' stories of dealing with chronically stressful situations revealed that those who burnt out had a sense of purpose revolving around a desire for recognition, fame and respect. Career advancement was an oft-quoted motive for their work and their reason for being. However, this was not an end in itself but a way of winning respect and recognition.

Many were profoundly motivated by the prospect of shining in front of others, and of developing their profile and reputations. Csilla told us: 'In the past when I did something I always wanted it to stand out, so that people would remember – I was always pushing myself to do that'. Suresh described what kept him going during the really stressful times:

> *There were occasions which really boosted me. For example, I got to present to the CEO for about an hour, and to talk to him about what we were trying to do. So along with the stress came some confidence that people higher up were actually looking at the project and giving us recognition. I really needed that. Every Group Vice President who visited would make a point of coming to see us, and I was leading the communication. That was a high point – it made it worthwhile.*

These individuals had a strong need for accolades, for recognition of their achievements. All were willing to sacrifice their personal life for the sake of satisfying that need. Indeed, many felt it was acceptable to damage their life and relationships with colleagues or loved ones if it produced the acclaim they desired. This neediness for and dependence on recognition appeared narcissistic, and concealed deep feelings of insecurity.

Kylie talked about a very difficult period in her career when she felt obliged to inform senior management about her immediate boss's behaviour:

*I guess there was part of me that thought: if I can do this and support the group and keep my boss in her box and give the company the information it needs, if I can negotiate this awful path it will be recognized. I don't know if that was true but I believed it at the time. I was invited to the CEO's Christmas party and my boss's boss introduced me to one of his colleagues as the person who'd had kept him sane for the last six weeks. That made it worthwhile. I believed that what I was doing was being recognized.*

## Promotion as a signal of recognition

Some of these individuals held specific goals, such as promotion, so close to their hearts that it acted as a guiding light for their every move. They were even willing to mould their personalities to achieve it. Often this short-term focus came over almost as goal achievement for the sake of goal achievement – a sort of 'because it's there' mentality. 'Without clarity of purpose – about what I/we are really here for – action can be chancy or erratic, driven by short-term, or even random, influences.'[23]

Svetlana, a high-flying manager in one of the big accounting firms, talked about wanting to become a Partner, even though she knew the level of stress for Partners was even higher than her current intense level of pressure:

*You become ambitious, and you find out that people respect you and you want that respect. The thing that has helped me progress is my determination. The minute I see the goal I'm, say, 80% sure I can reach it. But like any thought process, it requires lots of energy. So you just need to make the choice. It's the same with my engagement – once I'd made the decision to get married it was simple, but before making that decision, it was just really frustrating. It's the same with becoming a Partner. I'm 31, I need to think about my kids as well, future kids. I need to leave some time for myself. For women in this company it's even worse – no time for the kids.*

During our interview with Svetlana we asked her if she had mixed feelings about this. She replied:

*Svetlana*: You want recognition, but on the other hand you realize the price you have to pay for that.

*Researcher*: And how do you feel about the price you need to pay?

*Svetlana*: I'm not sure it's going to be unacceptably high for me. My experience tells me there's always going to be a way out of the situation. I can manage the situation and I think I'll find a way through it.

### Fixation on goals

We are reminded of a story told by our colleagues Mike Pedler, John Burgoyne and Tom Boydell in their book *A Manager's Guide to Leadership*: 'There was a traveller who, on arriving in a small town and coming across some bricklayers working on site, asked each of them what he was doing: "Laying bricks" said the first. "Building a wall", said the second. "Creating a cathedral" said the third. But a fourth, who was working a little way off, said "Serving God".'[24]

A goal is the prosaic end of a purpose, and a purpose is the esoteric end of a goal – achieving a personally important but often short-term objective, as against answering the question, 'What is my life for?'. Those whose notion of purpose is about achieving a goal are more likely to burn out, because they have an insufficient sense of meaning in their lives and thus a diminished sense of identity. 'Laying bricks only serves as a narrow purpose in the situation where there are bricks and mortar to hand; serving God can act as a direction finder in all aspects of life.'[25]

For the high flyers who burnt out, a fixation with goals was often a poor substitute for meaningful action. This accords with Megginson and Clutterbuck's separate research on goals.[26] High flyers' attachment to goals promoted a sense of intense driven-ness and activity which failed to provide a meaningful outcome. Goals 'Can be an outward form which is substituted for the thing that they are meant to be part of' (i.e. a well-thought-through purpose to which one is committed).[27]

Suresh told us about taking on a new and very challenging assignment which involved living in a separate city from his wife. He had focused on a goal with a finite timeline, but this timeline became extended:

*It's not that I didn't know it would be high stress. And I knew it would be good for my career. I was willing to invest everything in terms of time and mental energy for a concentrated period, but it's gone beyond that now and I'll probably be in the same scenario for another six or seven months. That was something I didn't expect, and which has added to the stress.*

As Pedler et al put it, 'Goals alone are not enough…The feeling becomes "I know what the goal is, but what I am here for?"'.[28] But the reckless pursuit of goals can do much worse that that. It can unhinge us mentally and lead us down a path towards our own destruction as well as that of others. By narrowing our attention goals can 'cause us to dismiss cues that do not seem relevant or helpful to their achievement'.[29]

Holger reflected on his goal of becoming a manager, which led him to work 120-hour weeks and resulted in his burnout.

*A year ago I was considering whether I should just quit or go for promotion, and I decided to go for it, do it 100%. But I was saying 'yes' to a lot of things that year – I don't think I had time for it. I used to come in at four or five in the morning and work till ten at night. Then I got sick, then I came back to the office and worked again for three or four months, then I got sick again. I could have done it the easy way and quit, and maybe that would have been better for my CV, because it's easier to get a new job than explain why you didn't become a manager in [employer's name]. But I decided to try, and of course now I have a bigger problem, because when I try for a new job I have to try to explain why this happened. I took the chance because I believed in it, and all the people around me told me, yes, they believed in me.*

For many of those who burnt out, the pursuit of goals was symptomatic of the addiction to action we have talked about earlier in this chapter. Goals represented a substitute for meaningful action and, for some, 'the use of outward busyness was a distraction from difficult unconscious material'.[30] We suspect that many of those who were burning out were using this busyness to avoid dealing with their fragile sense of identity and the debilitating sense of insecurity that went with it. As Suresh put it: 'If your ambition is to really set yourself up for something big then you have to be seen to be doing more. So you end up volunteering for a lot of work which you probably wouldn't if you weren't so ambitious'.

## Collusion with absorptive organization culture

The addictive, work-fixated, absorptive culture of many organizations ideally suits those for whom there is not a great deal of inner sense of self and who want to run away from this realization. Do they choose the organization or does the organization choose them? As in the previous Microsoft example, we suspect there is complicity on both sides. For an organization looking for new ways to emotionally engage its employees – and which believes that 'the key to raising levels of performance is to create a sense of meaning for their employees'[31] – those who lack their own sense of purpose are blank canvasses upon which the corporate brand values can be written.

The problem for those whose sense of purpose and identity is based on the achievement of goals – or 'laying bricks', to use the previous analogy – is that they are vulnerable to manipulation by the unscrupulous, and to the corporate zeitgeist of quick decision making resulting in behaviour without compassion for themselves or anyone around them. 'And this is the problem – many people do not want to be moved; they want to continue pursuing their goals. Goals "harden" us'.[32] Blakeley reminds us of Hannah Arendt's explanation of how ordinary Germans committed some of the most heinous crimes in human history by simply following their own goals – an explanation she described as 'the banality of evil'. 'Arendt used the term to show how one of the greatest evils in history could be perpetrated by people just pursuing their own small goals, obeying, conforming, and doing their jobs without asking too many questions regarding the outcomes of their actions or their responsibility to others.'[33]

*Craving for credit*

Several of those who burnt out told stories of persevering in their jobs in the direst situations, even when they had the possibility of moving elsewhere. Their motivation? To hang on in order to get the credit, the fame, or the profile, and to ensure others did not get the accolades.

But they lost part of themselves along the way. Kylie's decision to go work for a boss with a confirmed reputation as a bully just because the department was high up on the CEO's agenda is one example. The story of Mike, a high-flying architect in a world-leading international firm, is another. Mike stayed with the firm after his burnout merely to preserve his reputation. He desperately wanted to leave, but stayed until the awards were collected, so that history could not be rewritten and the benefits of the projects be credited to someone else. He felt terrible doing this – he really worked for the love of the job – and staying on made him feel 'like a prostitute'. In fact he found himself committing to a second project, which he hated.

Looking back on it, Mike realized that his decision to stay was catastrophic. He discovered the hard way that for some there is a point to which ambition will take them, before they become blinded by the goal.[34]

## The purposes of those who did not burn out

But what of those research participants who did not burn out? What is most remarkable about those individuals is that none gave recognition or career advancement as their primary purpose, and nor could this be inferred from what they said or did.

*Fascination with challenging work*

For some, recognition was still important but had become subsidiary to a fascination with the inherently challenging nature of the work and a preoccupation with doing 'interesting stuff'. Evgenia, a high-flying tax adviser in the Russian subsidiary of a multinational professional services firm, explained:

> *The level of stress is in exact proportion to the level of challenge. But this is stress and challenge in a positive way. A lot of foreign professionals who come to*

*work in our office say we're lucky, and that in London at our level they would never be given this kind of challenging work to do. When people here consider a secondment outside Russia they know the work will be crap compared to what they can do in Moscow. So, if people go on secondment it's just for their CV, or to live in another country, but not for more interesting work. Stress is the price you pay for interesting work.*

Joe provided an alternative perspective on this theme:

*The outlook is fantastic because the opportunity is so great. I've got probably the biggest single opportunity of anyone on the board – to add another £5 million of profit in the next 12 months. The opportunity is to take a department from having low stock, from being perceived as underperforming, to become one of the highest-performing teams in the business. It's huge, and that provides the motivation. As long as the motivation is there the stress can be dealt with.*

## Care for employees, family, contribution to society

Many asserted that their sense of purpose could not be primarily focused on the job because there were other, more significant calls on their reason for existing. For some this was their family; for some it was an acknowledgement that work was actually not that important of itself; others recognized that fate makes it impossible wholly to control one's career. For others it was about having a sense of service and responsibility for others, and giving back something of value to society. One of our participants explained:

*The important thing is to look after your employees, to help them solve this kind of problem [becoming over-committed]. I try to be hands-on with those who work for me, to make sure they aren't being pulled in too many directions. I always tell them to come to me before they say yes to anything, so that we can see if it fits in with the overall workload. When an exciting project comes in it's easy to say yes, but it's always good to have some support to give you some perspective.*

Joe explained why he was unwilling to stretch further an already over-stretched working day:

*I'd see less of my kids and my wife, which would be unacceptable. I've got a fantastic wife, great kids, and I'm just on the level where it's sustainable, so above all I will always maintain that. I'm very conscious of what could happen – it would be catastrophic if anything went wrong there. The real elements of stress for me comes in having to leave the office at 7 o'clock at the absolute latest, so I can spend half an hour with the kids before I read them a story and put them to bed. I can't leave work any later than that.*

Rick talked about how his sense of purpose changed after a particularly traumatic incident at work:

*Several months afterwards I realized that just because you're a bright, hardworking guy, doesn't mean everything good is going to happen to you. There are things outside your control. It was a maturing process for me: that air of invincibility was gone, and I just became more mature, and realized some of the realities of life.*

It became clear that some purposes underlying people's identities were burnout-proof, while others were more likely to lead to burnout. The former were, for instance, family, contribution to society; and the latter was typified by an ambitious desire for fame and distinction. It seems that having a purpose beyond oneself is a specific against burnout.

Because the majority of our interviewees were from the same age cohort, people's different sense of purpose cannot be put down to age or generational differences. We believe, based on our interviews with high flyers, that the differences can best be accounted for by people's level of maturation: the different developmental stage that each had reached.

## Reflexivity

In Chapter 2 we referred to the majority of those who burnt out as having poorly developed reflexivity or tending to interrupt quality self-interaction. Doing either was symptomatic of a pattern that prevented individuals from being in touch with their own needs, sensations and feelings.

We noticed that those who had been through burnout had the benefit of hindsight, and as a result were more able to make sense of the experience. But what, we wondered, happened to reflexivity during burnout? Was it performing as it should, or was it impaired in some way? We decided to focus on the reflexivity of those currently showing symptoms.

In determining people's level of reflexivity we encountered a considerable problem: reflexivity is inherently difficult to measure. Sometimes it can be detected by the general level of internal 'self-talk', as Hamish, a finance leader working for a large utility company, illustrates: 'I don't know it was saying anything to me. I don't think there was much of an internal dialogue. Lots of focus on a series of immediate problems without much time to reflect on them particularly deeply. I was physically very tired'. But generally, it is uncommon for people to reveal the nature or quality of the conversations they have with themselves.

We needed to find a way of operationalizing it in a research context. We based our exploration of high flyers' reflexivity on Torbert's model, which conceptualizes three dimensions of reflexivity: intentionality, relationality and momentary validity.[35] To this we added aspects of our own understanding of reflexivity which we felt were inadequately addressed by the original model – see Figure 4.4. These aspects mirror and build on our discussion of reflexivity at the beginning of this chapter. In particular we have focused on reflexivity not just being a rational act but needing to occur at an intellectual (head), emotional (heart) and impulse to act (gut) level. We have called this notion 'felt perception', a term that the 18th century poet and dramatist Friedrich von Schiller first came up with to mean that the manner of the act is as important as the act itself.[36]

We found that the reflexivity of many of the high flyers who burnt out appeared not to operate at all three levels – head, heart and gut – but only at one or two. Some appeared to evaluate the challenges in their environment intellectually, but there was no feeling or 'heart' assimilation of the data. Others made an emotional interpretation but seemed unable to make an intellectual or conceptual interpretation. Still others evaluated their situation at a heart and head level but failed to act on this evaluation.

Those who evaluated the challenges in their environment at an intellectual level only often came over as being very reflective. For instance, Keith demonstrated a great deal of self-awareness: 'That was a low moment, but whether I was that close to breaking point I don't know. I just absorb it and carry on. I think maybe my lack of self-perception means that if I do get to breaking point then basically it's going to have to be inflicted on me rather than something I'm going to do internally'. But this self-awareness failed to help him break his rigid pattern of not taking responsibility for his life. His reflections remained undigested.

Holger's reflections on his burnout experience indicate that he had begun to consider the possibility that his relationship with the job might be the cause of the experience. However, his reflections appear tentative and confused, and in this extract from the interview there is no sense of him owning his part of the responsibility for what has happened:

> *Researcher*: So, you took a long Christmas holiday and started to reflect on what was happening to you?
>
> *Holger*: Yes a little bit. It was the first time in seven years I thought that maybe I was working too much. But I don't think I

| Category | Positive | Neutral | Negative |
|---|---|---|---|
| **Scoring** | +1 | 0 | −1 |
| | Example | | Example |
| **Intentionality** Regards his activity as intentional on his part rather than as externally caused. One recognizes oneself as author or origin of one's behaviour even when environmental influences play a part. | I decided to do what my boss wanted, afraid of what would happen if I didn't. | | I can't help it if I get angry after a long day. |
| | +1 | 0 | −1 |
| | Example | | Example |
| **Relationality** Realizes his perceptions and behaviour change over time and in different contexts; that they influence and are influenced by others' view of a situation even in cases where his views are directly contradictory on a given issue. Will place differences within a relational context. It is possible to be very reflective and very self-absorbed. To be reflexive one needs to be aware of both self and the other. | I know, in a way that seems distant to me now, that my boss and I are both concerned to help these people, but I'm more aware right now of feeling angry with him for pressurizing me. I guess he felt I'm not concerned to help since he piled on the pressure and I wonder what I am doing to make him feel that was necessary. | | He just didn't care. His only interest was in getting the project delivered in time whatever the cost to my well-being or anyone else's. I had to protect the team from the worst of his demands. |
| | +1 | 0 | −1 |
| | Example | | Example |
| **Momentary validity** Recognition that the validity of one's behaviour extends to and is restricted to the moment of time of its performance. Concerned with whether its intentions are transformed into behaviour from moment to moment. | I felt a lot less anxious when I heard that others said they felt anxious, and I notice that I slipped back into the anxiety when I was 1:1 with my boss. | | I really think he ought to grow up and take responsibility for the mess he was causing. You shouldn't pay attention to people who try to tell you what to do. |
| | +1 | 0 | −1 |
| **Felt perception** In order to be effective, reflexivity needs to occur in the head (rationality), the heart (emotionality) and the gut (impulse to act). | I realized that although the strategy made sense, the team didn't have enough conviction to see it through, so I decided to do it myself. | | I know it was what I wanted, so I just did it. |

**Figure 4.4**  Model of reflexivity used to determine the level of reflexivity of high flyers involved in the research (based on the work of W.R. Torbert (1973) *Learning from Experience: Toward Consciousness*)

learnt anything, because I got back into my work in January and I forgot everything after a week. I started working a lot again.

*Researcher*: So what was the nature of the reflections you had over Christmas?

*Holger:* It was a bad year! I have tried many times to analyse what went wrong. Was it that things went wrong in my work? Maybe until May it could have been because of my girlfriend, because she was sick, but she died in June and I visited her family in August, which was good, so that excuse didn't exist any more. The problems with my sister didn't exist anymore because her life improved and everything was OK again. So I come back to my problems. When I started working again in September neither of these other issues existed and yet the same thing happened. I'm starting to think maybe I'm burnt out or maybe I am just very, very tired of my work and I need to change it. I'm tired of the people and everything that happened last year. Maybe it's because I can't work for them anymore because I'm just feeling that they didn't support me when I needed support – I don't know.

*Researcher:* How much of what happened to you was down to you and how much outside your control, do you think?

*Holger:* [long pause] It's a very difficult question. I don't know, I really don't know. In the beginning it was very easy to say the excuse was not me, it was things outside. It's very easy to say to your boss, 'No this problem is not the work, it's other things'. But maybe after a while you realize the problem is the job and not things outside. It's harder to tell yourself the problem is the job. It's much easier to say the problem is not the work, it's something else.

Curiously, there was little difference in how those currently experiencing burnout and those not experiencing burnout scored themselves on 'reflecting' when completing the Work Stress Survey. Indeed, those currently burning out scored themselves marginally higher than those not burning out – an average of 2.80 compared to 2.66 across the entire research sample on a 0 to 6 scale of frequency (in which zero meant that an individual never thought about their own work-related behaviour to gain understanding and insight, and six meant they did this every day). These scores also suggest that both those experiencing burnout and those not experiencing burnout perceived themselves as not being particularly frequent reflectors, since the scores indicate the behaviour taking place less than a few times a month.

Some of the high flyers who burnt out appeared very reflective, but at the same time very self-absorbed. To be reflexive one needs to be aware of both oneself and the other person. Torbert's model of reflexivity takes this into account through the dimension of relationality.

Keith's overdeveloped sense of responsibility led him into a fantasy world in which other people's real motives were not taken into account:

*That's me feeling responsible. I don't want to let other people down. Is it going to be any better if you take a day off and go in the next day? Probably not. Is it going to be any worse? Probably not. But if I start dropping days then other people who maybe feel exactly the same may start dropping days, and then the whole thing will just fall apart. It's like going down a slope: you're not quite sure where you're going to end up, but you might as well stay on the sledge going down the slope, rather than jumping off and not knowing what's going to happen.*

## Anger

Several of our high flyers – both those who burnt out and those who didn't – talked about losing their temper with colleagues and clients. Anger can be used reflexively – to usefully establish boundaries and make the seriousness of one's purpose and position clear to others, and it can also be used dysfunctionally. In the latter an individual 'loses it' and loses any subsidiary awareness of those around them, as well as any sense that they are using anger for a purpose. As a result, relationships are damaged. In a business context this can have serious financial consequences.

Earlier in this book we said that in some national, cultural or organizational contexts the expression of anger is more acceptable than in others. In exploring the use of anger in relation to reflexivity it is therefore important to compare behaviour from similar contexts. Both the following examples are taken from the same organization in Greece.

In the first example Yiannis talks about his response to a difficult client, and demonstrates a loss of relationality as well as little sense of intentionality or momentary validity:

*The client was pressing to get the report early, but I was trying to buy time. I was putting pressure on the Balkan office to send the report so I could review it before it went to the client. They sent it to me five minutes before it needed to go to the client. I said [to the client], 'I've only just got the report'. They said, 'We don't care. We don't care if it's very draft. We want it now'. So they got it. And we had a conference call with them the next day, and I still hadn't seen it. One of the people on the call – Mr K – I didn't know who he was. Next thing I know Mr K is screaming down the phone, 'What kind of a report is this?! Where are your results? This is complete nonsense!!', at which point I lost it and I started screaming back, 'Wait a second! I told you it was a working draft. I asked you to give me some more time. You said no!', and he screamed, 'Who are you to say these things! You're too young to be screaming at me!'. He didn't know who he was talking to either because at some point he said, 'Who is this person I'm speaking to?'. And I actually had to ask the same question. He got very upset and he said, 'Don't scream at me!'. I said, 'I don't appreciate being screamed at either', and that's where we left it. In retrospect, I was defending a report I hadn't read. When I read it I found out the client was right, but then I wasn't going to go against another office and say, 'Yes they did a crap job and you're right to be screaming'. The client knew me as the primary contact, which was a very bad position to be in. In order to mend the situation we had to prepare new presentations, new summaries and so on. Our costs ended up at 40,000 euros, which was a complete write off.*

In the second example Nefeli demonstrates the functional use of anger, and in the process demonstrates considerable reflexivity in all three aspects:

*In October one of the managers decided to transfer to the UK. Everyone in the office knew about this. He left at Christmas, then 15 days went past and on the 12th of January I got an e-mail from a partner saying, 'You're now the manager of one of his jobs'. I said to them, 'Why on earth, when you first found out that this person was leaving, didn't you give out his jobs at the commencement of the audit?!'. They let 15 days go by before deciding they needed a manager! I had to tell them how we'd deal with it – it was my responsibility – I couldn't just go in there just scream at them. I did scream, but I told them what I believed would be best to rectify things. I explained to them the risks of me having to complete work two months later.*

## Desensitization

Individuals experiencing burnout interrupted their reflexivity in a variety of ways, the most common being desensitization. Larissa's description of feeling robotic during her burnout experience illustrates a lack of reflexivity and lack of awareness of the moment, brought on by going without sleep and working under extreme stress:

*I kind of didn't feel myself, you know? It was me and not me, and I kind of saw myself from somewhere there, and another part of me was somewhere else! It wasn't pleasant. I was just working, travelling around all these projects. Sometimes my fiancé would bring my clothes and stuff to the airport or the train station. I didn't even go home. But you don't really feel alive. You just do it, and you don't think about your health or your emotional state or anything like that. People said it was like I was in a box. I didn't really see other people. Normally I smile and joke with people, but I didn't anymore. When I finally came into the office at the end of April, the manager said I had the syndrome of people coming back from a war! You don't get sick, or if you do you get back to work fast. I got a high temperature, up to 40°C, and I was really sick, but in three days everything was fine. The doctor said this was because of stress – how the body deals with it. You react only technically, and kind of emotionally, but it's not emotions – your emotions as a person – but your emotions as the manager, the technical person, the person responsible. It's the manager who has to do this. 'If I tell you to do this you have to – how can you not obey my orders?' It's crazy, really. And all the problems start when you lose the feeling of being human, being a person who has a life, hobbies, interests and whatever. I was lucky enough to stop and start to think about it from a different perspective. But I had to get into this trouble first, to start thinking about it in that way.*

Larissa failed to check in with herself. For instance, she did not question the idea of her fiancé bringing her clothes to the airport so she could move onto the next project. In addition, she often spoke to herself in the third person. The description of her coming back from a war is a mirror of her desensitization.

## Beating oneself up

Another common way for high flyers to disrupt their reflexivity was to beat themselves up. Jack told us how he'd assumed, incorrectly, he was in the wrong in a difficult meeting:

*I am very hard on myself. At the end of the day it did get done on time and everyone was very pleased, but I do tend to over-analyse things and always think about how I could have done something better, rather than congratulate myself on what I've done well. It doesn't help the stress side if you're beating yourself up over not doing something right. I guess then I started questioning myself, and thinking, well maybe I didn't do a very good job of this, maybe I should have done it differently. After this particular meeting I thought about it, and actually there hadn't been an issue: the other guy had got it wrong. If only I'd been a bit more confident, I would have said, well no one's reported an issue to infrastructure – if you think there's an issue you've really got to come and tell us about it. If I'd said that I'd have come across a lot better, instead of being almost apologetic about how I'd missed it, when I hadn't.*

The act of beating oneself up tends to distract the individual from the important work of being reflexive. Csilla explained what it felt like for her when somebody saw fault in her reputation:

*I don't like it. I feel really, really bad. I feel you have a name, a reputation for producing quality work, for always doing your best and always meeting the external limit, even though there are only 24 hours in the day. At that time it was very frustrating, and I was kind of angry because although I made it clear to everyone that I was caught up in a situation and needed help, I didn't get that much help. I wasn't happy about that, but at the end of the day I put the blame on myself.*

## *Deflection by using humour*

We found that some of the high flyers who burnt out tended to avoid meaningful contact with us as researchers, sometimes by changing the subject of the conversation or introducing humour when it appeared to us that the situation was critical to their health and wellbeing. When asked challenging questions, Rodoula wanted to tell one anecdote after another and use humour to avoid a serious consideration of the issues. This had the effect of diluting the strength of her feelings, and that of her contact with the researcher:

> *Rodoula*: We had to make a presentation to the client the next morning, and we were very pressurized to get everything ready, so we stayed late. Next morning we were very tired, but we came in early to see the client, who'd been delaying the meeting due to prior arrangements. Finally the meeting started. Then the Finance Director left us to continue the conversation with his Assistant, but the Assistant says, 'Will you excuse me right now, because I have to go have my hair cut'. [laughing] And I said, 'Oh my God!' I was so surprised [laughing] 'What did you just say?' [laughing]. He said, 'I'm going to have my hair cut'. And I had kept my team working until 4:30 in the morning, even when I had promised them they could leave earlier, so that we could complete the presentation. It was like a joke – let's have a meeting, but you don't mind if I leave to get my hair cut [laughing].
>
> *Researcher*: So you'd worked through the night, and done all this work...
>
> *Rodoula*: [laughing] And the client went to get his hair cut [laughing]. It's very funny.
>
> *Researcher*: I guess if I had been in your shoes I would have just got angry at that stage.
>
> *Rodoula*: I told my Partner. When something goes badly, I phone for 'psychoanalysis', because it's important that you tell somebody, I think, and not burst out to the client.
>
> *Researcher*: So you phoned your Partner and...?
>
> *Rodoula*: [laughing]. The client went to cut his hair! [laughing].

*Researcher:* And what did the Partner say?
*Rodoula:* I can't remember. It was more, like, psychological – to get it out.

## The consequences of burnout for the individual

### Derail or develop?

For most of the high flyers we interviewed, burnout led to some kind of career derailment. This was either significant and permanent – involving the loss of health as well as the job – or a temporary setback, such as being passed over for promotion or temporarily dropping out of the high-potential talent pool.

For a very few, however – and we are talking about 6% of our research sample – burnout appeared to be a catalyst for transformational development. What determined whether high flyers derailed or developed? Our research points to the degree and the speed with which they were able to learn from the experience.

Acceptance of responsibility for their contribution to what befell them was critical to high flyers learning from burnout. Fiona told us about how she moved from feeling a victim to feeling responsible:

*I felt I had too much work, a rubbish boss and no support – I felt no one noticed or cared. I felt like a victim, I couldn't see my way out. So whilst I recognized that I had to change something – I had endless conversations with my husband about how to change – I didn't feel empowered to do it. I knew I had to change the way I was working, but the very recognition of that felt like more pressure, one more thing to deal with. It felt terribly hard. But as I eventually started resolving it, what started to give me hope was my beginning to realize I wasn't a victim, but that I actually had some choice and some responsibility in the situation.*

There appears to be some similarity between our research findings and those of derailed senior executives. The derailment studies showed that those who fell from power often attributed their fall to 'bad luck'. But their demise was actually less the result of fate than of the way they handled the predicament in which they found themselves.[37] Equally our research showed that high flyers who burn out did so because of *their response* to highly stressful external conditions, rather than the situation itself. Rodoula's unwillingness to see a viable alternative to a situation that ultimately left her at risk of burnout is a good illustration:

*Rodoula:* We had to work through the night for several months. I didn't have time to reflect. I was very close to the edge: if

I had continued for even a bit longer at the same level I would have collapsed for sure. But I delivered the project, and it was excellent. Then there was another project, and the Partner said to me, 'Rodoula, there is a possibility...' and I said, 'No way! There's no way!'. I needed time to rest, because I knew that if I didn't I would have a problem. I wouldn't want to do the same thing again, but on the other hand I'm not sure I could have changed anything. You can't say 'I can't do that' around here. The 'no' thing is a bit difficult.

*Researcher*: What else might you have done differently, other than saying no?

*Rodoula*: It would have been the only option. The workload was crazy. Could I have worked smarter – like two hours less? [laughing]. That wouldn't have been a solution.

The derailment studies found that the very qualities that helped to make someone a high flyer in the first place (see Figure 4.5) worked against them: 'the strengths that made the derailers successful had a darker side as well'. Our research discovered that under intense pressure three of these characteristics – 'Brilliance', 'Commitment/Sacrifice' and 'Ambition' became the cause of high flyer burnout.

A frequent characteristic of executives who later derailed was 'unusual analytical or technical ability, often described by others as "*brilliance*"'.[38] However, this admirable quality could sometimes lead to a patronizing attitude towards those believed to be less brilliant. In Chapter 2 we observed that high flyers are prone to thoughtlessness and insensitivity. Brilliant minds often do not suffer fools gladly, and at times this flaw was evident. In the white heat of burnout it became exaggerated, and morphed into outright arrogance, cynicism and rudeness.

Those who derailed made exceptional discretionary effort, working long hours and demonstrating intense emotional *commitment* to the achievement of objectives. The shadow side of such a strength was that their lives became defined by their work and they expected others to do the same. Our research showed that the commitment of those who burnt out led them to create an identity that was co-dependent with their job and consumed their entire existence.

Derailers tended to be very *ambitious*, but this sometimes led them to 'do whatever is necessary to achieve personal success, even at the expense of others or the organization'. As we have seen earlier in this chapter, those who burnt out had ambition built on a sense of purpose that sought

| Track record | Most people who make it into the executive ranks have a strong track record, consistently getting bottom-line results or making an impressive impact in a functional or technical area. |
|---|---|
| Brilliance | Being seen as uncommonly bright was a common reason for success. Brilliance might show in a technical or functional speciality, in analytic and problem-solving skills, or in a singular burst of genius in a specific situation. |
| Commitment/ Sacrifice | Many could list as a strength their loyalty to the organization, often expressed as a willingness to work long hours and to accept whatever assignments they were asked to take. |
| Charm | Some people are capable of considerable charm, charisma or personal warmth when dealing with others. Sometimes this quality was used selectively, and often it was expressed upward toward those who made performance judgements. |
| Ambition | Although some were 'drafted' into the management ranks, many others actively sought it out, doing whatever was required to achieve success. |

**Figure 4.5**  Sources of initial success (*Source*: Adapted from W.M. McCall, Jr and M.M. Lombardo (1983). *Off the Track: Why and How Successful Executives Get Derailed*. Technical Report 21, Greenboro, NC: Center for Creative Leadership, pp 2–3). Reprinted with permission of Harvard Business School Publishing

recognition and fame, which often led to a reckless pursuit of career goals at any cost.

So, characteristics regarded by the high flyers' organizations as strengths became sources of weakness. This phenomenon can be regarded as symptomatic of the individual's weak reflexivity – they failed to make sense of changes in the external environment, so learning was interrupted and adaptation failed to happen. Its effect was exacerbated (as we saw in Chapter 2) by a blind spot regarding their own performance downturns: identity was so closely tied up in job success, and experience of failure was so limited, that they simply did not know how to deal with setbacks.

Some coped by displaying a certain amount of arrogance, which may have been a defence mechanism against receiving data they did not know how to deal with.

## Accepting responsibility

It was the individual's willingness to accept their share of responsibility for the burnout that largely determined whether they developed rather than derailed: 'Accepting responsibility for one's actions, even when external circumstances play a part heavily, is a prerequisite for learning.'[39]

## Being held

There was one other factor that influenced the degree to which those who burnout derailed or developed. This was the extent to which they were 'held' through the burnout experience by someone else. We use the term 'held' for two reasons. First, to indicate the non-prescriptive contextual nature of this relationship – it could be formal or informal, performed by someone at work or outside work, by a work colleague or a significant other, by someone formally trained in coaching or counselling or by someone with no such qualifications. Second, to mean a relationship in which the person burning out is sustained, attended to but also challenged and held to account (we talk more about the nature of this relationship in the next chapter).

The act of being held, however, required an acceptance that help was needed. For many this was difficult, as Scott explained:

*My partner was very busy with her work, and wouldn't get home until maybe ten or eleven o'clock at night, and we wouldn't see each other for days. She didn't understand because we didn't really have the conversations – about how I needed sleep, and was really struggling at work and within the relationship. I needed some kind of help, but I wasn't good at saying or demonstrating it. I was frustrated that I wasn't letting anybody in to help. Part of that is about self-reliance and self-confidence – a bit of denial that I needed it. But also because my whole life was so dreadful, and was affecting me. In the end I found a counsellor who I could work with. But it took four months for me to actually have a meaningful conversation about what was going on. Then there was a real breakthrough.*

## *Change in identity*

As we have seen, burnout resulted in a redefined sense of self. Personal myths (the narrative that provides a sense of purpose, gives life meaning and defines identity) were significantly revised. The revision was irreversible, in as much as it was impossible to go back to an earlier, less complex and more naive or innocent account of the self.

We explored these changes in high flyers' sense of self using the model of identity discussed earlier in this chapter (See Figure 4.2). In particular we looked for the extent to which the experience of burnout changed:

- efforts of high flyers actively to form an identity
- the central narrative tone and content of their personal myths
- their social interaction
- their reflexivity
- the ongoing evolution of personal myths and the high flyers' experience of themselves over time.

Figure 4.6 provides examples of how high flyers' identities changed as a consequence of burnout.

## Negative consequences

There were a range of negative consequences including feeling stuck, loss of self-confidence, lack of self-respect, losing sight of oneself or depersonalizing others.

Many of those who burnt out experienced themselves as 'stuck'. Their stories had failed to evolve, and as a result were more like those of younger people. This 'stuckness' was often accompanied by feelings of powerlessness and confusion resulting in a sense of hopelessness and passivity. There was a sense of being caught in a spiralling loss of sense of self, and of not knowing what to do about it. Holger found himself in just such a situation:

*I hope I can change this experience into something positive, but I think I need to find another level before I can do that. Right now – I don't know – I sometimes feel I'm not here, and then I'm here again. And when I go to work this feeling gets even worse, because they're telling me stuff that doesn't build me up. I'm finding it very hard to get out of this downward spiral, it just keeps going down. I hope next year is going to be better than this.*

Our stories need to evolve as we evolve. If we fail to make sense of an experience we can become stuck in the unfinished business of that experience – the unresolved emotional and psychic aftermath of what happened. As a consequence we can't move on.

| Aspect of identity | Explanation | Examples of how identity changed as a consequence of burnout |
|---|---|---|
| Creation of identity requires a proactive stance to form oneself | Identity is not a given; it has to be proactively formed, actively created by the individual. It requires courage to be your own person and not simply a layer of bricks. | • Adoption of a passive, reactive stance – responsibility for what happens occurs outside of them<br>• Devastating loss of self-esteem, self-confidence and willingness to take risks ('fear in the soul')<br>• Greater sense of responsibility for self-authorship |
| Identity is created through story and somatic form | We come to know who we are through the stories we tell others and ourselves about ourselves, and how we embody this in our somatic form. These stories perform the task of giving our lives 'meaning, unity and purpose'. They answer the questions: Who am I? Why am I here? What is my purpose in life? | • From being someone people liked to being focused on the task, just getting the job done; sceptical<br>• Deviation from central narrative theme of the story – 'I wasn't myself; I needed to get back to myself'<br>• From being someone whose story is the job to being someone whose story is balanced between different aspects of their lives |
| Identity is created within a social context | Our stories and thus our identities are constructed within a social context; our sense of self is socially created. | • Withdrawn, introverted; emotionally distant and cut off from others<br>• Willing to reach out and ask for help |
| Identity is made possible by the ability to interact with oneself | Reflexivity is the process through which we construct our stories, our identities. | • Greater self-awareness of own unproductive behaviour in certain contexts<br>• Reflexivity is interrupted; loses connection with self<br>• Greater sense of own limitations<br>• Greater sense of perspective – 'this is only a job, it does not define me'<br>• Circular, reflective, internal conversations that fail to result in action<br>• A developing sense of self-control |
| Identity is in process | We revise our storied identity as we move through to a new stage of adult maturation and as the nature and patterning of our relations and interactions change over time.<br>On a day-to-day level we experience ourselves differently at different times depending on the quality of connection we have with ourselves, our environment and how we are relating to others. This will not affect our storied identity unless this experience of differentness is prolonged. | • Overly patterned, rigid structuring of one's story<br>• Greater sense of choice and volition<br>• Story has got stuck – still that of someone much younger<br>• More of a sense of being on 'a journey' |

**Figure 4.6** How burnout changed high flyers' identities

Burnout often led to a devastating loss of self-confidence and of willingness to take risks, which Kirill described as a 'fear in the soul' that assailed him whenever he started working with new people: 'I have less confidence in my professional life. And because of that I'm sure I don't give as good a service to clients'. Diantha put it in terms of self-respect: 'I think I didn't respect myself as much as I did before. And I believe that it affects other people as well – how they perceive you, their picture of you. I think it changed in my case. It took a lot of effort to get their respect back'.

It takes courage to be your own person rather than be what others want you to be, and this fear and lack of self-respect makes it difficult to form an independent sense of identity. Many of our high flyers spoke of becoming someone they no longer recognized and did not like, but realizing that they could not stay this way. Kirill was one of them:

*I ended up working in a different way from the way I normally work. It became very easy for me to start shouting at people, or to be not very loyal to the client. I also found myself more and more often just coming straight to the point and telling them how things needed to be done, instead of trying to persuade them. That's not me: it's very difficult to make me wild about something. I started to worry about myself. And people started to notice I'd changed, and a few said I was responding out of proportion to things. But more and more I'm starting to understand that I can't stay the person I am now…*

Waking up to find you've become someone you don't recognize represents a deviation from the individual's prevailing, central narrative theme. This was often accompanied by a strong sense of wanting to get back to the person they thought they were, as Scott described:

*I didn't like who I was and where I was, didn't quite recognize how I'd gone there. Little bit by little I'd ended up being someone and somewhere that I didn't recognize and I didn't like. Fairly quickly I turned away from that, and regained the real me and became the adult that I thought I would become – but having taken a quite huge detour. That probably sums it up. I can't say that I regret it, because if that hadn't happened I wouldn't be who I am today, which is somebody that I really like.*

Scott went on to say how, after many years of being told he had changed for the worse as the result of his burnout experience, he came to fully recognize what had happened to him:

*Until you can show yourself that what you've become is not what you want to be, you aren't going to believe it. One day I stared in the mirror and I said, 'Right. What you see now with your own eyes is what those around you have been telling you for a couple of years', and the penny dropped. Whether you call it a moment of clarity I don't know, but the rose-tinted spectacles came off when I took that cold, hard look in the mirror and didn't like what I saw.*

What appears to lie behind this process of losing sight of oneself in burnout is an interruption of reflexivity. Our research participants lost connection with the voice inside of them. Their power to evaluate and interpret critically what is happening to them became weaker.

Relationships with people around them also changed. They began to depersonalize others and deal in a high-handed, dictatorial or contemptuous way, which was different from before. This new mode of relating continued over the course of the burnout experience, which, as we know, extends over many months and sometimes years. Because identities are formed in a social context, this had the effect of changing identities – although our high flyers did not recognize this at the time. They appeared to ingest new facets of identity without critically evaluating them.

## Positive outcomes

But this change could also take a more positive turn. This included recognizing one's own limitations, humility, asking for help, finding boundaries and thawing a frozen sense of self.

Where this happened it nearly always revolved around a recognition of the individual's own limitations and fallibilities, accompanied by a more realistic sense of their capabilities. They gained more of a sense of humility, perspective and balance. Scott explained how his recovery from burnout really started when he learnt to ask for help:

*One of the biggest comments I was able to make early on in counselling was an admission that I wanted to change but couldn't do it on my own. For me to say openly 'I can't do this' was one of the biggest doors to open. Once I'd said it, and opened myself up to the opportunity of changing, the journey with the counsellor became much, much easier, and that was probably when the work really started. Saying 'I don't know' was part of this much more genuine me, rather than some kind of pretentious know-all.*

Dimitris talked about learning about his own limitations for the first time:

*When I started here I thought there were no limits, that I could work for months, for years or whatever without stopping. When I first understood that I did have limits, it was a big change. What led me to it was realizing that the consequences of a client problem, or whatever, are not so big as to justify me having a near breakdown.*

In an interview we conducted with Larissa two years after her burnout experience, she explained her view that finding boundaries is difficult early in one's career. Her account also provides insight into how people's stories can become stuck in a developmental stage that is not appropriate for the individual's current life context:

*At that time I had a youngster's broad vision of my boundaries. It wasn't realistic. I didn't know what I was getting into, and by the time I realized it was too late. It's really important for people to set their own boundaries, but in my opinion they can't really assess their own abilities in the early stages of their career. They think they can achieve, well, anything. The main conclusion for me is that you need more than just a job in your life. Burnout happens because you concentrate too much on one thing. You need something else in your life for there to be proper balance. But for this balance to exist in the beginning I think it's very important for the organization to allow it to appear in people's lives in the first place.*

Burnout appeared to have the effect of either freezing the growth of an identity or helping it thaw out and continue to develop. Freezing was often represented by taking on an overly-patterned, rigid structuring of one's story. Scott uses the analogy of demolishing a building to describe this:

*I think there was an element of self-destruction going on, that I was almost wanting myself to fail monumentally so that I could start again. I wasn't at absolute rock bottom – there was still a little bit further to go. The building was crumbling and falling, but the foundation pillars were still holding, and propping it all up. What I needed to happen was for those pillars to come down as well. Counselling was the means by which they came down. My intellectual ability to deny and to rationalize was supporting those pillars…*

By way of contrast, Larissa described being back onto the path of evolution: 'I would say I'm still on the journey. You can't get over it straightaway, and you can't forget it. You still remember it and reflect on it. But it's not painful. You don't fear it anymore. You just have it, and you take the best from it'.

## Characteristics of high flyers who don't burn out

In this section we explore how high flyers who don't burn out organize themselves differently from those who do.

As might be expected, many of the characteristics of these individuals are opposite to those of people who burn out. However, in our research the relative frequency of these characteristics ran contrary to our expectations. We also discovered that these individuals demonstrated a behavioural repertoire for managing high-stress situations which was somewhat different from that of those who burn out.

## Reflexivity and open self-examination

By far the most frequently demonstrated characteristic was a high degree of reflexivity and openness to self-examination. While these high flyers described themselves as no more reflective than those who burnt out, they appeared reflexive at a heart and gut level (emotional and impulse-to-act) and more able to learn and adapt to changes in their surrounding context.

There was a marked tendency to alternate between taking notice of external events and 'going inside themselves' to take notice of their own feelings, thoughts and sensations. They were also able to distance themselves from a situation by limiting their own emotional investment in it, thereby remaining genuinely disinterested (in the proper sense of the word – of being neutral) and so more able to take effective action in the face of highly stressful work conditions.

## Internally referenced identity

As might be expected, the second characteristic was a strong sense of their own, internally referenced identity. This was coupled with the self-confidence and self-belief that goes with an internally driven sense of being your own person, and with a high degree of self-knowledge and awareness. Joe told us how he dealt with the intense pressures of a high profile in a major multi-national: 'I think it's belief that the steps that you are taking are logical, clearly understood and are effective. It's believing that nobody could do it any better than it's being done. And with that self-belief comes, "Well, think what you like, but this is as good as it's going to get"'.

Chuck gave us a very different and dramatic example of strong, internally referenced identity from early on in his career:

*I felt I got ambushed by the client and got very little support from my boss on a couple of issues that we had solved weeks ago. I got angry and yelled at the client and at my boss. After about twenty seconds of shouting that we had solved this before, I sat down in my chair, closed my notebook and thought well, I'll go look for another job. I literally thought I was being fired. And to be frank with you, that was OK. If that's how the company was going to act, and if that's how we were going to be treated by that client, then I was OK with being fired. It had reached that point. I liked the job, but I had to make that stand.*

Although Chuck took a huge risk (he is now in a senior role within the organization), his sense of having to make a stand, together with his retention of subsidiary awareness, demonstrates the intentional use of anger and the continued functioning of his reflexive abilities. However, he was so emotionally invested in the situation that he ran the risk of not thinking clearly and being unable to curtail his anger. As he told us later, he had allowed the situation to run on for too long and get out of control. This was an important lesson for him:

*The lesson I learned from that experience was that I have to do what it takes to stop things ever getting to that point again. If there's a frustration level or a stress level that I can't control and I think it's important, then I have an obligation, if not to anybody else then at least to myself, to stand up and say: 'we need to deal with this issue'.*

## Perspective

The third most observed characteristic was an ability to put things into perspective. An example of this outlook is realising that the current situation will not last forever.

These characteristics appeared interdependent. A strong, internally referenced identity was reliant on reflexiveness; in the same way, a sense of perspective was based on the robust foundations of a strong sense of self. Without one, the other characteristics could not function.

## Behaviours of high flyers who do not burn out

As well as identifying these three characteristics, our research also identified six coping dimensions that distinguished the behaviour of those who did not burn out from those who did. These we called sharing, proactivity, boundary-setting, working smarter, hope and renewing (see Figure 4.7).

■ *Sharing* work experiences with others during high-stress periods was the most frequently reported behaviour, and in one way the most significant in that it represented the act of reaching out and asking for others' help. This required a sense of humility and an understanding of one's limitations, rather than the grandiose illusion of invulnerability adopted by other high flyers. James described how

| Coping dimension | Behaviour |
|---|---|
| **Sharing**<br>A willingness to share work experiences with others during high-stress periods | • Does not sit and stew on things – talks to the people they need to directly to resolve things<br>• Talks situation over with family and friends to get advice from those with more experience; uses this advice to put situation in perspective |
| **Proactivity**<br>Takes urgent action to resolve existing or anticipated situations that will result in severe stress | • Comes up with alternative solutions to problems to stop high stress from happening<br>• Focuses on controlling what is in their power to control, including own behaviour |
| **Boundary-setting**<br>Has a mature and realistic understanding of own capability; accurately assesses workload capable of delivering; sets clear boundaries around this; only flexes these boundaries on the basis of increased time or resources | • Sets clear boundaries – faces down those who try to usurp these<br>• Assesses the significance of deadlines they are given. Recognizes that some are unrealistic or unnecessary<br>• Asks for more time or assistance |
| **Working smarter**<br>Well-developed organizational skills, including the ability to prioritize, delegate and work towards a clear end point rather than working long hours and sacrificing personal and social activities | • Prioritizing and goal setting: sets small goals to the next destination and then reviews from there<br>• Takes the approach that 80% right is OK; perfection is a fantasy |
| **Hope**<br>Visualizing how things might be beyond the immediate, harsh reality of the situation | • Sees the opportunity in the situation more than the challenge |
| **Renewing**<br>Engaging in activities outside work that are personally renewing | • Does exercise and sport<br>• Learns what helps them to switch off completely<br>• Understands they need time to process what is happening |

**Figure 4.7**    Behaviours of high flyers who did not burn out

he dealt with an inherently stressful workplace and a boss who was a bully:

> *So to relieve that kind of stress I'd go home and talk to my parents, I'd talk to my brother, sister, friends. Sometimes I'd go out and have a beer and have a laugh about it. The more people you talked to about it, the more advice you'd*

*get on how to deal with the situation. My father was in business for 45 years, and he'd learnt how to deal with stress. So I'd sit down with him and we'd talk about it, and my dad would say, 'OK, here's the way to deal with him' and so on. So you learned from other people how to unwind, how to deal with stressful situations, so that they didn't overwhelm you.*

- *Proactivity* Investing energy in resolving an existing or anticipated high-stress situation – which we called 'proactivity' – was sometimes about focusing on what was within the high flyer's control, even if this was only their own behaviour. Chuck explained: 'To try and control what you can control and try and live as much of a normal life as you can. Just the act of getting out there and getting to work every day ultimately helps relieve some of that stress'.

- *Boundary-setting* This was by far the most complex of the coping dimensions. It required high flyers having an accurate picture of their limitations in order to judge how much work they could take on. They then needed to set clear, inviolable boundaries around what they were capable of delivering, pushing back on attempts to undermine these boundaries. They would only adjust these boundaries if they were given additional resources or time.

- *Working smarter* Being able to see the possibility of a better future beyond the cruel circumstances of a period of prolonged stress was a decisive ingredient in helping high flyers deal with severe stress. Despite a very challenging work environment, Joe talked with passion and excitement about what kept him going: 'You see the light at the end of the tunnel. I know as soon as I've got those guys, as soon as they're in place, things will start to change and I will be more effective and I'll be able to slice things up'.

- *Hope* As Boyatzis and McKee put it,

  *...perhaps it is hope, above all else, that may be the first real step on a path of healing and renewal. If we cannot envision a better future, how can we consciously make the choices that will get us there? That magical and life-giving quality called hope is more than just optimism. It is also the result of developing a combination of emotional intelligence, intellectual flexibility, the ability to read one's environment and see possibilities, and a basic belief in one's own and others' power to influence our lives.*[40]

- *Renewing* High flyers who did not burn out knew what it took to relax and switch off from work. For many this involved physical exercise. Joe knew what he needed to do to sustain himself but his reflections on his current dilemma show unresolved issues:

  *Until three months ago I was running 25 miles a week, I'd do half marathons, I'd do biathlons. I'd bought a couple of bikes and I would do quite a lot of road work on them. Now I get to the gym once a week if I'm lucky. I've put on a stone. I don't feel good. I used to get here for six thirty, do an hour in the gym, get in the office by eight, work until six, get home for eight, play with the kids, have dinner, go to bed. If I get six hours' sleep and get my exercise I'm happy, but now I'm not getting my exercise, I'm rarely getting six hours' sleep and I'm reading my Blackberry at midnight. So – I suppose the self-knowledge is such that I can see all of that, and understand what the triggers are, and I can see how it manifests itself and I'm trying to deal with it. But there are no easy solutions.* [Our emphasis]

## What burnout means, and what to do about it

We said at the beginning that this chapter would be particularly useful to the reader who believes they may be in danger of burning out. So before we set out our chapter conclusions, let us say here what we hope such a reader will have taken on board.

To the individual asking himself or herself, 'What does my burning out actually mean? – what does it signify about me?' we say: burnout is a wakeup call that your life and a career are unsustainable. The fact of burning out tells you that your current way of operating at work and in your career has become untenable. It indicates that the story you have constructed about who you are, your purpose in being here and what gives you meaning, is no longer appropriate for the context in which you find yourself.

For that same reader, who then asks, 'What should I do now?', we have three pieces of advice.

First, and most importantly, choose someone to talk to about what is happening to you. That person must be someone you trust implicitly. This could be a colleague or a significant other, someone formally trained in coaching or counselling or someone with no such qualifications. Your relationship could be formal or informal – either way this person must have your interests at heart. They will be invested in you learning from the experience and are likely to be the kind of person who will hold you to account with challenging questions from time to time (there will be more on this dual concept of 'holding' in the next chapter). If you are someone who finds it difficult to ask for help (like Fraser, who took four months to open up to his counsellor) then this first step may be very hard. But if you fail then it is likely that you will go on to burn out. You won't be able to deal with what's about to happen to you on your own, and any lack of awareness on your part about your own limitations will pretty much guarantee burnout.

Secondly, examine with this person your relationship with your job and your career. Has the job become all-consuming? Does it define who you are? Whose sense of purpose are you serving? – yours, or your employer's?

Finally (and we discuss this in more detail in the next chapter), consider the possibility that going all out to prevent burnout might not be the right strategy. Consider that burning out might in fact be a call to adventure, a way of allowing you to have a remarkable meeting with yourself.

## Conclusions

We have said that burnout can happen when an individual defines himself or herself in a way that makes it difficult to sustain a healthy relationship with their job and their work environment. In this chapter we saw how work can become the defining aspect of an individual's personal narrative, to the exclusion of all else. We looked at the co-dependent relationship with work that the individual enters, in which the story of the organization and their role within it becomes *their* story.

We concluded, however, that it is the high flyer's sense of purpose that holds the key to whether actual burnout takes place. Our research participants who burned out tended to focus their sense of purpose on nothing more substantive than their own career advancement, losing an important part of themselves along the way. A purpose fixated on career achievement was a mere distraction from the lack of substance in their life, and no substitute for a real sense of self. Without a clear notion of what they were trying to bring about in the world other than their own self-aggrandizement, such individuals were prone to self-destruction.

We began the chapter by reminding ourselves that although organizations create the conditions for burnout, it is individuals, through their choices, who determine whether they burn out. We defined identity as being actively created by the self from the stories we tell others and ourselves about ourselves, and reflexivity as the process of self-interaction by which we do it.

We then looked at what our own research told us about the personality traits of those who burned out or showed symptoms of doing so. We found their most widely shared characteristic to be over-identification with work and career, leading to little inner sense of self and a fragile sense of identity. These were perfectionists who ignored their own and their loved ones' needs in favour of work, never willing to say no to the demand of a client or employer, however unreasonable, and convinced that their job was on the line at all times. A 'dysfunctional closeness' with work drove them on.

We then wondered what part employers could be said to play in this phenomenon of over-identification. We found that some organizations did indeed attempt actively to form the personalities of high flyers to personify the values of the brand, and so could be said to be complicit. But we also found that the individuals themselves almost always colluded in their own downfall.

In almost every case, over-identification with work concealed deep feelings of insecurity. It also tended to manifest itself in over-emphasis on achievement of short-term work goals, rather than on any meaningful purpose, which again pointed to a diminished sense of identity. High flyers' attachment to goals promoted a sense of intense driven-ness and activity which was a mere substitute for a well-thought-through purpose. Their consequent busyness was merely a means of avoiding dealing with a fragile sense of identity and the debilitating sense of insecurity that went with it.

We wondered, also, what happened to reflexivity during burnout. We found that many who burned out did not operate on all three of Torbert's levels of reflexivity – head, heart and gut – but only on two of these, and that some who were incapable of reflexion while burning out later looked back astonished at their temporary lack of sense-making ability. The most common means of interrupting reflexivity during burnout were desensitization – failing to 'check in with oneself' – and beating oneself up. Some of our participants had continued in this avoiding mode, this time not with themselves but with us as researchers.

We then considered the question why some individuals who burned out derailed, while others heard the wakeup call and managed to turn potential disaster into development. The degree and speed with which some were able to learn from the experience was key, but a willingness to accept share of responsibility in what happened to them seemed largely to determine whether individuals burned out or also derailed. The other major factor was the degree to which they were 'held' (as we have noted above).

We then looked at the changes in identity – the redefined sense of self – that came about as a result of burnout. Many experienced a sense of 'stuckness', their life story having ceased to evolve. There was devastating loss of self-confidence and willingness to take risks, feelings of having turned into someone else, changed relationships with others – all brought about by interruption in reflexivity, and usually taking place without self-knowledge at the time. However, recovery from burnout could yield a sense of perspective and balance, along with a new and valuable understanding of personal limitations.

We concluded the chapter by asking in what ways high flyers who burnt out differed from those who didn't. By far the most important characteristic of the latter group was reflexivity, and openness to self-examination. Reflexive high flyers may have described themselves as no more reflexive than those who burned out, but they were markedly more able to distance themselves from a situation by remaining genuinely disinterested, and were so more able to take effective action in the face of immense stress. They also shared a second characteristic of self-belief – a strong, internally-referenced identity – with the ability to maintain perspective as the third. We took the reader through the six coping dimensions that distinguished the behaviour of those who did not burn out: sharing, proactivity, boundary-setting, working smarter, hope and renewing.

In this chapter we have made many passing references to the notion of learning from burnout. But in the next chapter, 'The hero's journey', we will look at that learning experience in depth. We will look at the opportunities and the possible outcomes, and we will focus on the important concept, merely touched on in this chapter, of being 'held' through the process.

## End notes

1  McCrae, R.R. and John, O.P. (1992). 'An introduction to the Five Factor Model and its applications.' *Journal of Personality*, vol. 60, pp175–215
2  Taylor, H. and Cooper, C.L. (1989). 'The stress prone personality: A review of research in the context of occupational stress.' *Stress Medicine*, vol. 5, pp17–27
3  Schaufeli, W. and Enzman, D. (1998). *The Burnout Companion to Study and Practice*. London: Taylor and Francis
4  Freudenberger, H.J. and Richelson, G. (1980). *Burn Out: The High Cost of Success and How to Cope with It*. London: Arrow Books
5  Fischer, H.J. (1983). 'A psychoanalytic view of burnout', in B.A. Farber (ed.), *Stress and Burnout in the Human Service Professions*. New York: Pergamon
6  Glickauf-Hughes, C. and Mehlman, E. (1995). 'Narcissistic issues in therapists: Diagnostic and treatment considerations.' *Psychotherapy*, vol. 32, pp213–21
7  Pines, A.M., Ben-Ari, A., Utasi, A. and Larson, D. (2002) 'A cross-cultural investigation of social support and burnout.' *European Psychologist*, vol. 7, pp256–64
8  Keleman, S. (1987). *Embodying Experience: Forming a Personal Life*. Berkeley: Center Press
9  McAdams, D.P. (1993). *The Stories We Live By: Personal Myths and the Making of the Self*. New York: Guilford Press
10  McAdams, D.P. (1993). *The Stories We Live By: Personal Myths and the Making of the Self*. New York: Guilford Press
11  Blumer, H. (1998). *Symbolic Interactionism: Perspective and Method*. Berkeley: University of California Press

12  Charon, J.M. (2001). *Symbolic Interactionism: An Introduction, an Interpretation, an Integration.* New Jersey: Prentice Hall

13  Quoted in Senge, P., Scharmer, C.O., Jaworski, J. and Flowers, B.S. (2005). *Presence: Exploring Profound Change in People, Organizations and Society.* London: Brealey

14  Shaw, P. (2002). *Changing Conversations in Organisations: A Complexity Approach to Change.* London: Routledge

15  Clarkson, P. (1989). *Gestalt Counselling in Action.* London: Sage

16  Tsoukas, H. (2003). 'Commentary: Vulnerability, moral responsibility, and reflexive thinking.' *Reflections*, vol. 4, pp14–15

17  Covaleski, M.A., Dirsmith M.W., Heian J.B. and Samuel S. (1998). 'The calculated and the avowed: Techniques of discipline and struggles over identity in Big Six public accounting firms.' *Administrative Science Quarterly*, vol. 43, pp293–327

18  Murlis, H. and Schubert, P. (2002). 'Engage employees and boost performance.' Hay Group Working Paper. Quoted in M. Bunting (2005), *Willing Slaves: How the Overwork Culture is Ruling our Lives.* London: Harper Perennial

19  Harrison, R. (1997). 'Consultant as healer in an addictive world of work: Life on earth remembering earth's wisdom.' Unpublished article

20  McAdams, D.P. (1993). *The Stories We Live By: Personal Myths and the Making of the Self.* New York: Guilford Press

21  Pedler, M.L. Burgoyne, J. and Boydell, T. (2004). *A Manager's Guide to Leadership.* Maidenhead: McGraw-Hill

22  Pedler, M., Burgoyne, J. and Boydell, T. (2004). *A Manager's Guide to Leadership.* Maidenhead: McGraw-Hill

23  Pedler, M., Burgoyne, J. and Boydell, T. (2004). *A Manager's Guide to Leadership.* Maidenhead: McGraw-Hill

24  Pedler, M., Burgoyne, J. and, Boydell, T. (2004). *A Manager's Guide to Leadership.* Maidenhead: McGraw-Hill

25  Pedler, M., Burgoyne, J. and Boydell, T. (2004). *A Manager's Guide to Leadership.* Maidenhead: McGraw-Hill

26  Megginson, D., Clutterbuck, D. and English, P. (2008). 'An own goal for coaching.' Unpublished article

27  Megginson D., Clutterbuck, D. and English, P. (2008). 'An own goal for coaching.' Unpublished article

28  Pedler, M., Burgoyne, J. and Boydell, T. (2004). *A Manager's Guide to Leadership.* Maidenhead: McGraw-Hill

29  Blakeley, K. (2007). *Leadership Blind Spots and What to do About Them.* San Francisco: Jossey-Bass

30  Megginson, D., Clutterbuck, D. and English, P. (2008). 'An own goal for coaching.' Unpublished article

31  Bains, G. et al (2007). *Meaning Inc. The Blueprint for Business Success in the 21st Century.* London: Profile Books

32  Blakeley, K. (2007). *Leadership Blind Spots and What to do About Them.* San Francisco: Jossey-Bass

33  Blakeley, K. (2007). *Leadership Blind Spots and What to do About Them.* San Francisco: Jossey-Bass

34  Kayes, D.C. (2006). *Destructive Goal Pursuit: the Mount Everest Disaster*. Basingstoke: Palgrave Macmillan

35  Torbert, W.R. (1973). *Learning from Experience: Toward Consciousness*. New York: Columbia University Press

36  von Schiller, F. (1983). *On the Aesthetic Education of Man* (E.M. Wilkinson and L.A. Willoughby (eds)). Oxford: Oxford University Press

37  McCall, M. (1998). *High Flyers: Developing the Next Generation of Leaders*. Boston: Harvard Business School Press

38  McCall, M. (1998). *High Flyers: Developing the Next Generation of Leaders*. Boston: Harvard Business School Press

39  McCall, M. (1998). *High Flyers: Developing the Next Generation of Leaders*. Boston: Harvard Business School Press

40  Boyatzis, R. and McKee, A. (2005). *Resonant Leadership: Renewing Yourself and Connecting with Others Through Mindfulness, Hope and Compassion*. Boston: Harvard Business School Press

# 5

# The hero's journey

*A man may perform astonishing feats and comprehend a vast amount of knowledge, and yet have no understanding of himself. But suffering directs a man to look within. If it succeeds, then, there, within him, is the beginning of his learning.*

SØREN KIERKEGAARD

*Ironically, the very situations that most often lead to derailment can as readily lead to development. Put another way, experience can do one in or it can teach important lessons. The trick is to know how to influence which way it goes.*

PROFESSOR MORGAN McCALL

It may seem bizarre to think of burnout as a hero's journey – a call to deep and urgent learning about oneself. And yet this is the potential that burnout holds for those who experience it. In the process of writing this book, Tim looked back on what emerged from him out of the experience of burning out:

*I remember the epiphany of grasping, for the first time, that my burnout was the consequence of the personal myth I had created. I've since come to call that persona 'the masked stranger' – the tough, unstoppable, macho figure on whom others depended but who never needed their help. I was so incredibly invested in that particular story about myself. It helped me move ahead in my career and deliver against objectives in the most challenging circumstances. I invented it to protect myself. It helped me desensitize from others' emotions and my own – a useful trick to have if you're very ambitious but also easily hurt by brickbats, or for that matter if you're fighting a war. Burnout confronted – in a way nothing else could have done – the relevance of this part of my personal myth. It made me realize it had come to define me instead of being something I could use when I chose. It was living me rather than I living it.*

It is our belief that, contrary to what other authors might say,[1] it's not a matter of avoiding burnout, or banishing it or doing anything else with it. It's about allowing it and recognizing it as a natural process. Indeed we'd go as far as to say that sometimes the worst thing you can do for a high flyer is to prevent them from burning out. To do so not only stops them from making critical adjustments in the way in which they relate to the world, but also postpones the inevitable, potentially resulting in a far worse outcome both for the individual and their organization. Instead, the objective should be to 'hold' them in a way that enables them to learn from the experience. This learning is likely to be profound and transformational. Like the mythical hero's journey, the trials of burnout offer the possibility of transforming high flyers' consciousness and in the process creating vital leaders distinguished by their depth, their humanity and their ability to add value through learning and insight.

In this chapter we explain how the learning emerging from burnout fits in with that from other developmental experiences, as well as the specific lessons burnout can teach. We go on to justify the use of burnout developmentally, both at an individual, business and social level. We then focus on the key factors required for high flyers to learn from burnout. We conclude by looking at what the research tells us about the nature of the relationship in which high flyers were held through burnout.

## Burnout as significant developmental experience

Outside of those who have a vested interest in pretending otherwise – namely management trainers – there are few people nowadays who would claim that leadership is learned in the classroom. Since the pioneering work of Reg Revans, the founder of action learning in the 1940s, there have been countless studies demonstrating the primacy of on-the-job experience in the development of leadership skills. Leaders learn by doing. They learn their art through the performance of their roles, particularly those aspects which involve significant challenge and adversity. In the words of Aristotle, often quoted by Revans, 'That which we must learn to do, we learn by doing'.

The question of which experiences hold the most developmental potential has been widely researched. In their groundbreaking book *The Lessons of Experience* involving data from 191 successful executives from six major corporations, McCall, Lombardo and Morrison identified three categories of such experiences – job assignments, bosses – both good and bad – and hardships and setbacks (see Figure 5.1).[2]

Hardships involved distressing events, both in and outside work, in which 'Managers accepted appropriate responsibility for the mess they were in; during the worst of it they experienced a strong sense of aloneness or lack of control over events; and the situation forced them to confront

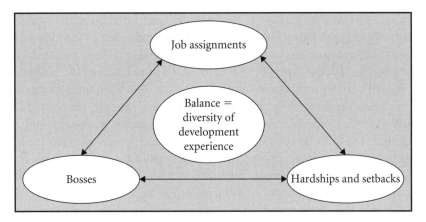

**Figure 5.1**   Experiences which hold the most developmental potential

| 1 | A *personal trauma* threatening the health and wellbeing of the executive or the executive's family. |
| 2 | A *career setback* involving demotions and missed promotions. |
| 3 | *Changing jobs*, in which some executives risked their careers to get out of a dead-end job. |
| 4 | *Business mistakes*, in which bad judgement and poor decisions led to failure. |
| 5 | A *subordinate performance problem* forcing the executive to confront people with issues of incompetence or with problems such as alcoholism.[4] |

**Figure 5.2**   Types of hardship developmental experiences

themselves. It was this struggle with "who (or what) I am" that made these events unique and triggered intensely personal learning'.[3] McCall et al listed five such events (see Figure 5.2).

Each type of experience provided executives with different learning: 'Assignments are the primary source of independence, knowledge of the business, confidence, leadership, toughness, handling relationships. Bosses are a primary source of managerial and human values and lessons of politics. Hardships expose personal limits and perspective on self'.[5] 'Balance' comes about through a diversity of developmental experiences across all three areas: 'The confidence spawned by success in tough assignments may need the balance engendered by a hardship that confronts a manager with his or her limits. Toughness may evolve into insensitivity if not balanced by basic values around the treatment of others'.[6]

The issue, of course, is how to ensure leaders gain this diversity of experience. While organizations can attempt to determine job assignments and bosses through succession planning and job rotation, they cannot do the same for hardships: 'Most of the hardships are not amenable, physically or morally, to organizational manipulation for developmental purposes'.[7] It is our contention that burnout falls into the category of a hardship developmental experience – specifically one involving personal trauma – and that it should be considered legitimate developmental material. It is legitimate because it is situated in the relationship between the high flyer and their work environment; both the individual and the organization contribute to the occurrence of burnout. We lay out the moral case for this later in this chapter and discuss the practical implications in the next.

The issue with learning from hardship is its unpredictability. As McCall et al put it,

> Of all the developmental events, hardships (and traumas in particular) guard their lessons best. The temptation to distance oneself from the event can be compelling. There is always someone or something else one can blame. Disclaiming responsibility for the event can set up a chain reaction in which one also denies the response to it. A trauma can be used to justify cynicism or fatalism or withdrawal or overcompensation. The choice between relying on one's less mature defences or looking inward to find lessons is one in which immaturity often wins out because it provides pat explanations.[8]

Evidently, there are very clear parallels between learning from personal trauma and learning from burnout.

For the organization committed to developing balanced, mature leaders this presents a considerable dilemma. How does one get leaders to learn the lessons emerging from hardship when these lessons are so open to chance? Organizations need to make use of every legitimate hardship opportunity that comes their way. Burnout is such an opportunity, and as such can – in the right hands – yield lessons that are transformative of individuals and their organizations.

## The potential (constituent) lessons of burnout

For those who develop as a result of burning out, the learning is profound. The high flyers in our study were forced into a confrontation with an old identity which had outlived its usefulness. Their understanding of who they were and what they stood for was fundamentally challenged. They experienced an inner shift which transformed their consciousness about their place in the world. Over time this shift became embedded.

They developed a new story about themselves. This converted into new neural pathways or associations which in turn translated themselves into new patterns and habits. When asked if they thought of themselves differently after their burnout experience, they answered with a resounding yes.

There were four major themes to this learning. Each is described below and summarized in Figure 5.3. The advantage of this kind of reductionist analysis is that it helps the reader understand the components of the learning that arose as a result of burnout. But there are also distinct disadvantages. Namely that we mislead the reader into thinking that an atomized list of lessons is an honest representation of the broader, systemic learning that emerged. In order to avoid this pitfall we discuss this systemic learning and its significance for the development of leaders later in this chapter.

### Recognition of own limitations and fallibilities – humility

Like Tim's story of the masked stranger, many of those who learnt from burnout talked about giving up an old image in which their power to take whatever was thrown at them was limitless. Like invincible super-beings they neither suffered from the frailties that afflicted mere mortals, nor did they need to live by the same laws that others followed. An illustration of this in the last chapter was Dimitris thinking he had no limits and was unstoppable. Burnout caused them to do the previously unthinkable. They reached out for help. They admitted they simply did not know what to do. They confessed there might be more for them to learn. They reeled in their estimation of their capabilities. Scott's story in the last chapter of asking for help is one such example. Here he continues the story:

*When I was in the middle of it I felt that I was managing. I felt that I was coping. I felt that I could turn things around. I was acutely embarrassed about being in the position I was in. I had such a high opinion of myself that it was inconceivable that I couldn't cope. I felt I could fix it and that people would look at me and say 'Was in a grim situation, but he turned that round, what a guy! Did it on his own. Self-reliant. What a trouper'. All the time, around the edges, family and friends were saying 'Let us help. We can see you're in crisis. We can see you are sinking. Let us help'. And either it wasn't getting through this shield of embarrassment and self-reliance, or it was getting through but I was rationalizing it away. 'No, I don't need that. I'm doing fine, thanks. I'm fine.' Looking back now I can see that there were so many pairs of helping hands desperate to help, desperate to get involved. I learned through the counselling that there was no shame in admitting weaknesses, admitting doing bad things, thinking bad thoughts, being vengeful and resentful. Just talking that through and getting somebody's opinion, when opinion matters, was a vital tool of healthy self-awareness and healthy living.*

William talked about basing his estimation of his abilities on a more realistic footing:

*It was the most difficult thing that has ever happened to me. I've been taken hostage, I've been mortared, I've been shot at and I still would do all of those things rather than go into that again...It took a massive chunk of confidence away, but I think that confidence was more brash and arrogant and I think now my confidence is placed more in what I'm able to do rather than what I think I'm able to do.*

## Greater sense of perspective

Not surprisingly for those who previously suffered from an over-identification with work to the exclusion of all other facets of life, the high flyers who learnt from burnout talked about gaining a sense of perspective. This could indeed be manifest by a more grounded approach to work and its place in their lives, but it could also make itself known through more balanced business decision making or having a clearer sense of what's important for them. Dimitris told us he had managed to control his tendency to overestimate the impact of events at work:

*The other thing I learned to do when I am very stressed is to ask myself what will be the impact if this happens? In most cases stress is the result of a lot of ifs. A lot of ifs which, when you put them together, can give you a breakdown. Often you overestimate the possible impact of what is really just a hypothetical event. So I try to list all the possible events that might happen and come up with the real consequences of each. That way the stress is minimized. And when you compare the consequences of one of these events happening with having a breakdown, you stop worrying about what might happen.*

Burnout had the effect of pulling back the curtains to reveal a much wider stage than the one on which the high flyers thought they were performing. Larissa talked about recovering from her burnout experience: 'We went on vacation to a quiet place, far away from the city. We were on our own. I started to understand that this is also life! This is really life. I started to feel like myself again. I started to realize that I really do enjoy something else other than work!'. This revelation often had the effect of reminding high flyers about a forgotten, more profound sense of purpose, as Li-Ying illustrates:

*My aim in life is to be happy. It [burnout] made me realize that I forgot about that goal. And that made me pause a while and think about my career, where I am, in terms of why I am alive and everything. It made me ask if I'm doing something I want to do. Is this the right company that I'm working for? Nowadays I set two rules for myself. If I'm not happy for a prolonged period of time, it may be time to move. Either move job or move out of the company. Secondly, if I don't believe in the leadership – in the direction that the company is heading, then it's time to move. At the moment I still believe in the direction the company is going, I still believe in what the company is doing, and I still believe in the leadership in general. So I can still feel the passion in me, and I'm someone who likes to be passionate about things. I don't want to lose that. I don't want to lose myself just because of my career. Whatever I do and however I progress in this company, I always want to be myself, to be happy and to believe in what I'm doing.*

## Self-management and self-responsibility

An important part of forming a more robust identity is taking one's share of responsibility for what happens in one's life while at the same time defining and managing clear boundaries around what one is willing to do and not do. In the last chapter Fiona looked back on her burnout experience with disbelief that she did not take more responsibility for the relationship with her boss, which ultimately led to her downfall. Stratos gave us the following example of creating much firmer boundaries following his burnout experience.

*My self-esteem is better now. Before [I burnt out] I was very polite with all of the colleagues, deal arrangers and bankers. I was very polite. I did whatever they told me to do 'cos I didn't actually know what was the norm. But I am more demanding now. I am not so polite and I do not do whatever they tell me to do. Definitely not. I negotiate more efficiently and I don't spend twenty-four hours a day just doing things for them.*

Another common theme for those that learnt from burnout was becoming more integrated with the whole of themselves – their bodies and emotions as well as their minds – learning to read themselves and better attend to their needs as a result. Li-Ying described how,

*I didn't take proper breaks for five years of working, in a very intensive, fast-paced and very demanding environment. Always pushing myself. I loved to be pushed and being challenged, and that's why I didn't mind at all. But there are times when you have to step away from it to give your body and your mind a rest and I didn't do that. My body was telling me, 'look I think it's time for you to take a rest. Hang on and pause for a while and just take a break'.*

She explained how she had previously kept her feelings to herself, 'I was bottling it up, and I realized that bottling things up doesn't help, it just becomes a time bomb, waiting to explode so from that I learnt to voice out my frustration whether it's at work or anything'. Being more connected with their own needs from moment to moment meant that the high flyers were able to exercise greater self-control, particularly during periods of high stress. Stratos described his approach to managing stress:

> *Stratos*: I have developed this defence mechanism of my own. I laugh. I laugh every day. If my colleagues see me and I'm not laughing, they say what's going on with you? Maybe it's a form of denial, I don't know. But after two or three days I stop thinking about the stress.
> *Researcher*: Because you're laughing at it?
> *Stratos*: Yes, I am trying to make light of it. I stop thinking of what might happen. It helps me to move on.

## Compassion for self and others

Learning to accept and forgive themselves for their foibles meant that the high flyers who burnt out were more able to show compassion towards others. Dimitris told us how his approach to people management had changed after his experience of burnout:

> *I have become a much more mature manager and better people manager. When I came here I couldn't imagine that someone could have a psychological problem or a breakdown. I came here to succeed. I didn't think such situations existed. If it wasn't for this experience I would be much more aggressive and really bad with people. Now, for example, I've had two or three situations where I've been the manager of someone who's got very stressed. I've asked them to take a week's leave and to come back when they're ready. I've come to understand that this is a very, very common situation in our firm. It's important you give them the necessary relaxation and the necessary time to balance. Otherwise they will leave and you will never learn the reason for them leaving because most of them don't feel close enough to senior staff to discuss these situations.*

Both Larissa and Li-Ying talked about how much more attuned they were to their team over committing themselves, and the importance of passing on their learning in this regard to others.

> *Li-Ying*: If somebody seems to be stressed out or overworking, I go to them, I won't wait for them to come to me. 'Why don't we go out for a coffee, a drink or a meal' kind of thing. Just check in with them. Usually things come out from that conversation. It's great because I'm able to share with them, and give them my view of things, if there are things I can help with or advise. And so far people who I've done that with have been very appreciative of it.

*Larissa:* It's important to talk to them [her team members] as soon as you see them making the same mistakes as you. It's so essential to have somebody telling you this in time, and helping you. Not just telling you that you shouldn't do this, but suggesting two or three different ways to do it that they can choose from. This is the most important role for any manager. It is so important that someone supports you, because nobody helped me when I was going into this.

| Key development themes | Examples of how this was manifest |
|---|---|
| Recognition of own limitations and fallibilities; humility | • More realistic sense of own capabilities<br>• Willing to reach out and ask for help<br>• Willing to admit they don't know what to do in a given situation<br>• Knowing when one's body needs a rest and taking it<br>• A greater sense of there being more to learn; a belief that one has not arrived but is on a journey<br>• Greater openness to learning the new: behaviour, beliefs, values |
| Greater sense of perspective | • Realistic assessment of the consequences of work issues<br>• More balanced approach to work and its place in their lives<br>• More mature, more balanced business decision making<br>• Being clear about what's important to them in their lives and their working lives |
| Self-management and self-responsibility | • Defining own boundaries<br>• Not repeating dysfunctional patterns and falling back into an old identity with limited relevance in the present context<br>• Taking their share of responsibility for situations and relationships<br>• Greater sense of self-authorship – improved sense of choice and volition<br>• Greater self-awareness of own unproductive behaviour in certain contexts<br>• Greater sense of self-control<br>• Realizing the importance of voicing feelings and concerns and not bottling them up<br>• Understanding the need to check-in with oneself in order to keep in balance |
| Compassion for self and others | • Greater sensitivity to others<br>• Greater sense of fairness and justice in the work place and managing people accordingly<br>• Greater focus on the development of others |

**Figure 5.3**   The potential (component) lessons of burnout

| The potential lessons of personal traumas | The potential lessons of burnout |
|---|---|
| 'Sensitivity to others' – learning the 'lessons of compassion as a result of pain' | Compassion for self and others |
| 'Coping with events beyond one's control – no-one can control events, but we can control how we respond' | Self-management and self-responsibility |
| 'Recognition of personal limits/The balance between work and personal life – being brought up short was the central theme of personal traumas, and reflecting on one's inadequacies and blind spots often led to a decision to reconsider how one lives one's life'[9] | • Recognition of own limitations and fallibilities; humility<br><br>• Greater sense of perspective |

**Figure 5.4**  Comparison of potential lessons emerging from personal traumas and those from burnout

## Comparisons with other studies

These lessons are similar to those McCall et al found in their research into the learning that arose from personal trauma (see Figure 5.4).

There are, however, some significant differences between the respective lessons of what McCall et al refer to as 'Coping with events beyond one's control' and the category of 'Self-management and self-responsibility' in our research. While the two studies agree that managers/high flyers learn to control their behaviour when unable to control the situation, McCall et al's finding that 'Hanging in and persevering through the event were common refrains' is not supported by our study. As we have seen, 'hanging in and persevering' was – in part – what got high flyers into trouble in the first place. Instead we discovered that those who learned from burnout learned to establish better responsibility-taking and self-management strategies, such as boundary setting and self-control. In other words they found that a 'more of the same' strategy only served to intensify their problem rather than solve it.[10]

## Suffering from burnout

Because the learning from burnout was profound, it was also distressing. Reflecting on the learning that came out of his burnout experience, Scott told us,

*It was terribly painful. There was disappointment, frustration, anger, resentment, but although I had all of these feelings I didn't recognize them for what they were at the time. There was a real prolonged period of passivity which I think was all a necessary part of the process. Earlier this year I had a conversation with a friend who asked, where did you go for five years? I said I don't know. But I didn't like who I was or where I was. And I didn't recognize how I'd got there.*

Hamish talked about his burnout as shattering '…any illusions that I had about being able to cope with anything and everything. That dose of reality is probably not a bad thing, but it was fairly smartly and painfully delivered'.

Experiences which hold the potential to make people question their very sense of identity inevitably bring suffering in their wake. We have referred to this kind of learning as profound. It could equally be called a 'dark night of the soul', the title of a treatise written by Roman Catholic mystic St John of the Cross to refer to a period in which one suffers a crisis of faith on the journey towards spiritual enlightenment.[11] What it is not is incremental learning. It does not involve the simple acquisition of new concepts or information that we can readily assimilate alongside other such data. Profound learning involves challenging deeply-held beliefs – in the case of burnout the nature of the very story we have constructed about ourselves. As Blakeley puts it, 'Learning (as opposed to information processing) often involves some psychological pain or discomfort. The greater the degree of learning, the greater the emotional intensity and, often, pain'.[12] This is a far cry from the sanitized 'information processing' version of learning held by many people in organizations and energetically peddled by the management training industry. In this world of fantasy and make-believe, happy learners eagerly swallow pre-digested information which is downloaded into their heads like pieces of software. Positive psychologists would have us believe that we spend far too much time contemplating what might be wrong with us, and far too little focusing on what we are already good at. Some organizations have even gone so far as to build their entire approach to developing leaders on such a premise. One of the messages of this book is that learning to lead entails a degree of suffering and inward examination. Without it we are left with 'bricklayers' rather than leaders; people who do not know themselves or what is important to them and who, as a consequence, lack self-integrity.

## Systemic learning and its significance for leadership development

Burnout is a systemic condition and it should come as no surprise therefore that the learning emerging from it is also systemic. When it occurs, learning from burnout brings about whole-person change. The development themes we have outlined above and the ways in which they are manifest underlie the evolution towards full adult maturity. At an individual level this means the growth of identity and sense of purpose. Personal myths are revised or comprehensively recreated. Purposes are grounded in a profound sense of the fundamental reason for existence. Consciousness is transformed such that the way in which the high flyer makes sense of their world broadens and deepens.

In many ways such a transformation of consciousness represents the holy grail of leadership development. How often have the bosses of rising stars struggled with issues of maturity and balance? How often have human resources professionals been tasked with developing high-potential employees who are seen as hot-headed, insensitive, exercising poor judgement, arrogant, poor team workers, risk averse or lacking the courage of their convictions? As far as organizations are concerned the lessons of burnout are systemic because they:

- develop wisdom in the sense of more balanced decision making, a greater sense of perspective and an awareness of the consequential nature of one's actions
- accelerate maturity and develop humility in the sense that high flyers have a deep understanding of their limitations and the patterns which can derail them
- develop compassionate and human leaders who inspire followership
- engender sustainable, balanced approach to leadership and the pursuit of one's career
- create independent thinkers whose leadership is based on strongly-held personal values
- develop emotionally robust individuals with their own distinct, vital identity which they are not afraid of expressing.

In the introduction we outlined some practices of good leadership which we believe to be universal and timeless. We said these practices describe what leaders do rather than what they are – their praxis rather than their characteristics, if you will. We explained that burnout offers the potential of teaching many aspects of these practices. Indeed, as can be seen from Figure 5.5, the learning from burnout contributes to the development of every one of these universal practices. This depth of learning cannot be bought, nor can it be engineered or manipulated. And perhaps this, above all, is the most compelling reason for organizations to take the issue of burnout seriously. Not because of the damage it might cause them, but because of the value it can bring.

| Universal practices of leadership | Systemic learning emerging from burnout | Constituent lessons |
|---|---|---|
| Form and sustain the enterprise they are leading so that it endures over time | Maturity and humility in the sense that high flyers have a deep understanding of their limitations and the patterns which can derail them | • Recognition of own limitations and fallibilities; humility<br>• Self-management and self-responsibility |
| Bring value (more often than not, insight or learning) not just to their followers but to the wider community of which they are a part | • Independent thinkers whose leadership is based on strongly held personal values<br>• Emotionally robust individuals with their own distinct, vital identity which they are not afraid of expressing | • Greater sense of perspective<br>• Self-management and self-responsibility |
| Hold and protect their followers, providing them with inspiration to continue on the journey | • Compassionate and human leaders who inspire followership<br>• Emotionally robust individuals with their own distinct, vital identity which they are not afraid of expressing | • Compassion for self and others<br>• Self-management and self-responsibility |
| Create a climate of balance in which the collective contribution of all is sought and creativity, learning and trade can flourish | Sustainable, balanced approaches to leadership and the pursuit of one's career | • Self-management and self-responsibility<br>• Recognition of own limitations and fallibilities; humility |
| Embody mature, vital humanity and compassion that sustains their followers through the most challenging times | • Compassionate and human leaders who inspire followership<br>• Emotionally robust individuals with their own distinct, vital identity which they are not afraid of expressing | • Compassion for self and others<br>• Self-management and self-responsibility |
| Are a great source of wisdom, sound judgement and balanced decision making | Wisdom in the sense of more balanced decision making, a greater sense of perspective and an awareness of the consequential nature of one's actions | • Greater sense of perspective<br>• Recognition of own limitations and fallibilities; humility<br>• Self-management and self-responsibility |

**Figure 5.5** Linkage between the systemic and constituent learning emerging from burnout and the universal practices of leadership

## The case for using burnout as developmental experience

Earlier in this chapter we said that the fact that burnout arises from the nature of the relationship between the high flyer and their work environment legitimizes its use by the organization as developmental material. However, some readers may be concerned that such use may leave high flyers vulnerable to attempts by organizations to, in Madeleine Bunting's words, '...mould and manipulate our inner lives through new styles of invasive management which sponsor our "personal growth".'[13] So in this section we develop the moral case for using burnout developmentally further, first in terms of the relationship between the individual high flyer and their organization and then in terms of the relationship between organizations and society.

Before doing that we want to make it clear what we are, and are not, proposing. We are making the case for the use of the learning that emerges from burnout as a legitimate way of developing the leaders of the future. Specifically we are suggesting that high flyers are 'held' while they go through burnout so that they do not derail but rather learn from the experience. The beneficiaries of this learning are both the individual high flyer and their organization. What we are *not* proposing is yet another thinly-veiled attempt at employee engagement or mind control or creating corporate clones. We are deeply apprehensive, if not a little queasy, about efforts to use personal transformation (what one well-known institute is calling 'enlightenment') to elicit discretionary effort and motivate people to give more of themselves at work.[14] The learning that emerges from burnout certainly holds the potential of developing better leaders. It would be deeply ironic (and as we have seen, highly unlikely) if it persuaded these same leaders to give even more of themselves to the organization!

### *The individual high flyer/organization relationship*

Both the organization and the individual high flyer contribute to the occurrence of burnout. Organizations create impossibly high-pressure working environments that foster burnout. In addition, the very programmes that are designed to develop high flyers are inherently likely to cause them to burn out. High flyers collude with these dysfunctional conditions and some possess characteristics that make them more vulnerable to burnout than others. Because there is shared responsibility for the creation of burnout, there is also shared responsibility for dealing with the consequences. One normally assumes that dealing with the consequences of something requires selecting the best strategy from a range of alternatives. However, in the case of burnout, the only effective response is to deal with it developmentally. Why? Because burnout is a natural process and is not preventable in the long term. The act of preventing someone from burning out may only create a temporary respite. They are just as likely to burn out again when the right combination of workplace conditions and pressures present themselves. The only real way, therefore, of supporting someone who is burning out is to help them negotiate the transition burnout is urging them to make. Organizations, by virtue of their culpability in causing burnout and their duty to develop the best version of leadership they can, have a moral responsibility to help individuals make this transition. High flyers, by virtue of their contribution to their own burnout and their responsibility for their own development, have a moral duty to negotiate the transition.

Our purpose in making this case is to avoid the dystopian future that those who want to banish burnout or prevent it believe they are achieving. Going through burnout without self-destructing is to learn life- and career-transforming lessons that ensure burnout does not recur.

## The relationship between organizations and society

Since the Second World War we have witnessed the rise of organizations to become what they are today – the single, most influential force on the planet. This new world order has yet to invest itself in many of the responsibilities that come with great power. Repeated examples of declining ethical standards, as well as the approach many organizations adopt towards burnout, show that organizations' sense of responsibility simply has not caught up with their new-found ascendancy.

Running in parallel with this phenomenon has been the decline in many parts of the world of institutions traditionally entrusted with helping people to form an adult life – the church and the family as well as the local community. This has created a vacuum in which some have over-invested in their jobs to the extent that they spend more time, psychic and emotional energy at work than they do in any other part of their lives, and indeed than all the other parts of their lives put together. What lies behind this is the use of work as a substitute for identity – for meaning and purpose in one's life. The quest for something bigger than just 'me' – what Viktor Frankl referred to as 'Man's search for meaning'[15] – is increasingly found through work.

Our research shows high flyers use work in this way. In Chapter 3 we described those coming into the labour market as seeking meaning beyond mere wealth creation. A Spring 2008 survey of more than 1500 UK employees working for a variety of organizations throws more light on this. It revealed that 'more than 60% of 18 to 25-year-olds [working for private sector organizations] and almost half overall [across all sectors] are looking for what they call "more worthwhile work".[16] By 'worthwhile' respondents meant work had 'to do two things: contribute to society (in the widest sense) and make the most of their talents'.[17] This search for worthwhile work demonstrates an admirable concern with making a contribution to social improvement. But it also reveals that increasing numbers of generation Y employees are focused on finding meaning through their work, in much the same way that high flyers do. As Madeleine Bunting puts it,

*We look to work for a sense of integration and connection to society, while our grandparents would have been able to look to their neighbourhood, their church, their political party, perhaps also an extended family nearby. This gives employers unprecedented purchase over our lives: how they are organized, how we perceive ourselves, and how we shape our relationships with others – both colleagues at work and personal relationships outside it.[18]*

Work has always played a role in satisfying our emotional dependency needs, but never to this extent.

Some believe the answer is for organizations to rise to the challenge of providing worthwhile work by giving employees 'an invigorating sense of purpose that goes beyond business success and which makes people feel they are changing society as opposed to just servicing needs'.[19] Others feel it's a matter of proving to these pesky ingrates that what they are doing for a living is genuinely worthwhile.[20] The first course of action has significant potential for abuse in the hands of less responsible employers, as it leaves employees vulnerable to corporate exploitation of their need for identity and purpose. The second assumes that organizations are simply not doing a good enough job of selling the inherent worthwhileness of their enterprise in the first place. What neither perspective grasps is that this search for meaning has to be satisfied at an individual level and cannot either practically or ethically be satisfied at a collective level. As Frankl puts it, 'Man's search for meaning is the primary motivation in his life and not a "secondary rationalization" of instinctual drives. This meaning is unique and specific in that it must and can be fulfilled by him alone; only then does it achieve a significance which will satisfy his own *will* to meaning'. It is not for organizations to 'create a sense of meaning for their employees'[21] in order to raise levels of performance to ever-more stellar levels, but for organizations to support employees in finding their own meaning and purpose – an identity by any other name. As might have become obvious by now, for those who experience it, burnout represents this journey towards identity.

Why should organizations help employees find their own meaning and in so doing, form an adult identity? We believe there are four very good reasons:

- First and foremost, if organizations want to develop leaders rather than 'bricklayers', they need to set about developing high flyers with a strong, authentic sense of their own identity.
- Secondly, the inevitable consequence of people spending most of their lives at work is that the workplace has become the primary milieu in which people mature and individuate. Simply by virtue of the fact that people spend so long *at work* means that the process of individuation will take place largely *through work*.
- Thirdly, organizations are literally trillions of dollars in debt to their employees in terms of additional working hours and discretionary emotional investment. Once organizations start seeing their people as investors rather than assets to be sweated, they will realize that they need to find a way of giving a 'worthwhile' return.
- Finally, with great power comes great responsibility. Organizations' ascendancy means they have – like it or not – inherited a role formerly performed by other declining social institutions.

## What it takes for high flyers to learn from burnout

Having considered what high flyers learn from burnout and why they should learn it, it remains for us to return to the theme we explored in Chapter 4, namely the key factors determining whether high flyers learn from burnout. In the last chapter we pointed to high flyers' willingness to accept responsibility for their role in causing burnout as the key determinant. But what lay underneath this willingness?

Other authors have referred to managers having two layers of defence against learning from hardship, the first being denial – 'refusing to believe it had really happened or to accept responsibility for what happened' – and the second being a feeling of powerlessness, 'a misplaced belief that nothing can be done about it'.[22] We found that most of those who did not learn from burnout were in denial and attributed their experience to factors outside their control. However half of those who did learn, did exactly the same thing. The same was broadly true for feelings of powerlessness.

Maybe, we thought, high flyers who learnt from burnout interrupted quality self-interaction less than those who didn't learn. So we took a look at the different dimensions of reflexivity discussed in Chapter 4 to see if this was the case. We discovered that there were some differences in intentionality and felt perception. Seventy per cent of those who did not learn had a negative intentionality compared to 50% of those who did learn. More intriguingly, the felt perception of those who did learn operated at both a rational and emotional level, but only at a rational level for the majority of those who didn't. It is important to note here that positive intentionality does not equate to accepting responsibility. It is possible to have a positive intentionality such as, 'I decided to take on more work, afraid of what would happen if I didn't', which does not demonstrate responsibility-taking for one's role in bringing about burnout.

As interesting as all this was, it didn't seem to supply a compelling reason for why some learnt whilst others didn't. We decided to turn our attention to the actual events that took place during the burnout experience of each of the high flyers we interviewed. Many of these events had the potential to make high flyers stop and reflect on their contribution to the experience. We found that those who learnt from burnout responded to these external stimuli differently from the majority of those who did not. First, they had a moment of truth conversation with themselves in which they confronted their current version of who they were. All of them could tie this down to a particular point in time, a moment of awareness that was burnt into their memory. Secondly, this conversation took place in the moment – during the event in question or immediately afterwards, but not several days or weeks subsequently. Thirdly, they made sense of things at an emotional and an intuitive level as well as an intellectual one. This involved the three-step reflexive process we described in Chapter 4:

1 Creating meaning of the conversation we are having with ourselves about our experience.
2 Listening to ourselves making this meaning.
3 Finding the will to act on the meaning we have created.

We also discovered there was something that happened to 'learners' that didn't happen to 'non-learners'. They were 'held' by someone invested in helping them learn from the experience.

Fiona's experience illustrates this process. In the gap between her old boss leaving and her new boss coming into the job, she took on many of her superior's responsibilities. Despite finding herself overwhelmed she held onto these after her new boss arrived. She felt she had to prove herself to the incoming leader, but also her pride stopped her from letting go of the work. Her moment of truth came one day in February:

*I can point to a time when I suddenly realized how deeply affected I'd been. As the result of being nominated as a high potential I'd gone to an assessment course for three days. That was in the February, after she [the new boss] arrived in September. By then I was a long way into feeling pretty stressed. I went to the assessment event but my confidence was so low I really felt 'what am I doing here? This is a disaster!'. And I didn't do at all well. I felt I'd really let myself down because I just wasn't able to be myself. So I think that was the start of the realization. The guy who fed back my results at the end asked, 'Is there something happening to affect your perform-ance at the moment?'. I told him, 'I can't talk to you about it, but yes, there is. My confidence is at rock bottom and I've only just realized that.' I was able to make a connection between how I felt at that event and what was going on with the work. So there was a dawning. (Our emphasis)*

Fiona was able to relate her experience to her internal process. In so doing she began to question what this meant for her sense of identity. The question she asked herself was not 'What is happening to me?' (an inter-nal dialogue that frequently occurred in those who did not learn from burnout), but 'Who is the me that this is happening to?'. This moment of truth conversation led to a dawning awareness that the story she had cre-ated about herself – her personal myth which formed her identity – was no longer 'a good story to live by'.[23] This represented the first stage of the reflexive process outlined above.

However, this recognition led to feelings of powerlessness and being overwhelmed which lasted several months, 'Whilst I recognized that I had to change something – I remember endless conversations with my husband about how do I change – I didn't feel empowered to change. I didn't feel good that I'd recognized the issue – it felt like even more chal-lenge – one more thing I now had to deal with…'. Fiona's husband – who happened to be a trained counsellor – held his wife through the experi-ence. He shared with her the changes he noticed in her behaviour, chal-lenging her lack of perspective and balance. He encouraged her to think of herself as having choice and responsibility. He supported her in tak-ing small steps to re-establish her self-confidence. His holding increased Fiona's experience of the suffering – she began to fully absorb its emo-tional intensity – and in so doing she began to listen to the meaning she had made of her experience (the second stage of the reflexive pro-cess). She started to assimilate the realization that her story (or personal myth) had become stagnant and lacked relevance for her current stage of development.

The turning point came when Fiona found herself buried in work as a result of trying to pull together a project involving her boss and a colleague who were not communicating properly. She took responsibility for her predicament – found the will to act on the meaning she had created about her experience, the third stage of the reflexive process – and went to see the HR manager to ask for help. Thereafter she had a conversation with her boss about reallocating some of her responsibilities.

Fiona's approach to work and life in general was transformed as a result of her experience. She became more aware of her limitations and her patterns – what triggers her and in what situations, her need to reconnect with herself to stay in balance. She is also more aware of how she impacts her team and consciously gives them more space to perform. Essentially, Fiona has revised and reconstructed her personal myth to make sense of changing circumstances and new developmental issues that have arisen in her life:

> *Fiona*: Looking back from where I am now, in a position of fairly good health and wellbeing, I can't believe I got myself into it. I can't believe that I didn't go and have constructive conversations with my boss when she arrived, to say 'Right, here's what I've been doing. How are we going to work this out?'. I just didn't – in fact almost quite the opposite, I tried to keep it, to make myself feel good, you know? I had a huge amount of responsibility and I ignored that, which was wrong. My relationship with my boss may not ever have been brilliant, but it could have been a whole heap better if I'd taken some responsibility for being more challenging of her. I think now I would have much more confidence to go and do that.
>
> *Researcher*: So, what impact do you think that experience had on your development?
>
> *Fiona*: It gave me an understanding of myself and what made me tick, and the things that I do. Some of my weaknesses, if you like. I'm not saying I can always get it right, but I manage things a lot better now. So, more self-awareness, better coping strategies for managing certain behaviours, I guess. I've done some reflection on what triggers particular situations since then, and it's probably influenced me a little bit in my own leadership style – how I am with other people. I recognize this driven-ness and this tendency to keep doing more and more and more – how does that impact others? And a growing awareness of how I need to recognize that

and allow others space. Nowadays I have check-in conversations with my team about how they're feeling and how they're doing. I am much more sensitive now to how my own leadership style can be affected by my driven-ness.

*Researcher:* Do you think of yourself any differently now compared to how you thought of yourself before you had this experience?

*Fiona:* I think of myself as a bit older and wiser for it (the burnout experience), though I don't say 'Oh gosh it was the best thing that could have ever happened to me'. I don't look at myself and say, 'You have this weakness that you carry and it could happen at any time'. I've been able to take the positives from it, I think, and build on it. I just see it as something that's contributed to my experience of life, not just work. It took me a while to get there though, that sense of learning didn't come immediately. I went through the next role, which had its own stresses, and it was probably only when I got into this role that I've been able to put some of that learning in. I'm now back into a leadership position and I can see the learning coming through in how I'm being. It's been a process of about two years to be able to reflect on it in that way. I think what contributes to stress often for me is not taking time out to reflect. So one of my learnings is that I'm not very good at putting in the time to keep reflecting – I need to force that time in.

Fiona's story also illustrates how those who have burned out need the time and the opportunity to contemplate what has happened to them. Then having done so, they often look back with wonder on the experience, astonished that they had lacked or temporarily suspended their sense-making ability.

Figure 5.6 summarizes the learning pattern of learners outlined above. Appendix 2 provides descriptions of 'the moment of truth conversations' for the other learners, in their own words.

Fiona's story is an illustration of developmental change – she had, to paraphrase the words of McAdams,[24] in some sense fallen behind in the growth of her personal identity. But more than half of the 'learners' faced the daunting task of 'personological change'.[25] They discovered either that their personal myth had never served them well or that it simply did not exist. The former meant that their myth was deeply and fundamentally flawed in some way; the latter that there was no inner sense of self, no identity other than the one painted onto them, superimposed by others. Scott,

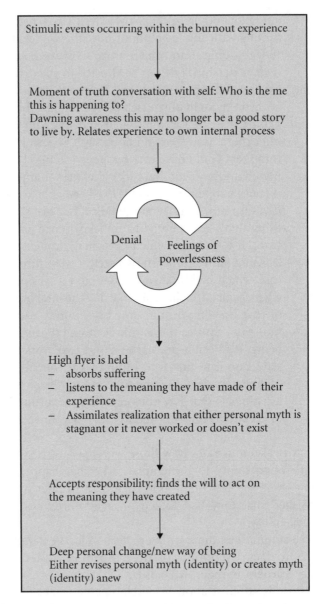

**Figure 5.6**    Learning pattern of those who learnt from burnout

for example, uses the metaphor of dismantling the foundations of a house to describe how he – supported by the person holding him – erased the old myth he had swallowed before creating a new myth of his own making,

*I was very concerned that we actually dismantled the pillars completely, so that when the building was reconfigured and my character and my personality was*

*reconfigured, I wasn't simply rebuilding the same attitudes, the same behaviours, the same approaches, and it would just become this repeating cycle. The image I remember using was a pitchfork and a straw. I'd taken the bold decision to shove the pitchfork into the straw and chuck it up in the air, and it took a long time for the straw to settle. I was very anxious that it didn't reconfigure.*

The majority of non-learners didn't have a moment of truth conversation with themselves and continued to believe theirs was still a good story to live by. As we mentioned earlier, most were in denial about what was happening and consequently were unlikely to experience a moment of insight. The felt perception of 80% of them functioned at an intellectual level only. The remainder processed experience at an intellectual and emotional level, but at no point in the burnout experience did this also embrace the will to act. To a large extent they were impervious to outer experience penetrating their inner experience of themselves. In the words of McCall et al, 'The inability to relate one's experience to what lies inside oneself, severely restricts one's ability to learn'.[26]

There were a few non-learners who did experience a moment of illumination, however. These individuals realized theirs was no longer a good story to live by, but this realization lacked clarity. They tended to veer wildly between grasping their role in causing burnout and believing others to be wholly responsible. This ambiguity meant that they engaged at a rational and emotional level but their determination to do something about it flickered on and off like a faulty light bulb. Some began to question the relevance of their current personal myth but lacking conviction failed to follow this through and fell back into their old familiar patterns. They failed to listen to the meaning they had made of their experience. Sadly they were not held, and so lacked an external agency that could encourage them to listen to themselves. Ultimately, their internal dialogue defaulted to a 'What is happening to me?' conversation.

What motivated the learning of those who learnt as opposed to those who didn't? Even though they were aware of just how incredibly painful this learning was going to be, they chose to commit themselves to what Scott Peck calls 'The road less travelled',[27] the road of trials. In doing this they were not driven by most of the things cognitive psychologists would have us believe motivate us to learn. Namely, they were not trying to preserve their self-esteem or their need for self-enhancement, they were not trying to maintain a positive self-concept; they were not trying to protect positive perceptions of self-efficacy – in fact, quite the opposite; nor were they trying to sustain coherence and continuity of their self-image – they were in fact doing the reverse.[28] Why did they follow such a seemingly counter-intuitive path? Each had discovered to a greater or lesser extent there was little meaning to their lives, that their lives lacked purpose. What they thought of as their identity turned out to be little more than straw blowing in the wind. They were motivated not by the pursuit of psychological comfort or happiness but by the search for meaning and purpose. In the words of Viktor Frankl, 'Between stimulus and response there is a space. In that space is our power to choose our response. In our response lies our growth and freedom'.[29] Of course happiness is not just assumed (by cognitive psychologists of a certain persuasion) to be one of the primary goals of learning but of life generally. Western society has lionized the idea we should aspire to a perpetual state of happiness, that indeed there is some inherent meaning to be gained from this pursuit. The heroic stories of those who struggle with burnout show such thinking to be not only simplistic but also patronizing.

*Happiness is only one of many goals in human life...To justify everything in terms of happiness reduces human life to that of the animals. If the search for meaning is a unique feature of the human species, then it would seem advisable to consider meaning's merits on their own...Meaning enriches and enhances our time on earth. It gives life a certain quality that happiness itself cannot assure.*

## Holding high flyers through burnout

The act of 'holding' helped high flyers listen to the emerging sense they were making of burnout and ultimately to accept responsibility for their role in bringing it about. We have described the person doing the holding as someone who is invested in helping the high flyer learn from the experience. In Chapter 4 we began to describe the nature of this relationship. We said it could be formal or informal, performed by someone inside the high-flyer's organization or outside it. We described the role of the person doing the holding as sustaining the high flyer but also confronting their behaviour and perspective.

Only a minority of the high flyers who burnt out were held by those inside their organizations. Offers of help more often than not came from family members or loved ones, rather than anyone at work. This applied whether or not the high flyer had an existing coach or mentor. One possible reason for this was high flyers' skill at hiding the true extent of their distress in the work environment. Fiona told us, 'Emotionally I struggled to cope with stuff. I managed not to show it at work, but lots of tears and emotion at home...I'm pretty good at covering up. My immediate colleagues might have seen me looking tired and a bit frantic but they wouldn't have noticed much else'. When asked to explain why they didn't approach anyone in the organization, high flyers pointed to their colleagues' lack of interest in their condition: 'I was working very, very long hours and becoming incredibly tired and nobody noticed', said Fiona. 'That was a pressure in itself. It really pissed me off. When I tried to talk to [my boss] about it, she didn't seem interested...' Elsewhere in this book we have talked about the extent to which burnout stigmatizes those who experience it. This sense of shame as well as anxiety about the consequences for one's career, may also have contributed to high flyers avoiding a work-based relationship to support them through burnout.

Those doing the holding appeared to participate in the suffering of the high flyer to the degree that they temporarily forgot their own needs and acted instinctively out of compassion. Fiona recalled her husband,

*Challenging me on that sense of victim. He reflected back to me that I did have a choice, that I could take some responsibility. He was incredibly supportive, at a time when he could have said, 'This is absolutely crap! I don't ever see you. You're working all the time and there's nothing left for our relationship. There's no time left to do anything fun any more'. He could have really chucked it at me. But he didn't. He was very supportive, but definitely challenging me to change.*

There was also a quality of participating in the development of the high flyer without being invested in the outcome – understanding that the responsibility for development lay with them and not with the one doing the holding. This was coupled with a commitment to speak the truth, but it came out of a sense of compassion and hence the timing with which the truth was spoken was chosen carefully. Larissa talked about being held by her fiancé,

*He was very supportive and he was very understanding. He was just working on – kind of on me, but he wasn't pushing me, he wasn't upset with me or anything like that. He was wise enough not to say anything before the completion of the project. Then, when I started to think about what had been going on, he said to me that it's not everything you have in life...*

The intentionality[30] of the one doing the holding appeared wholly focused on the learning of the high flyer. This required a high degree of selflessness on their part as well as the exercise of 'ruthless compassion'[31] – a willingness to 'sit with' and encourage the exploration of the other's pain for the sake of the deep personal learning that would emerge.

One of the few high flyers who sought help within their organization commented on her mentor,

*He helped me find clarity around what the issue was; what it was I was feeling and why I was feeling that way. That made it easier because it gave me a model of*

*what I need to work through. And so I started moving from sort of passive, it's all happening to me, to how do I want to respond to this and what are my options. And so it became a process of management rather than things happening to you...I trusted him implicitly. He helped me find clarity in a completely selfless way. He was great at being a mirror – he just reflected things back at me until I could work it out for myself, which was very, very helpful.*

The exercise of ruthless compassion – the willingness to sit with the suffering of another for the sake of their development, rather than try and rescue them – was described in an article written by our much-missed colleague David Casey some years ago, 'There is a level of learning, particularly about oneself, which can be reached only through some level of pain... Kahlil Gibran wrote, "Your pain is the breaking of the shell that encloses your understanding".[32]

David was writing about the deep learning that can occur within an action learning set or small learning group of peers. Later on in the article he refers to the role of the group facilitator in bringing about this learning,

*Unless the atmosphere is one of trust and love, the chance for self-understanding would never arise...but unless the set adviser is also Jesuitical enough to hold onto his belief that the only way to help at the moment of truth is to push the learner through the shell of his own pain, no amount of supportive understanding will really do the trick. This conspiracy of love with truth is a formidable alliance and a potent source of help.[33]*

His description appears equally applicable to the kind of relationship which holds a high flyer through burnout.

Is it naive to expect this quality of coaching relationship to exist within an organization? Our research findings, albeit based on limited numbers of in-company coaching relationships, say otherwise, and our experience as coaching practitioners in organizations supports this. However, such relationships are less likely to survive in toxic organizational cultures – those characterized by intense competition and murderous politics. Those who dismiss the idea of selfless coaching as hopelessly idealistic are more than likely working in this kind of environment. Organizations with more nurturing climates have the legitimate opportunity to take advantage of the potency of burnout's learning potential.

## Conclusions

We started this chapter by saying that the focus on preventing burnout is delusional and ultimately unproductive. Instead, organizations – at least those with developmentally orientated cultures – should concentrate their efforts on allowing and managing burnout by holding high flyers through the experience. We described burnout as the hero's journey. Indeed, burnout is a manifestation of the hero's journey in the very sense that Joseph Campbell intended it.[34] Campbell talked about the consciousness of the hero being 'transformed through trials or certain illuminating revelations'.[35] Burnout represents the road of trials wherein the high flyer's consciousness is transformed. It has the power to catalyze maturation and personal identity. Precisely the journey that Campbell was suggesting. The fact that it does this in a work environment is neither here nor there.

We then went on to look at the research on experiences which hold the most developmental potential, positing burnout within the category of hardship experience, specifically that concerned with personal trauma. We explored the constituent lessons of burnout, explaining that we had arrived by these through reductionist logic and they should not be confused with systemic learning from burnout. In terms of constituent lessons we identified four major learning themes: recognition of own limitations and fallibilities, a greater sense of perspective, self-management and self-responsibility, and compassion for self and others. We compared these lessons with those from other studies of hardship and found there was a remarkable similarity. However, they differed in respect of self-management. Those in the McCall study were seen as soldiering through hardship, whereas those in ours learnt to establish better responsibility-taking and self-management. We noted that suffering was inherent in learning from burnout by nature of its profundity and compared it to what St John of the Cross referred to as a 'dark night of the soul'. We mused on the difference between this and the sanitized version of learning peddled by the management training industry, and reinforced one of the key messages of this book which is that learning to lead necessarily entails a degree of suffering and inward examination.

We explained that the learning emerging from burnout was systemic in as much as it concerned whole-person change and the transformation of identity and purpose towards full adult maturity. We said this kind of learning represented the holy grail of leadership development. We described it as concerned with the development of wisdom, the acceleration of maturity, the development of compassion and sustainable approaches to leadership and one's career, the fostering of independent thought and the establishment of emotionally robust identity. We showed how this learning contributed to the development of the universal practices of leadership we introduced at the beginning of this book, saying that this was probably the most compelling reason for organizations to take burnout seriously. It is worth pausing for a moment to reflect on the fact that learning from burnout produces 'responsible leaders'. They are responsible in the sense that they are cognisant of the consequential nature of their actions, reflect on the limits of what they feel responsible for in the world, and act on this responsibility. Many of the world's largest organizations are currently engaged in the quest to develop such leaders, as a response to declining levels of public trust. They would be wise to seriously consider what the lessons of burnout can offer in this area.

We then presented the case for using high flyers' experience of burnout as valid developmental material. We explained it was legitimate to use burnout developmentally within the relationship between the high flyer and their organization because of their shared responsibility for causing burnout. We pointed out that since it was not possible to prevent high flyers from burning out the only possible strategy was to use the developmental potential of the burnout experience. At a social level we noted the trend for not just high flyers but generation Y employees generally to find meaning through their work, and that this left them vulnerable to abuse by irresponsible employers. We concluded that it was not for organizations to supply employees with ready-made identities and purposes, but for them to support individuals in finding their own identity and purpose.

In turning our attention to what it takes for high flyers to learn, we outlined our findings that those who learn from burnout respond to external stimuli within the experience differently from those who don't. We described this different response as having a moment of truth conversation with themselves during the experience and making sense of this at an emotional and intuitive level as well as an intellectual one. We said the other key differentiating factor between learners and non-learners was that the former were held by someone investing in helping them learn from the experience. This enabled them to absorb the suffering, assimilate the realization that their personal myth had either become stagnant or didn't exist and ultimately accept responsibility for their role in the burnout. There were a few non-learners who also had a moment of truth conversation with themselves but their sense-making lacked lucidity and the lack of someone holding them meant they fell back into old and dysfunctional patterns.

We went on to explore the motivation of learners and discovered they were driven by a search for meaning rather than the nostrums of cognitive psychology.

Finally we took a look at the notion of holding. Most learners accepted offers of help from outside their organizations, probably due to their prowess at hiding their feelings at work, the indifference of colleagues and the stigma attached to burnout. The research revealed the key practices of effective holding as participating in the development of the high flyer without being invested in the outcome, the intentionality of the holder being wholly focused on the other's learning, and the exercise of ruthless compassion or 'breaking the shell that encloses your understanding'.

Suffering – to paraphrase the quotation from Kierkegaard at the beginning of this chapter – turns people to look within themselves. In the case of burnout it sends high flyers on a quest for meaning to their lives. While there is a clear distinction between a life based on the futile pursuit of happiness and one based on the search for meaning, 'few people are happy if their lives are empty and pointless'.[36]

Where does burnout's learning potency come from? We believe it to be connected in some way to a deep impulse within us 'to experience traumatic events as if they were in some sense divine'.[37] 'The truth,' as Scott Peck says, 'is that our finest moments, more often than not, occur precisely when we are uncomfortable, when we're not feeling happy or fulfilled, when we're struggling and searching'.[38]

In the next chapter we describe what it would take for organizations to recognize this struggle.

## End notes

1 We think it significant that most researchers and authors in the burnout field have never experienced burnout.

2 McCall, M.W., Lombardo, M.M. and Morrison, A.M. (1988). *The Lessons of Experience: How Successful Executives Develop on the Job*. New York: The Free Press

3 Lindsey, E., Holmes, V. and McCall, M. (1987). 'Key events in executives' lives.' Technical Report 32, Centre for Creative Leadership

4 McCall, M.W., Lombardo, M.M. and Morrison, A.M. (1988). *The Lessons of Experience: How Successful Executives Develop on the Job*. New York: The Free Press

5 McCall, M.W., Lombardo, M.M. and Morrison, A.M. (1988). *The Lessons of Experience: How Successful Executives Develop on the Job*. New York: The Free Press

6 McCall, M.W., Lombardo, M.M. and Morrison, A.M. (1988). *The Lessons of Experience: How Successful Executives Develop on the Job*. New York: The Free Press

7 McCall, M. (1998). *High Flyers: Developing the Next Generation of Leaders*. Boston: Harvard Business School Press

8 McCall, M.W., Lombardo, M.M. and Morrison, A.M. (1988). *The Lessons of Experience: How Successful Executives Develop on the Job*. New York: The Free Press

9 Lindsey, E., Holmes, V. and McCall, M. (1987). 'Key events in executives' lives.' Technical Report 32, Centre for Creative Leadership. Quoted in M.W. McCall, M.M. Lombardo and A.M. Morrison (1988), *The Lessons of Experience: How Successful Executives Develop on the Job*. New York: The Free Press

10 Watzlawick, P., Weakland, J., Fisch, R. (1974). *Change: Principles of Problem Formation and Problem Resolution.* New York: Norton

11 St John of the Cross (2003). *Dark Night of the Soul.* New York: Dover

12 Blakeley, K. (2007). *Leadership Blind Spots and What to do About Them.* San Francisco: Jossey-Bass

13 Bunting, M. (2005). *Willing Slaves: How the Overwork Culture is Ruling our Lives.* London: Harper Perennial

14 Roffey Park (2007). 'Roffey Park reports on research project into enlightenment at work.' Roffey Park press release, 9 May 2007

15 Frankl, V.E. (1946). *Man's Search for Meaning.* New York: Rider

16 Stern, S. (2008). 'The meaning of life at work and other employee perks.' *Financial Times,* 11 March

17 CHA (2008). 'Worthwhile work: A CHA report.' See CHA website www.chapr.co.uk

18 Bunting, M. (2005). *Willing Slaves: How the Overwork Culture is Ruling our Lives.* London: Harper Perennial

19 Bains, G. et al (2007). *Meaning Inc. The Blueprint for Business Success in the 21st Century.* London: Profile Books

20 CHA (2008). 'Worthwhile work: A CHA report.' See CHA website www.chapr.co.uk

21 Bains, G. et al (2007). *Meaning Inc. The Blueprint for Business Success in the 21st Century.* London: Profile Books

22 McCall, M.W., Lombardo, M.M. and Morrison, A.M. (1988). *The Lessons of Experience: How Successful Executives Develop on the Job.* New York: The Free Press

23 McAdams, D.P. (1993). *The Stories We Live By: Personal Myths and the Making of the Self.* New York: Guilford Press

24 McAdams, D.P. (1993). *The Stories We Live By: Personal Myths and the Making of the Self.* New York: Guilford Press

25 McAdams, D.P. (1993). *The Stories We Live By: Personal Myths and the Making of the Self.* New York: Guilford Press

26 McCall, M.W., Lombardo, M.M. and Morrison, A.M. (1988). *The Lessons of Experience: How Successful Executives Develop on the Job.* New York: The Free Press

27 Scott Peck, M. (1997). *The Road Less Travelled and Beyond: Spiritual Growth in an Age of Anxiety.* New York: Rider

28 Erez, M. and Earley, P.C. (1993). *Culture, Self-Identity, and Work.* Oxford: Oxford University Press; Blakeley, K. (2007). *Leadership Blind Spots and What to do About Them.* San Francisco: Jossey-Bass

29 Frankl, V.E. (1946). *Man's Search for Meaning.* New York: Rider

30 We are deliberately using the term 'intentionality' here rather than intention. Intentionality is a concept often used in psychotherapy which means much more than mere purpose or voluntary intention. 'Intention is a conscious, psychological state; I can set myself voluntarily to do this or that. Intentionality, rather, refers to a state of being, and involves to a greater or lesser degree the *totality* of the person's orientation to the world at that time. This may be *opposite* to conscious intention.'[1] May, R. (1965). 'Intentionality, the heart of human will.' *The Journal of Humanistic Psychology,* vol. 5, pp202–209

31  Rightly or wrongly we attribute this term originally to Zen Buddism: 'It is difficult, if not impossible, to resist what is happening, to know when to be assertive and tough and to know when to yield, to give in, and let all things go as they go. Sometimes saying NO is actually YES, is very affirmative. Don't give in to idiot compassion. For example, you spoil your kids and they run out into the street and get hit by a car . . . Even Jesus did his thing with the money changers, driving them out of the holy temple. You might have to do something that looks very forceful, but you do it because it is appropriate and done out of love, not out of aggression. That is *ruthless compassion*'. Tibetan Buddhist monk, Lama Surya Das, quoted by R. Peterson (2004), 'Ruthless compassion: Reflections on the treatment of an alcoholic.' *Clinical Case Studies*, vol. 3, pp234–49

32  Gibran, K. (1926). *The Prophet.* London: Penguin, quoted by D. Casey (1987), 'Breaking the shell that encloses your understanding.' *Journal of Management Development,* vol. 6, no. 2, pp30–7

33  Casey, D. (1987). 'Breaking the shell that encloses your understanding.' *Journal of Management Development,* vol. 6, no. 2, pp30–7

34  Campbell, J. (1949). *The Hero with a Thousand Faces.* London: Fontana

35  *Joseph Campbell and the Power of Myth with Bill Moyers* (1988). Mystic Fire Video

36  Baumeister, R. (1991). *Meanings of Life.* New York: Guilford Press. Quoted in McAdams, D.P. (1993). *The Stories We Live By: Personal Myths and the Making of the Self.* New York: Guilford Press

37  Stromer, R.S. (2003). 'Faith in the journey: Personal mythology as pathway to the sacred.' Phd dissertation, Pacifica Graduate Institute.

38  Scott Peck, M. (1997). *The Road Less Travelled and Beyond: Spiritual Growth in an Age of Anxiety.* New York: Rider

# 6

# A ledge beyond the edge

*There's a ledge beyond the edge. Keith landed on it! Lucky bloke. Lot of people missed the ledge.*

BILL HICKS

In Chapter 5 we put forward the radical argument for allowing high flyers to go to the edge without falling off it. We presented a case for 'holding' them while they go through the burnout experience. By 'holding' we mean supporting the high flyer within a relationship that does not try to prevent them from burning out but allows them to experience and learn from it. At the same time, the holding contains and manages the experience so that the worst extremes of career derailment and self-destruction do not occur.

In this chapter we describe what it will take for organizations to support this approach, together with some of the key issues that need to be addressed in order for it to be implemented successfully. We focus specifically on two of these. We discuss the kind of organizational culture required to support people learning from burnout. Secondly, we look at what 'holding' looks like within a coaching relationship – what coaches need to do and need not to do in order to coach high flyers in burnout effectively. We conclude with a discussion of the larger-scale implications for organizations of following this path.

But before we get there, we need to answer the question 'Why?'. Why should organizational leadership teams even consider going down this path? What organization in its right mind would accept its brightest and best going to the edge to learn abject and transformational lessons about themselves that may make them truly stellar performers?

## The business case for working with burnout

An impossibly idealistic proposition suggested by a couple of old hippies? We think not. We believe there are three, broad, strategic reasons that would drive organizations in this direction: the crisis in leadership development, empowering lessons for high flyers from acknowledging limitations and the need for leaders to individuate.

Despite the millions of dollars spent on developing executive talent, there is a widely perceived *leadership crisis*. Put simply, there is a shortage of good leaders capable of effectively handling the kinds of challenges facing 21st century organizations. Now, there are several factors contributing to this perceived shortfall, not least of which is the way organizations have traditionally gone about developing their leaders. Specifically, we point to the continuing and unerring faith that many otherwise intelligent HR folk have in the power of classroom-based training to develop leadership skill. Experience is the primary way in which human beings assimilate leadership skill. Robots and trained apes are excellent subjects for having pre-digested information downloaded into their heads, though even then it's unlikely they will pick up anything that looks much like leadership. As lamentable as this state of affairs is, our focus is actually on another organizational trend which we believe is also a contributory factor to the crisis of leadership. This is what we call the 'normalization' of leadership. The belief that there is an ideal set of leadership characteristics that can be identified and against which leaders can be measured to work out whether they have, in Morgan McCall's words, 'the right stuff'.[1] These characteristics are generally known as 'competencies' and organizations employ a multitude of sophisticated tools to search for them, including psychometric instruments and assessment centres. Those deemed to have the requisite qualities are then entered into an accelerated development programme with the aim of enhancing their mastery of them. The problem with all of this[2] is that it tends to reject those who might not readily fit a 'normal' profile and is intolerant of diversity, particularly psychological or emotional diversity. It is highly unlikely that such a system would embrace those who might be burning out, whether or not the burnout experience is destined to be transformational for them in terms of their development. Inevitably, then, organizations tend to steer away from anything which might pose a potential risk and instead head towards the perceived safety of the mainstream, and in so doing create an army of corporate clones.

A second reason for considering the use of burnout as valid developmental material is the *empowering lessons it can teach high flyers about their own limitations and fallibilities*. In Chapter 5 we positioned burnout as a double-edged sword. On the one hand it can derail a career, on the other it can lead to a transformation of consciousness. We talked about burnout in terms of it being 'hardship' developmental experience. We know from the work of McCall and others that the most frequently reported flaw leading to executive derailment is arrogance and insensitivity. In the boardroom this is often referred to as CEO disease – a condition which leaves top executives isolated from disconfirming feedback because their subordinates are either too scared, or too sycophantic to deliver it. For high flyers climbing their way to the top of the organization self-assurance and confidence morph into a belief that they have become intergalactic time lords, unfettered by the normal constraints bestowed on others. Burnout is a powerful leveller. Not only does it offer the possibility of bringing the high flyer back into normal, adult contact with those around him or her, it also teaches them to adopt sustainable approaches to the pursuit of their careers.

The final reason for organizations taking burnout seriously is *to kick start individuation*. This is a somewhat more philosophical and esoteric point, but important none the less. Earlier in this book we referred to burnout being caused at an individual psychological level by a sense of fragile identity and purpose. We explained that those who burn out often have an identity which is largely externally referenced. Their sense of self and meaning in life is derived from success in their jobs and careers. It is as if they do not have an identity separate from this. Their capacity for reflexivity – to interact with themselves and to critically evaluate how they form their personalities – is underdeveloped or stuck. In such circumstances, burnout offers the opportunity to kick start the process of individuation. It is a vehicle through which high flyers may discover their authentic, inner identity.

Other authors have argued that organizations have a responsibility to provide their people with a sense of meaning and purpose.[3] This is fine so long as the objective is to find a way of connecting people's hearts to some higher purpose other than the somewhat vacuous and ultimately self-defeating one of increasing shareholder value above anything else. But people cannot derive their meaning and purpose from the companies they work for. They have to do this for themselves. Believing your meaning is one and the same as the organization you work for is at best an excuse for an identity and at worst a recipe for poor mental health, and indeed burnout.

What is the payoff for organizations? It is simply this. Soulless organizational 'wastelands' are populated by those who profess beliefs they do not have, loyalty to those they do not like, claim identities they do not own and pursue career advancement above all other considerations. They are ciphers not leaders. Vital leaders living authentic, intentional lives are what organizations need. Why? Because they bring passion, a sense of integrity, commitment and humanity to their stewardship. And they make money. Lots of it.

## What organizations need to do to support this approach

The legendary stand-up comedian Bill Hicks used to joke that Keith Richards of the Rolling Stones had gone to the edge and found a ledge just beyond it, on which he sat playing his guitar.[4] The joke was based on the premise that Keith had lived a life of such unprecedented excess that by all rights he should have fallen off the edge of existence, but somehow had managed to remain a fully-functioning member of one of the world's most successful rock bands.[5]

What will it take for organizations to embrace an approach that allows their high flyers to learn from burnout? It will require them to create their own ledge beyond the edge. In doing so they will need to incorporate the following into their thinking about how they develop leaders.

- It is imperative that those at the top of organizations along with the HR professionals that advise them hold the belief that *leaders are largely made rather than born*. The importance of 'genetic material' has been greatly overstated thanks to the combined forces of Freudian psychology, simplistic popular thinking and Christian fundamentalism. Human (and leadership) identity is formed primarily through social interaction in relationship with others, during the course of a life. It can and does change as adults mature. It is not static. But it can and often will get stuck. What such a worldview offers is the possibility of transformation – at any age and in any circumstances. We are not merely the products of our parents, nor need we be the products of our contexts. We have choice and can decide our own destinies. In the words of personality theorist George Kelly, 'No one needs to paint themselves into a corner; no one needs to be completely hemmed in by circumstances; no one needs to be the victim of their biography'.[6]
- Developing leaders is primarily concerned with *developing them strategically*, in a profound sense, rather than incrementally. It's about changing the way in which leaders view reality, the perspectives they use to make sense of the world, helping them to broaden their horizon about what they pay attention to and therefore can influence and integrate. This kind of development improves the wisdom and quality of leaders' decisions and actions. They are more able to understand the consequential nature of their actions because they are making more and more relevant connections with disparate data. Development in this sense is about transformation of consciousness.

- Leadership is a *whole-person activity* where emotional maturity and physical wellbeing are as important as intellectual competence. Since leaders have to bring the whole of themselves to the leadership task, their development must be holistic. It must combine a concern for the leader's physical self and health, their emotional and psychological integration, their stage of development in life, the quality of their thinking and their intellect. This will not be an easy task for many organizations. A lot of leadership development is firmly rooted in a second generation leadership model developed from mid-20th-century thinking and attitudes. To pay serious attention to aspects of leadership outside the intellectual domain will be a bridge too far for some. But for those of us who have grown old witnessing the quietly courageous struggles of people as they wrestle with their growth as leaders, this is the very essence of leadership. As Warren Bennis puts it, 'The process of becoming a leader is much the same as the process of becoming an integrated human being...becoming a leader is synonymous with becoming yourself. It's precisely that simple, and it's also that difficult'.[7]
- Leadership is *performed within a specific context* and set of challenges. To be at all effective, leadership development needs to start from here, rather than a finite set of leadership characteristics. In essence the leader's context should drive the characteristics required of him or her, not the other way round!

In summary, the business case for engaging with burnout (the leadership crisis, the empowerment through acknowledging limitations and a focus on discovering authenticity in leaders) is realized by organizations following some holistic principles of development, that leaders make themselves; that their function is to integrate a broad range of issues, that their whole selves (including mind, body and emotions) are engaged and that their choice of leadership behaviours is embedded in a particular context. This leads us to propose an agenda for developing leaders, which is spelled out in the next section.

## A new agenda for leadership development

We envisage that the assimilation of these concepts would lead an organization towards a certain set of interrelated development activities for their high flyers. This would include the introduction of a multidisciplinary programme that accelerates wisdom and maturity and helps to develop their own sense of leadership and individual identity; the allocation of a coach skilled in working with hardship and the development of identity; the assessment of physiological wellbeing, together with an understanding of the individual's current level of psychological integration and their developmental stage in life; the identification of the context and environment creating the conditions in which burnout occurs, including the degree to which the organization's current talent culture and strategy is contributing to this.

For organizations, the product of such activities would be far-reaching. Far greater numbers of more skilful, well-grounded leaders would emerge as a result. These leaders would be more capable of handling change effectively, more able to think strategically and better at making wiser and more informed decisions. A more robust sense of self-identity and ability to establish clear boundaries would make them potent Board material, and their ability to handle uncertainty and ambiguity would be powerful and unusual. Because they would lead as much with their heart as their head, they would develop more balanced, more productive relationships with those who work with and for them. They would instil genuine commitment and engagement because that which gives them authentic meaning and purpose is connected[8] to what the organization stands for – its mission and values.

In a nutshell, organizations would witness significant improvements in leadership pipeline and succession, greater retention of high flyers as well as enhanced performance, wellbeing and long-term health. And more of them would actually achieve their highest potential, without derailing along the way.

Our confidence in making these assertions is based on experience of implementing many of the above elements in global multinational organizations over the last 10 years. In particular we have created high flyer 'experiences' which have explored psychological integration, the development of authentic identity and the ability to think strategically. Each of these experiences involved working extensively with high flyers going through burnout and integrated many of the concepts discussed previously. One participant talked about how this experience had brought about, 'more a change of consciousness and awareness' than anything else, '…but I have seen a change in my own decision making – I have shifted my focus towards what values I follow and who am I'. Another commented, 'It was like a curtain falling down in front of you. Before I was pursuing life from an individual perspective and now I see the greater landscape – it gave me strength to do even bigger things and to expand my ambitions'. Our work involved a particular emphasis on supporting high flyers' maturation and their understanding that leadership is in service to a wider community rather than their own ambition.

Commenting on this aspect, one participant said, 'My whole perception of leadership has changed. I used to be someone who got somewhere at any cost – but now to be successful in today's environment, you have to be more focused on people, recognizing their values, and more human…'.

Working with our colleagues in burnout in talent consultancy Edge Equilibrium™ we have put all of these ideas together into a personal development programme aimed at helping high flyers realize their highest ambitions while remaining true to themselves and their individual purpose.

## Key issues in implementing the vision of leadership development

We believe there are a number of key issues which organizations will need to address in order to implement this approach effectively. These include dealing with the stigmatization of burnout and establishing its use as valid developmental material, and the qualities required of those supporting high flyers in burnout. Our views on these issues are informed by our work with high flyers in burnout, but they have not formed the major thrust of our research, and consequently they present areas for future possible research. We have considerably more to say from a research perspective on the organizational culture required to support learning from burnout and the approach to coaching necessary to achieve this. Each of these latter areas is dealt with in what follows.

What can be done to *deal with the stigma of burnout* and legitimize it as valid developmental material? We recommend that organizations ensure that their entire high-flyer population participate in the kind of interrelated development activities we outlined above, whether or not they are deemed at risk of burnout. This gets round the issue of identifying and thereby stigmatizing those who are experiencing burnout. Equally importantly, it avoids the organization making inaccurate decisions based on invalid data. After all, few organizations will have, or be capable of, amassing the kind of information which will enable them to make an accurate assessment. Nor will most self-respecting high flyers be willing or happy to disclose such information. Nevertheless, our experience shows there is often pressure from human resources professionals – more often than not, those with a background in occupational psychology – to entrust them with making such an evaluation. Our firm recommendation to organizations is not to bow to such pressure as it is likely to lead to some fairly disastrous consequences for the retention and commitment of your talent pool. There is certainly no harm done and a great deal of benefit accruing from the entire high-flyer population participating in this approach. Working on authentic identity, physiological well-being, psychological integration and learning from hardship are things all leaders need to apply themselves to.

What of *establishing burnout as valid developmental material*? Our colleagues Tommy Hutchinson and Mike Ward, of social marketing agency Equator Media, propose getting high flyers to identify their current level of burnout by completing a quiz called, 'How burnt out am I?'. In the same way that sexuality can be perceived as a spectrum – not I am straight or I am gay, but how gay or how straight am I? – so burnout can be presented in a similar fashion. As a result burnout becomes a little closer to what people regard as 'normal' and it becomes easier for those experiencing burnout to 'come out' and talk about their experience. This approach is also part of the thinking behind the development of a typology of burnout that ranges from total devastation ('crashing and burning') to a pattern of chronic self-destruction to careers lived unsustainably. Our intention is to encourage people to regard burnout as being both more pervasive and closer to their own lived experience, while at the same time avoiding the trap of trivializing it. Campaigning to de-stigmatize burnout and getting individuals and organizations to recognize the developmental value of the experience are part of the overall mission of Edge Equilibrium.

Another important issue is the qualities required of the coach and those entrusted with running the development activities for high flyers. One very clear requirement of the coach or mentor is that he or she is *operating at a developmental stage beyond those they are coaching*. It is equally a requirement of those leading the overall programme of high-flyer development. While age is an unreliable ally in this regard – how often has one met people in their forties, fifties and even sixties in the business world who have clearly not worked their way past young adulthood – it is more likely such people will be in their forties and above than the same age or younger than the high flyers with whom they are working. Of course, paradoxically, how one correctly identifies whether someone is at a higher level of maturity than those they are working with, depends on the observer's own level of maturation!

## Coaching people in burnout

We explored the nature of the relationship in which high flyers are held while they are in burnout in the previous chapter. How does this translate into the context of a coaching relationship? In this section we lay out our approach to coaching high flyers in burnout and what informs it, as well as a model of coaching practice.

First and foremost it is important to clarify the purpose of the coaching. Despite exhortations to the contrary, the coach is not there to prevent the high flyer from burning out but to enable them to learn from the burnout experience, while simultaneously ensuring they do not derail.

Such an approach is informed by the coach working with their client systemically and avoiding the temptation of reifying burnout, ensuring that the 'solution' emerges for the client. It is also informed by the coach approaching burnout, learning and change as natural. Since both of these notions are relatively complex it is worth exploring each in more detail.

## *Working with the client systemically*

Burnout is a *systemic condition*; it follows that coaching people in burnout or at risk of burnout needs to come from a systemic perspective. This means working with the client's mind, body and identity (or what some might call 'spirit') as an interactive system. A change in any area effects change in every other area to differing extents. If there is a shift in the client's mind, there will be a shift somewhere in their body. Since our bodies are the seat of our emotions, a shift in the client's body – how they somatically organize themselves – will lead to a shift in how they feel about themselves.

One of the biggest barriers to working with high flyers in burnout as a whole system, is the temptation to treat burnout as if it was a thing, rather than seeing it as an understanding used to describe something that seems to be happening. This reification – making something abstract (burnout) into an entity/thing – leads to unhelpful ways of approaching burnout on the part of both coach and high flyer:

- It encourages the coach to think of the high flyer in burnout as something they can fix, and they search for a solution to their client's burnout. Of course, those coaches who pursue such a purpose are doing little more than indulging grandiose and arrogant illusions. The solution will *emerge* for the high flyer in burnout. The role of the coach is merely to increase the high flyer's experience of themselves in burnout, giving them more choice about the decision they might take.
- It can lead to self-pity and inaction on the part of the high flyer – 'I can't help it, I'm in burnout'.
- And on the basis of our findings it is inappropriate as there are different manifestations of burnout (crash and burn, chronic self-destruction and joyless depletion).

## Burnout, learning and change as natural

Burnout is the inevitable consequence of an identity (or personal myth) that has stopped evolving and has become stuck in habitualized patterns and ways of being that are no longer relevant for the individual. In normal circumstances, we and our personal myths are constantly evolving. We are constantly learning to adapt to life as it comes our way. Rather than always relying on ingrained patterns and ways of behaving which may no longer be relevant, we are able creatively to organize a response to the present moment. Change and learning are natural phenomena. Death marks the point at which this process of change ends (at least on a temporal level).

*Reflexivity* – the ability to make meaning from the disparate information that comes our way – is the process whereby we evolve our personal myth. We are hard-wired to do this and in a balanced, healthy state do so without effort. But when we become unbalanced or ungrounded, as in the case of burnout, we tend to interrupt this process and our sense-making – and our ability to evolve – becomes stuck.

The task of the coach is therefore to help the high flyer understand how they are interrupting this natural process.

These principles are served by the following *fundamental coaching practices* required to help high flyers learn from burnout. They apply universally, regardless of the particular experience of the person burning out.

## Fundamental practices

There are some fundamental practices required in coaching people to learn from burnout, which apply universally, regardless of the particular experience of the person burning out. These 'fundamentals' include:

- The coach 'holding the space' for the client – allowing them to work things out for themselves. It follows that the coach needs to keep their interventions to a minimum.
- The coach 'running a clean system' both at a personal and interpersonal level. By running a clean system we mean that the coach is fully present – somatically, cognitively and emotionally – so that they are able to notice their own thoughts, feelings and bodily sensations and can use this as a data source in their work with the client. Running a clean system also means coaches are fully engaged, adult to adult, in the interaction with the client. It means not indulging in fantasies about being superior to the client or different from

them. It means flushing out and admitting (to oneself, if not to the client) assumptions, prejudices or preconceived notions about the client. It requires the coach continually checking-in with themselves to ensure they are relating to the client from their centre.

- The coach maintaining their boundaries and keeping a distinct identity, separate from the client. This is particularly important when working with people who are experiencing powerful emotions. It is very easy to get lost in those feelings, particularly as Western culture tends to pathologize emotions like anger and sadness as negative. When dealing with powerful emotions in the client, it is important that the coach keeps breathing, keeps pulsating back and forth by imagining these emotions flowing through the client, flowing through them, and then returning back into the client again.

- The coach having the courage to try out new things with the client without fully knowing where they might lead. This requires the coach to adopt a child-like approach of giving it a go – ensuring at the same time that they are honest and transparent with the client when doing this. Sometimes we understand things only after we have done them. One of the failings of Western thinking is that we won't try anything out until we absolutely know how to do it.

## Model of coaching practices that enables learning from burnout

Our model of coaching high flyers in burnout is built on our research findings.

We have identified nine characteristics of those vulnerable to burnout as the basis of this model (see Figure 6.1).

These characteristics are described in detail in chapters 2 and 4. In this chapter we have linked each of these to the corresponding behaviours and practices required of the coach in order to facilitate learning in the client. As some of this practice is counter-intuitive, we have also identified traps for coaches to avoid. The result is a model of coaching practice that enables learning from burnout. Figure 6.2 provides a summary of this model, which is then described in detail in much of the rest of this chapter. Within these nine practices we introduce a range of models and frameworks that we have found to be useful in working with those burning out. These include the drama triangle, models of identity formation and identity development, the hero's journey and Rosinski's ethno-relative approach. We now examine each of the nine practices in turn.

| 1 | Over-identification with work; lost distinct identity |
|---|---|
| 2 | Sense of purpose based on recognition and fame |
| 3 | Undeveloped or stuc k' reflexivity |
| 4 | More committed to jobs/careers than to organization; to the individual than to the collective |
| 5 | Burnout is contextualized within a specific life stage (early career) |
| 6 | Is unaware or unwilling to recognize reduced effectiveness |
| 7 | Sense of identity is in flux |
| 8 | Unwilling to take responsibility for consequences of own action; addictive behaviour |
| 9 | Burnout not particularly culturally sensitive, but its manifestation is |

**Figure 6.1**     Burnout characteristics and correlates that form the basis of the coaching model

## *Exploring over-identification with work: lost distinct identity*

There are two coaching practices without which the task of seeking to enable people to learn from burnout is a fruitless one. These are, first, to hold the client rather than support them, and, second, to focus the coaching on the development of identity rather than anything else.

We talked about the difference between holding and supporting in Chapter 5. It is a critical one. One could easily assume that if someone is in burnout the coaching response should be to start from emotional support and only get into holding as the client emerges from the experience. But by offering support without challenge the coach falls into the trap of mirroring the same unbounded process manifested by the client. They reinforce the high flyer's pattern of confluence – their inability to tolerate difference between self and other or self and organization. By seeking to stand beside or stand up for the client, they can prevent the client making the necessary distance between their own intentions and that of their boss, or their sense of what the organization requires of them. This can happen so easily outside of the coach's awareness. It is an insidious process in which the coach often fails to notice what is happening until it is too late. If we slow it down it looks something like this. The coach feels the client's pain and wants to save them from it. They want to help the

| Characteristics | Coaching behaviour/practice | Traps to avoid |
|---|---|---|
| Over-identification with work; lost distinct identity | • Hold the client<br>• Focus on the development of identity through personal myth, quality of social interaction, physical form and the client's sense of life purpose | • Offering only support<br>• Trying to rescue the client<br>• Using performance coaching |
| Sense of purpose based on recognition and fame | • Ruthless compassion: break through the shell of their understanding by confronting the externally referenced nature of their identity<br>• Use questions to get at 'ultimate concern' | |
| Undeveloped or 'stuck' reflexivity | • Get the client to narrate their story of burnout; help them to notice their own sense-making process<br>• Intentionality of the coach wholly focused on the client's learning<br>• Holding the space – allow the client to work it out for themselves<br>• Minimal intervention | • Mistaking reflection for reflexivity<br>• Becoming heroically interventionist |
| More committed to jobs/careers than to organization; to the individual than to the collective | Use the Law of Three Clients and focus the client on their relationship with the organization | |
| Burnout is contextualized within a specific life stage (early career) | • Focus on the development of inner identity<br>• Use developmental models based on the development of personal identity to guide intervention<br>• Give the client a challenge which confounds their current level of thinking and being<br>• Explain the transition process in terms of a call to adventure | Using developmental models focused on career developmental stages |
| Is unaware or unwilling to recognize reduced effectiveness | • Suggest the client obtains feedback on current performance<br>• Paradoxical interventions which combine unconditional support and super challenge | |
| Sense of identity is in flux | • Engage the client in conversation about what transition might look and feel like<br>• Enable the client to trust their own process and remain independent of outside influences<br>• Support the client in taking their own time to form a new identity | The coach interrupts the client's process by intervening out of a need to feel useful or to prove their value |
| Unwilling to take responsibility for consequences of own action; addictive behaviour | Coach models responsibility-taking by taking responsibility for how they are responding to the client and by setting clear boundaries in the relationship | |
| Burnout not particularly culturally sensitive, but its manifestation is | • Coach works from an 'ethnorelative' stance rather than an 'ethnocentric' one<br>• Coach creatively adapts to the different cultural and ideological perspectives presented by the client | Coach assumes their worldview is common to everyone and imposes it on the client |

**Figure 6.2**   Learning from burnout coaching model: how the nine characteristics determine coaching behaviour and practice

high flyer become whole (again) but are worried about challenging their addiction to work. Perhaps the coach is also worried about losing the client's trust or increasing their emotional turmoil by challenging the addiction. Maybe they are frightened of losing the client. At this point the coach is caught in precisely the same bind as their client. In the same way that the client is unable to establish boundaries between them and their job, so the coach has become unable to establish boundaries between them and the client. If this continues the relationship will become co-dependent. Once this happens burnout is no longer the primary problem, rather it is the coaching relationship itself which has become the problem. The coach has become 'the person in the addict's life who is so scared to lose the addict's love that they don't dare challenge the addict's addiction'.[9] Any possibility of learning from the burnout experience is brought to a sudden, grinding halt. Never, at any stage in the coaching relationship can the coach *ever* afford to offer support without challenge.

There is another big trap that coaches can fall into by showing support rather than holding the client. When someone is in pain it is natural to want to rescue them. Coaches may find themselves feeling this way as they witness the torment of burnout unfolding in front of them. Their hearts go out to the client as a fellow human being in need. When the coach notices this happening it is time to stop and take a breath. The coach's desire to help, to take care of the client, leads to another kind of unequal relationship, this time one in which the client becomes dependent on the coach. The coach is now in the position of knowing better than the client. The power in the relationship is in the hands of the coach. This is no longer a relationship of equals. The coach has become the expert who will rescue the client from their terrible condition. In effect the coach's misplaced eagerness to help the other has infantilized the client. And at the same time they have rendered themselves utterly and completely useless to them.

Karpman's drama triangle (see Figure 6.3) takes this pattern of interaction one step further. In trying to rescue their clients coaches often have covert and sometimes unconscious motives. They may be driven by a sense of their own grandiosity for instance, or a need to feel good about

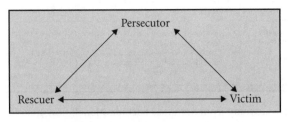

**Figure 6.3**    Karpman's drama triangle

themselves. As a consequence they become heroically interventionist. However, as the drama plays out, either the coach or the client may switch roles. For example, the client/victim turns on the rescuer and becomes persecutor or the coach/rescuer switches to persecuting.

Whatever the eventual outcomes of the dyadic relationship that ensues, the coach has once again reinforced a pattern of confluence in their client. What coaches need to do and do well is to develop a profound sense of humility. They are not there to be the hero of the hour. Rather they are there largely to witness a personal change process.

Burnout is fundamentally an issue of individual identity, meaning and purpose. In enabling the high flyer to develop a sense of internal identity it is important to start with their current identity and what gives them purpose and work out from there. This will lead to improved performance over time. The primary focus should be on the ways in which identities are formed and expressed – the stories the client tells themselves about themselves, the way they embody their identity physically, the manner in which they interact with others and the sense of meaning and purpose that emerges from the interaction of these dimensions (see Figure 6.4).

In our coaching practice, we use an adapted version of the research interview to discover the client's story, focusing specifically on periods of prolonged and intense stress as well as turning points in their understanding and definition of themselves. Using the work of Keleman and others we notice how people somatically respond to the situations and challenges that confront them. We explore how these deeply encoded, habitual somatic patterns affect people's sense of who they are. And at an interactive level we notice how we are responding to what is happening in the coaching relationship and

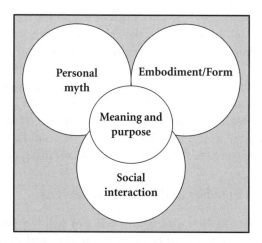

**Figure 6.4**   How identity is both formed and expressed

use this as valid data in working with the client. We also focus on the quality of contact – of interaction – we are experiencing with the client, bringing this information into the coaching relationship. By understanding the quality of relationship they are having with their coach, the client will better understand the quality of contact they have with themselves.

Coaching those in burnout is up front and personal. It requires coaches to bring the whole of themselves into the coaching relationship. Since an undeveloped sense of identity is often manifested by a lack of boundaries, the coach may want to problematize boundary setting within the coaching relationship. This might involve keeping strictly to time boundaries, for instance, or ensuring that the client accepts responsibility for their actions. Equally, since confluent individuals find it difficult to tolerate difference, the coach may legitimately rock the boat by provoking the client into disagreement. There are as many ways of doing this as there are coaches, but one way we have found to be effective is to repeatedly ask the client to define who they are.

## Developing from a sense of purpose based on recognition and fame

In Chapter 5 we talked about the use of ruthless compassion and the coach needing to break the shell of the client's understanding. In this context the 'shell' is the high flyer's identity built on work and career and a sense of purpose based on fame and recognition. Breaking through this shell means helping them to see their current identity and purpose for what it really is. In other words, the coach needs to find a way of confronting the client's complicity with the organization and their identity based on career success. Asking the client questions about their sense of purpose, what they stand for and why they are here in this world is one obvious route. Another, less obvious, possibility is to use Paul Tillich's concept of 'ultimate concern' by helping the client to 'the simple yet profound personal realization that there is "something in life for which you would give your life", something that as a result, "you take with ultimate seriousness".[10] Thus the coach might enquire whether there was anything in the client's life that they would be willing to suffer or even die for, and then to explore the significance of their response to the meaning of their life.

## Addressing disrupted or undeveloped reflexivity

There is much in the literature about ways of helping people to reflect and thereby increase the quality of their insights and decision making, but little on how to help them improve their reflexivity. There are two reasons for this. The first is that many people do not understand the difference between reflection and reflexivity, confounding the two concepts to the extent that there is no daylight between them. The second is that the process of helping someone to improve the quality of their self-interaction is indeed a very complex one.

Our approach to the development of reflexivity is based on the notions of identity and reflexivity we presented in Chapter 4. In essence these were that we come to know who we are through the stories we ourselves and others tell about ourselves, and that reflexivity is the process through which we construct our identities. Reflection produces the raw material for reflexivity to work on. Someone who is very reflective may think a great deal but their thinking will have little impact on their story, which fails to evolve, as do they.

High flyers in burnout may appear very reflective but this does not mean they have a well-developed reflexive process. As we have seen, the opposite is more likely. It follows that the experience of burnout will not really live for them until they tell someone about it. We believe the starting point, therefore, is to get the high flyer to talk about their current and past experiences of severe stress and burnout. More often than not, this will be the first time they have ever told these stories as an intact whole. In the telling, the high flyer will need to create a narrative story line that relates events, actions and experience to one another. In doing so they will make connections. They will emphasize certain aspects of the experience rather than others. They will choose a certain kind of language to describe the experience. The coach's task is to notice this, and to discuss what they are noticing with their client. As this interaction goes back and forth, the client will begin to make new sense of the experience. The meaning of the story will evolve for them and new sense will be made of it. As new sense evolves so will the significance of the story in the client's life, and their understanding of their own identity. The hope is that over time, this gentle conversational process will stimulate the client's reflexive capability.

The intentionality of the coach during this process has a profound impact on the client. When it is wholly focused on the learning of the high flyer it can help them to make the identity shifts that they need to function in their post-burnout world. Nancy Kline talks about, 'Attention, the art of listening with palatable respect and fascination, is the key to the Thinking Environment. Listening of this calibre is enzymatic. When you are listening to someone, much of the quality of what you are hearing is *your effect on them*. Giving good attention to people makes them more intelligent'.[11] Intentionality consumes considerable emotional energy and requires constant monitoring. To remain focused, the coach needs to periodically tune into themselves and check on their intentionality during the coaching session with the client.

Finally, there is much to be said for the coach using conventional approaches to develop 'ordinary' reflectiveness in the client, not least because we know that those who burn out need time and space to learn from the experience. After all, reflection is, as we have said, getting to first base, even if it isn't the real thing. The requirement on the coach is to practise minimal intervention, stay out of the client's way and 'hold the space' for the client: 'Real help, professionally or personally, consists of listening to people, of paying respectful attention to people so that they can access their own ideas first'.[12] The coach may need to sit with what Nancy Kline calls 'busy silence', allowing the client time and space to find the words to express themselves. She describes 'busy silence' as the point when someone goes quiet when they are talking, 'they are off on a solitary walk. You have not been invited to come along but it is assumed you will be there when they come back… Their walk is of high quality exactly because they know you are waiting, thinking about them, while they are gone'.[13]

## Challenging focus on own jobs/career rather than organization/others

As we have seen, the identities of those who burn out tend to be highly externally referenced. They are based on success and advancement in career more than being derived from personal unfolding or contributing to a wider community. As a result high flyers can be self-absorbed and more driven by their own self-interest than a duty of service to others or the organization. One of the ways in which the coach can work with this is by using what Hawkins and Smith call the 'Law of Three Clients'.[14] They hold that 'there is always more than one client, even if only one of them is in the room with you'.[15] The coach needs to ensure they are serving:

- the high flyer who is experiencing burnout
- the organization for which they work
- the 'purpose of their joint endeavour, to which they are both in service – their clients, customers, stakeholders',[16] including the community and social environment of which they are both part.

In particular, the coach needs to keep bringing the coachee back to focus on their relationship with the organization and what it is they and the organization are here to achieve, and to whom they are in service.

## Burnout contextualized within a specific development stage

Burnout normally occurs to high flyers within the first 10 years of a career. In large part this is due to the high flyer being at an early development stage in which boundaries and identity are still being formed. Inevitably, then, coaching people in burnout requires an understanding of the process of individuation and the stages of development through which adults develop towards maturity. We agree with Hawkins and Smith's view that using developmental models can be immensely useful for the coach, because, 'They allow us to view present behaviours in a broader life context, and link the specific work around business issues with broader issues of personal maturity'.[17] However, we have found that in the case of coaching high flyers in burnout it is critically important to find developmental models which speak to the developmental issues faced by the high flyer. Models which present too narrow a focus on an individual's career stages, for instance, are less helpful to the coach because they do not address the development of personal identity and tend to reify developmental stages. Torbert's model of levels of leadership development provides a more useful approach as it is steeped in developmental psychology, particularly the work of personality theorists Loevinger and Blasi. Our preferred developmental model is based on the premise put forward by McAdams and others that human identity is constructed upon a story or 'personal myth' that each of us creates in order to provide our lives 'with unity or purpose' and 'to articulate a meaningful niche in the psychosocial world'.[18] McAdams posits that we create 'identities through narrative', beginning this work in late adolescence and continuing it into old age. Figure 6.5 represents our organization of the key stages described by McAdams in the development of personal identity. We have deliberately specified that each stage has a notional beginning point and deliberately not specified a stage of life when each of these stages might end. We humans are far too diverse and complex for any generalizations to be made about when a particular stage of development should begin or end, though we can make rough approximations based on prior experience.

In what we call the pre-mythic stage in early childhood, we gather 'material for the self-defining story we will someday compose'. Foundational mythmaking normally occurs from late adolescence. This is when we first begin to see our lives as a story with historical perspective and we 'become self-conscious mythmakers when we confront head-on the problem of identity in human lives'. We build a belief system at this stage of our development that often stays with us for the rest of our lives, and helps to contextualize our story within 'what we believe to be true and good'.

| Stage of identity development | Main theme | Notional point at which this begins |
| --- | --- | --- |
| Pre-mythic | Generating material on which personal myth is later built | Infancy/early childhood |
| Foundational mythmaking | Fo rmulate personally meaningful answers to ideological questions so that one's identity can be built on stable foundations' | Late adolescence/early adulthood |
| Imago development | 'Creation and refinement of main characters in our personal myth' | 20s and 30s |
| Integration | 'Bringing opposing parts of our story together into a vitalizing and harmonious whole'; beginning of 'generativity script' | Mid-adult years |
| Post-mythic/eldership | 'Generativity script' moves on to how we can pass on the torch to others to meet the needs of future generations; we review and pass judgement on our life story | Final years of life |

**Figure 6.5**   Model of identity development (based on the work of Dan P. McAdams (1993), *The Stories we Live By: personal myths and the making of the self*)

In the imago development stage we populate our story with characters who 'personify our basic desires for power and love'. These imagos are built out of 'actual or imagined personas' and manifest as archetypes such as 'the warrior, the sage, the lover, the caregiver, the humanist, the healer, and the survivor'. By this stage of our lives the stories we have created are too complex to be inhabited by just one main character. The nature of these characters 'determine the quality of our overall identity'.

During the integration stage our 'personal mythmaking becomes more integrative as we seek to bring opposing parts of our story together into a vitalizing and harmonious whole'. This involves 'integrating and making peace among conflicting imagoes', which is of itself 'a hallmark of mature identity'. At this stage we also become concerned 'with the anticipated ending of our life story and the new beginnings that we may be able to generate'. This is the point at which we begin to compose our 'generativity script'. 'The generativity script links the individual personal myth to the collective stories and myths of society as a whole and to the enterprise of promoting and improving human life and welfare from one generation to the next.'

Finally the post-mythic stage marks the point at which we 'begin to take final stock of what we have made'. We continue to develop our 'generativity script' focusing on we can 'pass on the torch' to others by enabling them to meet the demands of the future.

Most of those in burnout are likely to be in the imago development stage, though some may still be stuck at foundational mythmaking. However, it is highly unlikely any will be at the integration stage, given what we know about burnout's connection with a fragile sense of identity. The coach needs to identify which developmental stage the client has reached, what is preoccupying them at this stage and what, if anything, is getting in the way of their story evolving. Clearly, if the client is at the imago development stage, the coach needs to have an understanding of the characters of self-populating the client's story, as these will determine the quality of their identity.

Why is this important? Because burnout holds the potential of triggering an individual's transformation either to the next level within their current stage of identity development or to a new stage of developmental maturity altogether. In the case of the former, burnout can be the catalyst which helps a person excise a character that has outlived its usefulness and invent a new character that better serves their needs at this point in their lives.

For example, Tim developed an imago in his early adult years that was fiercely independent and powerful, but always at the margins of the social world. He came to call this character, 'the masked stranger'. He could trace its emergence back to a pivotal teenage conversation he had with his father who exhorted him never to follow the herd and to retain his independence. The imago came to absorb the qualities of quiet strength and being on the fringes of society from characters played by Clint Eastwood in films Tim remembers watching in his twenties. The character's strength helped him endure difficult and painful episodes in his twenties and thirties and as a result became more and more dominant as he grew older. While the character protected him, it also kept him apart from others and made it difficult for him to ask for help. He found himself increasingly isolated and unable to express compassion for himself. The coaching he received during his final cycle of burnout helped him see how this character was stopping him from evolving and he developed a more self-caring and loving approach to himself, and this led to him being able to do the same towards others.

At one point during this process of transition, Tim found himself working with David Casey who was facilitating the action learning set of which he was a member. When it came to Tim's turn to be the client he described how he was finding it increasingly difficult to meet the needs of his clients because of his level of over-commitment. He was unable to do work of quality any more and was not doing what he described as a 'proper job'. After finishing this tale of woe, Tim sat morosely in his chair, despairing of his ability to change the situation. David looked over at him and asked him what it would take for him to do a proper job? Tim felt stung by this remark. How could he do a proper job when he was so over-committed, for God's sake?! David replied, 'Tim, this is simply not good enough! You ought to be doing a proper, professional job! What will it take?!'.

Sometimes the only way of moving the high flyer in burnout to the next stage of consciousness is to do what David described as 'grabbing them by the hair and dragging them through a hedge backwards'. Others describe this process in more arcane fashion: 'To help a person shift levels of consciousness, one has to confound their current level of being and thinking, by giving them a challenge which they recognize as important or intriguing but that cannot be achieved within their current mode of operating. This challenge acts as a form of paradoxical double-bind, which is meant to create a "paradoxical seizure", fusing the old circuits of mind and forcing new connections to be created'.[19]

Such a challenge might be asking how the high flyer can do all that they are doing now, but at a much higher level of quality, or it might be asking them to think about how they would tackle their boss's job.

How does one support the transition of high flyers from one identity development stage to another? Conventionally consultants roll out one of many change or transition curves at this point, whose provenance is more often than not based on the work of Kubler-Ross. We have found it is useful for coaches to recognize specific steps or stages in the transition process, but once again, find that many of these models are described in rather dry, scientific terms that do not lend themselves to the lyrical work of evolving a new identity. More often than not, therefore, we prefer to use the stages outlined in Joseph Campbell's hero's journey[20] (see Figure 6.6). We have mapped these against Keleman's notion of somatic transition, represented by the three stages of endings, middle ground and formation, which is a worthy alternative and is outlined in the section dealing with the client's identity being in flux.

The hero's journey lends itself to working with clients around the development of identity because:

- it is metaphorical of the central narrative that underlines any story of personal growth or change
- it addresses the basic human need for story and narrative as a way of constructing our identities. It presents personal change as a vital,

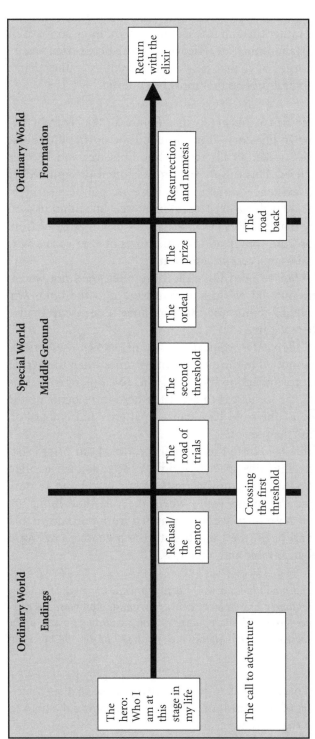

**Figure 6.6** The hero's journey and stages of somatic transition. (*Source*: Based on the work of Joseph Campbell, Stanley Keleman and Christopher Vogler)

vibrant process rather than an intellectual one. In doing so it avoids the client talking about their experience rather than experiencing it

- it frames the journey of change as a 'call to adventure' rather than a painful psychological process that must be endured.

The premise of the hero's journey is that we are all the central character or hero of our own life story. From time to time during the course of our lives we receive wakeup calls to redefine ourselves and become authors of our own lives. This *call to adventure* is often precipitated by living an inauthentic existence – one in which we are not being true to who we are and what we truly value. The call may well-up within us – an overwhelming feeling that our lives have to change – or it may come from outside of us, perhaps from conversations with others or a series of events which conspire to lead us in a certain direction.

But many of us *refuse* to heed this call. More often than not we are frightened of leaving our old world and venturing into the unknown. Perhaps we feel we will fail in our quest to find ourselves or we feel duty-bound to remain where we are.

A guide or helper ('*the mentor*') appears or becomes known – sometimes once the hero has committed to the quest or other times when the hero is still deciding whether to embark on the quest. This role can, of course, be fulfilled by the coach, whose task is to assist the hero in recognizing the call, help them let go of their old habitualized patterns and embark on the journey to redefine themselves.

*Crossing the first threshold* from the 'ordinary world' of our prior existence and self-identity into the 'special world' of the unknown is often a frightening one. We leave the known limits of our world and venture into an unknown and dangerous realm where the rules and limits are not known; a point of no return. We feel separated from our known, old world and old self and begin the transition to the potential new world and new self. We feel vulnerable and often lost,

*We enter a strange no man's land, a world between worlds, a zone of crossing that may be desolate and lonely, or, in places, crowded with life. You sense the presence of other beings, other forces with sharp thorns or claws, guarding the way to the treasure you seek. But there's no turning back now, we all feel it; the adventure has begun for good or ill.*[21]

At this point the coach's role is to provide reassurance that such feelings are a normal part of the transition as well as challenging the hero to remain committed to the journey.

*The road of trials* represents the experiences that the individual must undergo to begin the process of transformation. They are likely to be tested to the limit as they experiment with new ways of being and doing. These tests or ordeals help to shape the new identity that is being formed. By entering this stage the person shows their willingness to undergo a metamorphosis.

*Crossing the second threshold* represents entering the most dangerous spot in the special world – a place where the hero must face their greatest fear. In *the ordeal* the fortunes of the hero hit rock bottom in a direct confrontation with their greatest fear, death or supreme danger. This is a point where the hero has to die unto him/herself in order to be born again. If they are successful in overcoming the ordeal they are able to claim *the prize*, which is forming an identity that helps them evolve and serves the vision of who they want to become. The ordeal represents the lowest point in the journey. It is the point where the client will experience the greatest fear about failing in their quest to reinvent themselves. The prospect of severe personal hardship may emerge. But it is also the point of greatest learning. It is the place where the client discovers whether they are able to realize their new identity. The coach has their work cut out for them at this stage. Their role is to enable the client to explore what they are learning about themselves and their world. What is the emergent vision of the person they want to become? What will stop them from becoming this person? What do they most fear on this journey of evolution?

*The road back* to the hero's ordinary world is a tricky one. They have been born anew (*resurrection*) but at some point during the return to their ordinary world the *nemesis* raises its head. They are challenged to prove they have learnt the lessons of the ordeal – that, once and for all, they have let go of the old ways of being and doing that were holding them back. If they stumble at this point they risk falling back into their old identity; the learning from their quest will be squandered. If they succeed, they are transformed and return to ordinary life with the prize intact. The coach is there to help the client become more aware of the habitual patterns of behaviour that may undermine or tempt them from their path.

*Returning with the elixir* is in some ways the most difficult part of the journey. It means that somehow the hero has to find a way of retaining the wisdom gained on the quest (the elixir) and integrate it into their everyday lives. They also have to work out how to share the wisdom with their community, for unless they do so, their journey will have been meaningless. The problem is that the hero has gone through a fundamental transformation of consciousness and worldview. If they reveal their new self to the citizens of their ordinary world they may well get labelled as crazy and be ostracized (or even crucified). As a consequence, the coach's role is to help the client assimilate and integrate their learning into everyday life. How will they practise this new identity for instance, and how will they behave differently with others? What new value can they now bring to all the different stakeholders they serve, that they previously were unable to offer?

## Raising awareness of reduced effectiveness and performance

High flyers often do not recognize the downturn in their performance caused by burnout. How can the coach help to recognize this? One way is for the coach to invoke the Law of Three Clients, by suggesting it would be valuable for the client to receive feedback on the degree to which they are meeting the needs of their stakeholders. This is best done by the client supplying the names of key stakeholders whom the coach can interview on behalf of the high flyer. We advise against the use of the organization's formal 360-degree or upward feedback processes for this exercise. Formal survey tools are unlikely to provide the nuance that the coach will be able to pick up in direct contact with stakeholders. In addition, many of those responding to surveys tend towards positive bias. There is a great deal at stake here for the high flyer. Providing survey evidence which reinforces their ignorance or denial of their falling level of performance could be potentially disastrous for them. The coach needs to stick to their guns if either the high flyer or the HR department insist on the use of a pre-scribed feedback survey. Another alternative is for the coach to make the kind of paradoxical intervention which combines elements of unconditional support as well as super challenge. A colleague of David's described how he was asked to coach a senior manager whose co-workers described as a complete bastard. During their first meeting the coach explained his rationale for being there by saying he understood that the manager enjoyed being a complete bastard and he was there to help him in any way he could to continue being that person.

## Supporting the sense of self is in flux

People sometimes have overly-fixed or rigid identities that do not permit adaptation to new circumstances or the development of a new way of being. Such identities can often be perceived through the language used by the coachee. Their vocabulary will be liberally sprinkled with phrases

such as 'I always...' or 'I'm the kind of person that...' or false univer-
salities such as 'Everyone knows that...' or 'It's obvious that...'. Burnout
effectively opens a window into this world, loosening up the former fix-
edness and making identity more fluid. As burnout takes hold, the client's
language begins to become less certain and more tentative. It is up to the
coach to notice the change and engage the client in noticing this as well.

One way of engaging high flyers in conversation around their state
of transition is to develop their understanding of what transition might
look and feel like. This can prove valuable to them, given that they have
formerly invested themselves in retaining a state of rigidity. Keleman's
model of somatic transition lends itself to this task because it inherently
deals with the development of individual identity (or, in Keleman's terms,
'form'): 'All transitions require a period of separating, a time for waiting
and time for reorganizing new action'.[22] Keleman describes these periods
in terms of:

- endings – of embeddedness in a certain way of doing things
- middle ground – a period of being unformed and in flux
- formation – trying out new behaviour.

Endings signal that an aspect of our lives has become redundant,

> When familiar patterns of behaviour become invalid, they must be discarded.
> If we are to survive and go on to the next stage of our lives, we must first confront
> situations in a state of emerging helplessness and not fall back to old automatic
> responses which have become counter-productive or even destructive. Real wisdom
> is when we recognize an ending instead of clinging to delusions that there is safety in
> habitual static patterns.[23]

Part of what happens to us when we approach an ending of a particular way of being or pattern of behaviour is that we withdraw and reduce
our attachment and energy investment in the pattern. Endings tend to
be unstructured and as a result 'we go through an identity crisis, a crisis of self-recognition...when our patterns of self-recognition become
threatened we do almost anything to perpetuate them. The more energy
we have invested in a pattern, the more the threat of a loss of identity'.[24]
Ending something creates a vacuum where once there was substance.
Scared by the unknown, some people refuse to go through this process
and try and retain their former pattern. In doing so they maintain their
rigidity and stop themselves from growing. Coaches need to reassure
their clients that ending a pattern 'does not necessarily mean obliteration

or mutilation. Unbounding doesn't mean severing, forgetting or throwing everything out of the window. Rather it is like committing oneself back to the current of life. Endings are not oblivion. They mean taking a distance, changing a connection.'[25]

Middle ground represents a state where we give up aspects of our former identity and for a while remain less formed and structured. It is where we allow 'things to be brewed, to be reorganized in a less specialized way that forms a starting point for new form', it is 'the great creative soup originating social form from creative chaos. It is the central moment of turning points, the space where something has ended and something may form'. Middle ground is a scary place for many people because they experience powerful feelings and sensations. They feel less in control, 'Middle ground is difficult for people who cannot stand in between spaces'. It is important to recognize that people are in a vulnerable state when they are in middle ground; it is easy for others to manipulate them into changing in a particular way.

Tim's experience of middle ground as he emerged from burnout illustrates this. He found himself surrounded by people who wanted to help him. Most of these people seemed to appear and then, when he moved out of middle ground, disappear again. On one occasion a trainer on an executive retreat he was attending tried to impose his religious views by convincing Tim that his new identity should be founded on the rock of Jesus. Fortunately, Tim had a coach who helped him stay true to himself and not ingest others' doctrines. Tim describes this time in his life as, 'Really weird. I was aware there was only half of me there really, like I was firing on two cylinders and not on four. I didn't think it was affecting my work but it must have done. I knew I was a bit fucked up but it was like I couldn't just snap my fingers and change things. I had to wait it out, see what emerged. The worst thing was that it was like every other fucked up person in the world had some special kind of radar which meant they could home in on me'.

The coach needs to support the client to stay with and trust their own experience and process at this stage. In doing so they may need to challenge the client to remain independent of outside influences – including, paradoxically, the coach themselves.

Formation is the point where we begin to organize and structure our identity anew. New possibilities emerge for us as we experience the confusion of middle ground. We 'reform ourselves and live out our new vision'.

However, many of us become so scared of losing the security of familiar patterns of identity that we refuse the call to adventure and fall back into our habitual way of being. The coach's task is to support the high flyer in finding the confidence to take their own time in the difficult middle ground stage and not hurry to develop a new identity too quickly. This takes courage on the part of the coach because it means sitting quietly with the client's fear and uncertainty. The coach may feel a strong desire to intervene. It is essential they recognize this is more about their own need to feel useful than it is a need for the client.

## Challenging addictive behaviour/not taking responsibility

The most effective way of helping the client to take responsibility is for the coach to model taking responsibility for their own behaviour and emotions. This includes the coach talking about how they are responding to the client and being candid about what is happening in the room for them right now. It also involves the coach disclosing when they simply don't know what to do in their work with the client. This also serves to validate that it is OK not to know, and for the client not to know. Feelings of powerlessness should similarly be validated. Setting clearly-defined boundaries in the coaching relationship is another way the coach can help to create an environment that models responsibility-taking. For instance, in offering their support, coaches might offer that if the client needs to talk to them they should not hesitate to do so, at the same time making it clear that they may do so only at certain times of the day.

## Recognizing that the manifestation of burnout 'behaviour' depends on cultural context

Our research shows that it is important for coaches to integrate a cultural perspective into their practice, as well as having an individual psychological one. Earlier in this chapter we talked about the coach 'running a clean system'. As we have seen, it is all too easy for coaches to assume that their worldview – be it one that is informed by their national culture, religious beliefs, social class or corporate norms – is 'central to everyone's reality'. This is to fall into the trap of what Philippe Rosinski calls 'an ethnocentric view'. Instead, coaches need to 'perceive cultural differences as inevitable' by adopting an ethnorelative approach. Figure 6.7 illustrates the differences between ethnocentric and ethnorelative approaches to coaching.

Working from an ethnorelative perspective, the coach temporarily suspends their ideology and culturally informed beliefs and creatively adapts to the different perspectives presented by the coachee.

The coach also needs to adopt an ethnorelative stance because of the impact the cultural context of the high flyers can have on the manifestation

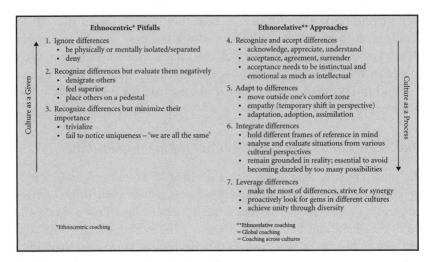

**Figure 6.7**    Dealing with cultural differences. *Sources*: Milton Bennett (1993), *Towards Ethnorelativism: A Developmental Model of Intercultural Sensitivity*, and Philippe Rosinski (1999), *Beyond Intercultural Sensitivity: Leveraging Cultural Differences*. Reprinted by Courtesy of Nicholas Brealey Publishing

of burnout. In Chapter 2 we saw that the nature and symptoms of burnout are similar across national and organizational boundaries but the manner in which they are manifested behaviourally can depend on the cultural context. For example, emotions are likely to be more extrovertly manifested in Mediterranean cultures as compared to Scandinavian ones.

## Summary

We have described the nine features of burnout and the coaching activities to address them one by one. In practice (and in theory) it is necessary to work holistically with all nine sets of practices. This is one of the features that makes coaching in this area both demanding and rewarding. In the next two sections we consider the type of intervention that can support this holistic approach to coaching and we look more widely at what research has shown about creating a coaching culture.

## Models of development that contribute to focus on the client's intentions

We are reluctant users of techniques and frameworks in coaching. If we do use them we are likely to create them spontaneously in a coaching conversation to address a particular issue or respond to a dilemma. Many of the approaches in the previous section are of this kind – emerging from experience. However there are some well-attested models stemming from the work of Chris Argyris and Peter Senge[26] which we find have a place in working with those burning out. These are grounded in Argyris's framework for exploring the reasoning and attitudes that underlie human action. He sees quality interaction as being based upon processes of advocacy and inquiry. In other words, if I am seeking to help someone burning out, I will encourage them to articulate their own position and to enquire about the position of others. I will be interested in the assumptions that clients make about themselves, and about others. Similarly I will be explicit about advocating my own assumptions and enquiring about the client's. This compassionate and clarifying process serves to provide a gentle but also implacable challenge, which can deepen the understanding that the client has of their situation. Paying attention to the balance of advocacy and enquiry in the interactions of the client can help them to notice which process they are neglecting – it can be either or indeed both – and this can lead to a spontaneous rebalancing as those burning out experience how they are not making themselves clear or not checking out the expectations of others.

David used another model described by Senge and colleagues, with a young high flyer, who was convinced that his Chief Executive was ignoring his advice. The energetic but exhausted executive took responsibility for facilitating a Board meeting, and in a coaching conversation afterwards he claimed that the Chief Executive had wilfully ignored his proposal for change. David asked him to write down as much as he could remember of the exchange in the right-hand column of a page divided in two with a vertical line. He then asked him to write anything in the left-hand column that he had thought, felt or wanted to do, but had not expressed. The high flyer realized that he had thought the proposal vividly, but had not actually articulated it. He had gone from the assumption that the Chief Executive would never accept it to feeling rejected without giving the proposal a chance. He was in a phase where he was neither enquiring nor advocating. The left-hand column process specifically highlighted this position and also left the high flyer with a pervasive sense of how he was being in the world and a will to change it.

Another client was locked into advocating that others smarten up their act and was hugely and skilfully adept at rejecting feedback from these others or taking responsibility for things going wrong. It was only when he thought through his communication in terms of advocacy and inquiry that he came to recognize that his reputation for being a 'Teflon man' had some substance and served to negate all the frantic work that he did fending off the negative data that he was being offered.

A further model that also comes from the Argyris/Senge stable is called the 'ladder of inference'. This is based on the notion that we take action based on our beliefs and we assume that our beliefs are a true representation of the world. We neglect to notice that the observable data of our interactions (as a tape recorder might capture it) are a long way from these beliefs. First the data are selected from; then we add meanings to those we select; then we make assumptions based on the meanings; then we draw conclusions from the assumptions. Only then do we adopt the beliefs about the world and people that we took to be facts. Once the rungs on this ladder have been explored we find that self-justifying leaders can begin to examine what leads them to engage in patterns that are ultimately self-defeating. Further details of these three core processes can be found in Senge's book.[27] They help maintain the clean communication we have spoken of earlier and embody the connectedness that burnees may crave but often lack.

## Creating a culture of respect and growth

We have identified throughout this chapter specific practices that coaches can adopt when working with someone close to the edge or on the ledge beyond the edge of burnout. However, the crucial learning from our research respondents is that what they need and want most to progress in their journey is a relationship which, as de Haan says, 'engenders feelings of well-being, recognition or solidarity between equal partners'.[28] The coach can offer this connectedness. But de Haan also says that the coach must exercise what the Greeks called *parrhesia*, or fearless speech.[29] The kind of coaching that is encouraged in an organization that supports people in burnout both recognizes and acknowledges the experience of the person on the edge, and also challenges their behaviour by not flinching from saying everything that the coach sees.

Clutterbuck and Megginson[30] show that in large organizations with many high flyers susceptible to burnout, there are features of organization culture that contribute to the possibility of using the burnout experience constructively. Of the 24 items in their model five stand out as crucial in setting the culture that we identify as being conducive to a developmental stance on burnout.

- *Encourage and trigger being a coachee*: the availability of help is crucial to those burning out as they are often highly resistant to seeking help or even to recognizing that they need it. Our research shows that those burning out will not want to admit any possibility of weakness to other people or indeed to themselves. They will have a lack of clarity about their goals and they may experience what is described as 'fog on the road'. This refers to the situation where the way ahead is unclear and they can hold off even starting because they are unsure of their first steps. A culture which encourages being a coachee goes some way towards reducing the likelihood of fog-bound isolation that can envelop those burning out.

- *You can challenge your boss to coach*: acknowledging the coach's potential to help and seeing the coaching as an opportunity to enhance the relationship can be useful behaviours to encourage in those at risk of burnout. Once someone is deep into the experience of burnout, it may be necessary for them to seek help from an external coach, but in the early stages a sympathetic boss may point out what they see as the unfolding or unravelling situation, and may either be able to help the high flyer to reflect on their experience or to point out sources of external help to develop a reflexive perspective.

- *Coaching is promoted as an investment in excellence*: a climate of openness to learning is a help. But for high flyers who are burning out it is also necessary for this help to be seen as something that contributes to the development of top talent. If coaching is seen in any way as remedial, then they will not touch it with a disinfected bargepole.

- *Organic not process-driven*: an organic approach to developing a coaching culture relies on word of mouth for its propagation. If other high flyers are able to share their own experience of burnout and of being helped through it, then this will have an impact on the acceptability of coaching. The experience of successful role models is powerfully influential in a way that HR interventions or the availability of assistance programmes simply are not. John Bailey of KPMG is quoted as saying[31] that 'a coaching culture is one where people are keen to ask for help and to give help – and that this makes a huge contribution to the management of risk'.

- *Constructive confrontation*: this calls for the coach to be indifferent about the outcome of the coaching. If coaches have a vested interest in one outcome or another, then they are into selling solutions or persuading, and they will not allow the individual who is burning out to become empowered to see and deal with their situation. Coaches need fearless speech, but they also need to subordinate their egos so that they do not interfere in the process of individuation by which the high flyer who has crashed in the jungle will come to recognize that they are on a journey. Once they recognize this, they can decide on the course to follow – going deeper into the jungle or heading straight for the nearest route back to civilization. David, when working in this situation and confronted with an individual making a choice which seems undesirable for the client in their own terms, suggests to them that they try out the path, and treat it as an experiment, rather than a definitive solution. In a sense, whether we are burning out or not, every decision can be seen as an experiment. And indeed the answers clients come up with are no more than eddies in the stream of possibilities opened up by finding better questions with which to interrogate their own lives.

More recent research[32] has shown that, in companies initiating a coaching culture, the three most important of 37 items to high flyers were:

1  The senior team leads the move to coaching.
2  Time to think and permission to speak are valued.
3  People know that help is available through coaching.

In creating a coaching culture where the experience of burnout is likely to be developmental we see these high flyers as saying that they call upon the Board of their organization to set a direction which encourages top talent to engage in reflexive one-to-one learning; where finding and developing one's voice is accepted as part of making a career and making a contribution to the good governance of the organization; and where the ready access to development support is built into the fabric of the organization.

The main outcome of our research is that individuals, with appropriate help, can use the experience of burnout constructively to broaden and deepen their lives and their identity. However, from the point of view of organizational practices, the dimensions of the coaching culture model outlined above can create the conditions in which individuals can increase the probability of achieving a developmental outcome.

## Conclusions

Clearly, having a 'ledge beyond the edge' relationship within the workplace is rife with difficulties. In high-performance, very task-orientated organizations no one has time to notice when a high flyer is on the edge; most of the people around them are emotionally not very switched on, and are driven by their own urgencies and fears. We have therefore in this chapter adopted a middle path of suggesting organizational benefits and conditions, but in devoting the bulk of the chapter to what coaches might do, we are acknowledging that outside help may be necessary. Some organizations have well-trained and highly-skilled internal coaches, and a small fraction of gifted and developed bosses may be able to take this role, but often it will fall to external coaches to deliver the holding that those burning out need. In any event, whether the holder is internal or external, this chapter seeks to provide principles, frameworks, models and practices that will guide the development of high flyers in burnout. It is worth adding that many of these principles and practices are also of the highest relevance to those members of the high-flyer population who are not burning out.

We have argued that using hardship as valid developmental experiences is legitimate and necessary and we have offered a way of achieving this that is grounded in our research and tested by experience. In particular we have shown that using coaching is a legitimate way of working with people on hardship.

The kinds of organizations which are more likely to go down this road are those that take their duty of care for their employees seriously; who have a model of mental health; who do not stigmatize employees for mental health issues; who do not believe that mental health equals incompetence; who understand that going to the edge, mentally, is part of a deep learning process and that this does not necessarily translate into disability, who accept that going to the edge is a normal part of adult development – of individuation.

We have argued a compelling business case for organizations learning to accept burnout as a normal part of adult maturation. First, the global shortage of good leaders – worsened by over-reliance on traditional classroom-based training and on competencies – would be abated. Secondly, leaders would be less prone to 'CEO disease' and more able to adopt sustainable approaches to their careers. And lastly, valuable high flyers would be more reflexive, committed, humane leaders.

We said that the benefits for any organization were considerable: improvements in succession pipeline, greater retention of high flyers, enhanced performance and less incidence of poor mental health and expensive derailment – with the potential for a very real impact on growth and profitability.

We began the chapter by describing the changes that organizations must undergo to embrace burnout as a learning process. The belief that leaders are born and not made must be abandoned. Leadership must be developed using an approach that is fundamental, not merely incremental. And faith in competencies as blueprints for leaders must be put aside. We said that an enlightened organization would have a programme on leadership and identity, the services of a psychologically-trained coach, regular assessments of psychological wellbeing and an understanding of the conditions that lead to burnout. (We developed our own programme, Edge Equilibrium, on these lines.)

We then looked at the destigmatization of burnout. We suggested that organizations should apply activities to all their high flyers, whether or not deemed at risk of burning out, as a means to this end. We also recommended that they refer to burnout not as an either/or condition, but as a tendency on a sliding scale.

Before going into detail on our own coaching model we looked at the broad notion of coaching during burnout. What does it entail? We noted that coaching in burnout needs to be systemic, focused on experience rather than on outcome, and supportive of reflexivity. We said that the coach must understand the importance of maintaining a 'holding' stance, of being fully present both cognitively and emotionally, of being able to keep within boundaries as a distinct and separate individual, and of being – perhaps above all – courageous.

We then went through our model, describing the behaviour and practice we believe appropriate when coaching a client exhibiting the characteristics of high flyers in burnout, and drawing attention to traps for the unwary.

- We began by emphasizing the importance of holding the client through their loss of identity, rather than merely supporting them. We said that the coach who gives in to the desire to solve the problem for the client, rather than with them, is worthless. We also stressed the need for the coach to focus on identity, meaning and purpose, while bringing their whole self to the process.
- We then talked about the 'ruthless compassion' required to confront the client's complicity with the organization and their identity based on career success. We recommended asking the client to describe what they were actually about, as a person, and what they might even die for.
- Next we looked at the role of the coach in helping improve reflexive capability. We warned against mistaking reflection for reflexivity. We noted the significance of the coach's intentionality, counselling them not to become heroically interventionist but to 'hold the space' for the client using Nancy Kline's 'busy silence'.
- To tackle the burned-out high flyer's tendency to self-interest over duty of service, we recommended using the Law of Three Clients.

We also counselled bringing the client's attention back repeatedly to what they and the organization were actually there to achieve.

- We then looked at some length at how the coach should address the contextualization of burnout within a specific development stage. We recommended McAdams' model of development, based on the concept of identity created through narrative. We took a lead from Campbell (the hero's journey) and Keleman in framing the passage of change as a call to adventure, with the coach in the role of guide or helper ('mentor'), there to provide the hero with reassurance, to challenge them to stand fast, and to help them understand.

- In the face of the client's inability to recognize their own down-turn in performance caused by burnout, we recommended getting feedback from key stakeholders. We recommended interview by the coach as preferable to 360-degree feedback or any other more restrictive, standard process.

- We then looked at how the coach should handle the high flyer's fluid sense of self during burnout. We said that the coach needs to provide reassurance that changing doesn't have to mean discarding, but rather engagement in the ebb and flow of life. The coach needs to support the client to remain independent – even of the coach himself – while taking care not to intervene out of a misplaced need to feel useful.

- In response to unwillingness to take responsibility for actions, or to recognize addictive behaviour, we said the coach's most effective route is to act as model, talking about their own responses and being candid about their experience of the current situation. We also recommended putting clear boundaries around the coaching interaction.

- Finally, we stressed the importance of the coach having cultural as well as psychological perspective, warning against the naive assumption that their own worldview is either appropriate or relevant.

Having gone through our own model of coaching, we then touched on some other techniques and frameworks that we believe have a place in coaching in burnout. We described several by Argyris and Senge, which are based on the notion that quality interaction comes as processes of advocacy and enquiry – a compassionate process which is nonetheless challenging.

We finished our examination of coaching in burnout by focusing on what a coaching culture within an organization actually entails. We highlighted five of Megginson and Clutterbuck's characteristics for special mention: the ready availability of coaching in the organization, the opportunity to challenge one's boss to coach, the promotion of coaching as an investment in excellence, an organic promulgation of coaching, and the use of constructive confrontation.

In the final chapter we draw these threads together and put forward their overall significance for the development of high flyers and leaders generally.

## End notes

1 McCall, M. (1998). *High Flyers: Developing the Next Generation of Leaders.* Boston: Harvard Business School Press. In using the phrase 'the right stuff' McCall quoted the title of a book written by Tom Wolfe in 1980 about the first seven astronauts selected for the NASA space programme.
2 We also agree with Morgan McCall's argument that such an approach is based on the fallacious assumption that leadership ability is innate and competencies are used to test for these innate skills.
3 Bains, G. et al (2007). *Meaning Inc. The Blueprint for Business Success in the 21st Century.* London: Profile Books
4 On the face of it, the worlds of rock 'n' roll and corporate organization have few things in common. Except in one respect – the intense pressure to perform experienced by high flyers in both worlds and the often self-defeating ways in which they attempt to manage the pressure. Whilst it appears to be acceptable for rock stars to go over the edge – often in a spectacular and very public way – it is generally thought to be pretty career limiting for most corporate high flyers to do the same. However, the consequences – sub-standard performance, damaged relationships and self-indulgent drivel masquerading as creative output – are pretty much identical.
5 Bill Hicks maintained that great rock 'n' roll is fuelled by a reliable drug habit (of course he didn't actually say it this way at all; we have paraphrased in order to side-step the laws of blasphemy). Others would probably add that great art is often created by those who society would perceive as living on its fringes or indeed having gone off the edge altogether. One thinks of Vincent Van Gogh, for example. We'd agree that serious art is more often created by those who frequently live their lives outside of social mores. This is what brings them their unique, often disturbing and beautiful, perspective on life. However, we'd equally argue that a life led at the bottom of a bottle, in perpetual heavy substance abuse or addicted to casual sexual encounters is unlikely to lead to great art, or even great rock 'n' roll.
6 Kelly, G. (1955). *A Theory of Personality.* New York: Norton
7 Bennis, W. (1998). *On Becoming a Leader.* London: Arrow Books
8 By 'connected' we mean an adult relationship in which commitment is given on condition that the other party performs its end of the bargain.
9 Kline, N. (1999). *Time to Think: Listening to Ignite the Human Mind.* London: Cassell Illustrated

10 Stromer, R.S. (2003). 'Faith in the journey: Personal mythology as pathway to the sacred.' Phd dissertation, Pacifica Graduate Institute.

11 Kline, N. (1999). *Time to Think: Listening to Ignite the Human Mind.* London: Cassell

12 Kline, N. (1999). *Time to Think: Listening to Ignite the Human Mind.* London: Cassell

13 Kline, N. (1999). *Time to Think: Listening to Ignite the Human Mind.* London: Cassell

14 Hawkins, P. and Smith, N. (2006). *Coaching, Mentoring and Organizational Consultancy.* Maidenhead: Open University Press. The Law of Three Clients was based on work by RELATE, the UK relationship counselling service

15 Hawkins, P. and Smith, N. (2006). *Coaching, Mentoring and Organizational Consultancy.* Maidenhead: Open University Press

16 Hawkins, P. and Smith, N. (2006). *Coaching, Mentoring and Organizational Consultancy.* Maidenhead: Open University Press

17 Hawkins, P. and Smith, N. (2006). *Coaching, Mentoring and Organizational Consultancy.* Maidenhead: Open University Press

18 McAdams, D.P. (1993). *The Stories We Live By: Personal Myths and the Making of the Self.* New York: Guilford Press

19 Hawkins, P. (1999). 'Organizational unlearning.' Learning Company Conference, University of Warwick. Hawkins, P. and Smith, N. (2006). *Coaching, Mentoring and Organizational Consultancy.* Maidenhead: Open University Press

20 Campbell, J. (1949). *The Hero with a Thousand Faces.* London: Fontana

21 Vogler, C. (1998). *The Writer's Journey: Mythic Structure for Storytellers and Screenwriters.* London: Pan Macmillan

22 Keleman, S. (1979). *Somatic Reality.* Berkeley: Center Press

23 Keleman, S. (1979). *Somatic Reality.* Berkeley: Center Press

24 Keleman, S. (1979). *Somatic Reality.* Berkeley: Center Press

25 Keleman, S. (1979). *Somatic Reality.* Berkeley: Center Press

26 Senge, P., Ross, R., Smith, B., Roberts, C. and Kleiner, A. (1994). *The Fifth Discipline Fieldbook.* London: Brealey

27 Senge, P., Ross, R., Smith, B., Roberts, C. and Kleiner, A. (1994). *The Fifth Discipline Fieldbook.* London: Brealey

28 de Haan, E. (2008). *Relational Coaching: Journeys Towards Mastering One-to-One Learning.* Chichester: Wiley

29 de Haan, E. (2008). *Relational Coaching: Journeys Towards Mastering One-to-One Learning.* Chichester: Wiley

30 Clutterbuck, D. and Megginson, D. (2005). *Making Coaching Work: Creating a Coaching Culture.* London: CIPD

31 Clutterbuck, D. and Megginson, D. (2005). *Making Coaching Work: Creating a Coaching Culture.* London: CIPD

32 Megginson, D. and Clutterbuck, D. (2008). 'What is new in creating a coaching culture?' Presentation at the 15th European Mentoring and Coaching Council Conference, Prague, December

# 7

# Developing leaders with purpose

Moyers:  Unlike [the classical heroes] we're not going on our journey
to save the world but to save ourselves.
Campbell:  But in doing that, you save the world. The influence of a vital
person vitalizes, there's no doubt about it. The world without spirit is a wasteland. People have the notion of saving
the world by shifting things around, changing the rules, and
who's on top and so forth. No, no! Any world is a valid world
if it's alive. The thing to do is to bring life to it, and the only
way to do that is to find in your own case where the life is and
become alive yourself.

THE POWER OF MYTH, JOSEPH CAMPBELL WITH
BILL MOYERS

We began this book by saying that our purpose was to question prevailing paradigms of leadership development and put forward new ways of
fostering leadership. We have done this through the prism of burnout
among high flyers. We have explained that burnout potentially represents
a significant development opportunity which can be used legitimately in
facilitating learning among high flyers. The learning that emerges from
burnout is equivalent to that which can emerge from personal trauma.
When it happens, this learning brings about systemic, whole-person
change that moves high flyers from one developmental stage to the next.
We are not saying – as a participant at one of our recent presentations
suggested – that all high flyers need to burn out in order to grow and
mature. We are saying that some burn out and some don't. Those who
do, have potential lessons to learn, that those who don't *appear* to have
already learned. We are making a virtue out of necessity. We are suggesting that those charged with developing organizational leadership are
opportunistic and take advantage of what naturally happens, a notion

that McCall et al call 'scrambling' – 'In executive development, the ability to scramble means knowing what kinds of experiences are potentially developmental for what, and being able at a moment's notice to tweak or nudge or leverage opportunities when they appear.[1]'

In this chapter we pull together those findings from our research which mark a substantial departure from previous burnout studies, before outlining the significance of them for organizations, high flyers and those who work with them. Based on these conclusions, we put forward a new paradigm of leadership development. We finish with some thoughts about the wider social implications of work and the development of identity.

## What we are saying that is different from existing research on burnout

There are nine key areas in which the results of our research are substantially different from prior research on burnout (summarized in Figure 7.1). Each of these areas is described below.

### *Burnout, high flyers and the see-saw perceptions of burnout*

Prior research correlates burnout with those who are in the early stages of their careers, are highly achievement focused and restlessly pursue success in their careers – in most organizations such people are regarded as high flyers. Our research found that burnout affected around 20% of the high-potential population during the first 10 years of career. This figure applies to those who are manifesting all of the symptoms of full-blown burnout. It does not take into account those who may be exhibiting some of the symptoms of burnout – a condition that we termed 'joyless depletion' in Chapter 2, and which we revisit later in this chapter.

Burnout's prevalence at this stage of career should not be a surprise. Those who are relatively new to the world of work are also those whose self-knowledge is at an early stage of development. As a result they are likely to have less sense of their limitations or their boundaries. There is often an inner fragility masked by arrogance or brash confidence.

But why do high flyers burn out up to 10 years into their careers? Surely they've had sufficient time to develop a greater understanding of themselves and the perils of organizational life? In explaining his theory of 'discrediting' – purposely turning one's back on what has worked in the past to avoid future traps – organizational theorist Karl Weick uses the example of fire-fighters. Weick says that firemen are most likely to get

| What's different from existing research | Source |
|---|---|
| 1 | Burnout affects 20% of high flyers in the first 10 years of their careers; it stigmatizes high flyers and their organizations | Chapters 2 and 6 |
| 2 | Symptomatology:<br>• Reduction in performance and productivity but unnoticed by high flyer<br>• Addictive behaviour<br>• Manifestation of symptoms are culturally sensitive | Chapters 2 and 4 |
| 3 | Burnout is caused by the nature of the relationship between high flyers and work: organizations create the conditions for burnout to occur, individuals determine whether they burn out or not as a result of how they handle the conditions | Chapters 2, 4 and 6 |
| 4 | The financial impact of burnout on organizations is calculable; there are substantial succession and reputation management risks | Chapter 3 |
| 5 | There are specific individual characteristics that make some high flyers more prone to burnout and others less | Chapters 2 and 4 |
| 6 | Burnout brings about a change in sense of self | Chapters 4 and 5 |
| 7 | Burnout offers the potential of significant, consciousness-changing development | Chapter 5 |
| 8 | Accepting responsibility for one's role in bringing about burnout, confronting oneself, being motivated by a quest for meaning and being held are the determinants of learning from burnout | Chapter 5 |
| 9 | Coaching high flyers in burnout means focusing on them learning from the experience *while* ensuring they do not derail. The learning is transformational – it concerns the development of identity. To be effective, coaches need to hold the client rather than simply support them, focus on identity through the development of narrative consciousness and adopt a systemic perspective | Chapter 6 |

**Figure 7.1**    How our research is different from existing studies of burnout

killed or injured in their tenth year on the job. They believe they've seen all there is to see in terms of dealing with fires. As a result they become less open to new information, and consequently base their decisions and actions on an old way of seeing the world.[2] High flyers appear to do the same thing, and as a result of hubris or believing they are infallible, make choices which ultimately lead to burnout.

Burnout stigmatizes individual high flyers and their organizations. Although it is not psychopathology, for some it has this resonance, and is seen as being on the cusp of mental illness. Despite mounting evidence about the incidence of mental health issues at work (see, for example, the social justice in the mental health charity, Stand to Reason,[3] and *Snakes in Suits: When Psychopaths Go To Work*[4]), mental illness remains one of

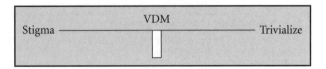

**Figure 7.2**   The see-saw perceptions of burnout

the last, great organizational taboos. High flyers believe their organizations see burnout as a sign, at best, of weakness or failure and, at worst, psychological disorder. Organizations run the risk of being perceived as 21st century sweat shops, and suffering untold damage to their brand and ability to attract and retain the brightest and best.

At the same time, the emergence of burnout as a popular, social notion and its use as a colloquial 'catch all' term, has devalued its meaning as a serious psychological condition. As a result, the term has – to all intents and purposes – become meaningless.

There is thus a delicate see-saw of concerns – with the stigma of burnout at one end, its trivialization at the other, and in the middle our notion of using the potentially derailing burnout experience as valid developmental material or VDM (see Figure 7.2).

## Symptomatology

Unlike other studies, we found that high flyers in burnout had little sense of reduced performance and productivity at work. However, there was evidence that their performance suffered as a result of burnout – they simply did not notice it. We concluded this was due to the dissonant nature of such information for high flyers' sense of identity, which was built on success after success. High flyers' way of coping with such disconfirming data was effectively to deny what was happening to them, an escape route that was also a pattern for those who did not learn from burnout. Denial has the added advantage of avoiding difficult and painful feelings of powerlessness. But it also requires the suspension of reflexiveness and this can lead to emergence of blind spots and eventually a loss of sense of self. Arrogance is sometimes employed by high flyers to cover up inner feelings of insecurity that emerge as a result.

We discovered that addictive behaviour was characteristic of those who burn out – in contradiction to other studies that deny correlations between burnout and addiction. High flyers in burnout appeared to be addicted to work and the pursuit of goals which helped them to avoid difficult unconscious material concerning their fragile sense of identity. Organizations sanctioned this addictive behaviour through the creation of highly-demanding psychological performance contracts for high flyers coupled with work fixated and absorptive business cultures. In the words of the Microsoft employee from Chapter 4, 'If you have an alcoholic in the house, you don't put a bottle of gin by the bed'. Unlike other addictions, there is no social stigma attached to working excessively – until you burn out, of course.

Like other researchers we found that burnout was a universal and pervasive phenomenon whose basic pattern was not strongly culturally dependent. But unlike them, we discovered that national cultural contexts influenced the way in which symptoms were manifest. We believe this to be a potentially fruitful area for future researchers to explore further.

## Burnout caused by nature of relationship between high flyers and their work

Our evidence points to burnout being the product of the relationship between the organization and individual high flyer, and implicates both parties in causing burnout. Organizations create the conditions for burnout to occur; individuals – through the choices they make and how they handle the challenges in the work environment – determine whether they burn out or not. We concluded that burnout ultimately arises as a result of the way in which the individual organizes themselves to deal with the work environment.

We identified two additional external drivers of burnout that are unmentioned by other researchers. Organizational approaches to the development of high-potential leaders, if based on a survival-of-the-fittest mentality, can generate a culture of burnout. Equally organizational attempts to provide employees with meaning and identity can hinder individuation and create a fertile environment for burnout to occur.

Our research identified a typology that extended the range of burnout experience beyond the commonly accepted one of total devastation (see Figure 7.3). Conventional approaches to burnout tend to view the condition as uniform and invariable. In addition to traditional notions of burnout (which we called 'crashing and burning') we distinguished two other variants – a chronic self-destructive pattern, and joyless depletion. The latter involved high flyers exhibiting some of the symptoms of burnout, always teetering on the edge of it, but never tipping over completely – a perpetual state of joylessness. There are strong similarities between this form of burnout and drug addiction, in as much as the 'high' only lasts as long as the latest fix – which in the case of burnout is represented by adrenalized and action-addicted work styles.

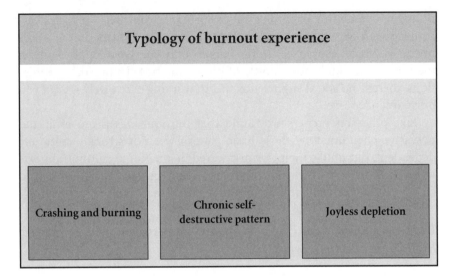

**Figure 7.3**  Typology of burnout experience

## The business impact of burnout in talent

Burnout represents a significant financial and reputational risk to organizations, and threatens management continuity. Using the example of a three- to four-year qualified professional services employee we calculated the financial exposure to be between £393,000 and £743,000 for partial withdrawal, £420,500 and £770,500 for full withdrawal, and £695,500 and £1.045 million for total loss, per employee. The range of these costs is driven by the complexity of the role held by the high flyer and whether or not they hold a sales position. Succession and reputation management risks are not easily calculable but are likely to be substantially more than this, particularly when one takes into account the cumulative damage to the brand and employee value proposition, and the impact on attracting and retaining high-value employees.

## Individual characteristics that make some high flyers more prone and others less

We found that high flyers who derived their identity primarily from work and career success, whose sense of purpose was rooted in the need for fame and recognition and who lacked quality self-interaction were vulnerable to burnout. Over-identification with work created a 'dysfunctional closeness' in which the high flyer could not distinguish between their work and personal needs. Identity was something that was painted onto them by work, the organization or career. It was externally referenced and there was little inner sense of self. Organizations' attempts to inculcate corporate values and performance standards were sometimes conscious, largely unwitting, but usually ineffective attempts to form high flyers' identities. However, many high flyers willingly colluded with them, spurred on by the work addiction we spoke of earlier, which shrouded emotional dependency needs.

The high flyers in our study who were in the midst of burnout appeared to lack a sense of purpose that was grounded in something deeper and more enduring than just the achievement of work or career goals. Although they could talk about events that had happened to them in the past, there was little meaning imbued in the telling of them. We derive a sense of purpose and meaning from the stories we construct about ourselves. In other words, it is not *what we experience* that has significance for us, so much as *our stories about what we experience,* 'By telling these stories we start to construct a meaning with which our experiences gain sense – the construction of meaning arises from the account, from the continuous actualizing of our story, of our narrative plot'.[5] Our story and the sense we make from it is dependent on the process of reflexivity. But those in burnout had either an underdeveloped reflexive ability – one which was operating only at an intellectual level rather than also at a feeling and intuitive level – or they had chosen to suspend their reflexivity. As a result they lacked a sense of story – or narrative consciousness – and appeared as though 'the lights were on but there was no one in the house'. There was a great deal of energy being spent on the living of a life, but little sense of what it was all leading to.

For some, the experience of burnout was clearly the first time they had considered their lives as having some kind of narrative theme or story. There was a sense in which life was living them, rather than them living it. Events were happening in their lives, but there was no sense of volition about these events – they were happening to them, rather than taking an active role in making them happen. As a result they appeared to be living out their lives without much conscious examination of their choices or what they were here for, 'What remains invisible to people is the inevitability of living out unconscious and ill-fitting mythologies if a conscious psychic process has not disclosed more meaningful ones to take their place'.[6]

Of course, lack of narrative consciousness can apply at any age and is certainly not the exclusive prerogative of high flyers. Its absence is significant because of the demanding roles and the responsibilities required of high flyers. As a consequence they need to learn these lessons earlier in life than others.

Organizations that fail to encourage high flyers to develop their own sense of purpose run the risk of producing 'bricklayers' rather than leaders, blank canvasses upon which the corporate brand values can be written, but who do not know themselves and who therefore lack conviction.

Those who did not burn out had a better functioning reflexive ability, identities that were more internally referenced and a greater sense of perspective than those who burnt out. Their stories were more coherent and connected. They had also developed a repertoire of coping behaviour that gave them the resources to deal with highly stressful working environments.

## Burnout brings about a change in sense of self

Because high flyers' identities were so closely tied up in success on the job, burnout brought about a change in their sense of self. For most, this change froze the growth of identity and they developed an overly patterned approach which – like Weick's fire-fighters – did not permit new data to challenge their rigid models. For a very few, the change accelerated their development and maturation, leading to systemic growth. By virtue of being a form of personal trauma, burnout holds the transformation-learning potential of other kinds of trauma which 'Tend to force this development along a much more rapid timeframe'.[7] We saw the results of this acceleration of maturity in Chapter 5. The most common concerned awakening high flyers to a need to be of service to others, which included teaching them the lessons that burnout had given them.

## Burnout as significant development experience

Burnout – as a form of personal trauma – has the potential to bring about systemic, whole-person change of untold value to both the individual high flyer and their organization. It does this by challenging high flyers' basic assumptions about life, on which their personal myth is built. In Chapter 4 we described how our personal myths or stories become embedded. They are not immutable but are resistant to reformulation other than through maturation or significant changes in our social context. Their resistance to change serves us well because our stories and their inherent assumptions are the means by which we make the world intelligible to us. Without them we cannot effectively respond to what happens around us. Burnout calls into question the validity of this story and the basic assumptions on which it is built, in particular those assumptions concerning meaning, unity and purpose. This, in turn, can lead to the reformulation of our personal myth. Like other forms of trauma, the learning that can emerge from burnout

> *involves giving up many things: old assumptions; hopes; belief systems; and, in particular, notions of invulnerability and personal power, and harsh judgements of self and others. Paradoxically, a new sense of power must be nurtured: the determination to extract the good from living and to actively contribute to it. Confronting spiritual issues is almost always an aspect of this process of transformation, and comfort is often found in decisions to accept and serve.*[8]

The learning that emerges from burnout benefits both organizations and the high flyers that work for them. It helps to develop universal practices of good leadership and moves individuals along the path of evolution towards full adult identity.

Burnout's contribution to the growth of wisdom is particularly striking. This has also been noted of other forms of personal trauma. Tedeschi and Calhoun, for instance, note that 'It appears that the growth that is perceived by those experiencing traumatic events produces the kind of thinking and perspective that is similar to what is described by those who are building models of wisdom'.[9] Wisdom is defined as 'knowledge of the world gained through experience of the world rather than through the prism of our intellectual conception of the world',[10] and includes the appreciation of paradox. High flyers who learned from burnout talked about taking away good things from the negative experience of burnout. They realized they were not invincible and needed the support of others, but ultimately their development was their own responsibility. They learned to accept their limitations and fallibilities while also developing the inner strength of their own purpose. 'This logic, based on contradiction and paradox (i.e. dialectical thinking), has been described as the cognitive component of wisdom, which is integrated with an affective component.'[11] Wisdom brought in its wake what Tedeschi and Calhoun call 'emotional serenity together with an acute appreciation for life and an exhilaration that can come from a recognition that the self is vulnerable yet strong'.[12] Those who learnt from burnout talked in terms of what Joseph Campbell called 'the rapture of being alive'. They saw the world with new eyes and committed to living a life on their own terms.

Burnout holds the potential of triggering an individual's transformation either to the next level within their current stage of identity development or to a new stage of developmental maturity altogether. In the case of the former, burnout can be the catalyst which helps a person excise a character that has outlived its usefulness and invent a new character that better serves their needs at this point in their lives. One such example from our research and our own lives was letting go of the old myth about persevering even in the direst situations. This was markedly different from McCall et al's conclusions about persevering being one of the lessons of hardship. We found not only was persevering not a virtue, but – when applied to a burnout situation – it served only to get the high flyer stuck. The solution – persistence – had now become the problem. Persistence represented a first-order change approach to a second-order change problem – or what Watzlawick et al call a 'more of the same' strategy, in which more of the wrong solution is applied.[13] The only way to deal with a burnout situation is to tackle it from a second-order change level – either by attempting to change the structure and functioning of the workplace or by changing one's own approach to being under extreme work pressure.

Like the learning that accrues from trauma, learning and growing from burnout had both an intrapersonal and an interpersonal aspect to it. 'The intrapersonal aspects occur during the process of acceptance and wrestling with the possible meaning of what has happened. The interpersonal aspects occur during times when help from others is accepted...The interpersonal realm also plays a role during the time when your life narrative is reshaped.'[14]

## Determinants of learning from burnout

We identified three factors which determined whether high flyers learnt from burnout: accepting responsibility for their role in making burnout happen, being motivated in learning from the experience by a quest for meaning in their lives, and being held by someone who was invested in them learning from the experience.

We found that learners had a moment of illumination – a moment of truth conversation with themselves which marked the beginning of their reflexive process towards accepting responsibility – both for the burnout and their own development. This conversation involved them confronting their current version of themselves and finding they were uncomfortable with what they saw. The question they appeared to be asking themselves was 'Who is the me this is happening to?', which led to a dawning awareness that theirs was no longer a good story to live by. This conversation was a memorable event which occurred during the burnout experience, not after, and kicked off a sense-making process that awakened them at an emotional and intuitive level.

The high flyers in our study realized that there was not as much meaning to their lives as they had thought, and it was this discovery that motivated them to learn and change as a result of burnout:

*The evidence to date suggests that when trauma throws into question the explicit or implicit meaning of life that a person has developed, the event may be perceived as meaningful to the extent that it provokes the development of new meanings. These new meanings may be found when people have to reorder their schemas [their basic assumptions about life], their behaviour, or both. A final step in the process of giving meaning to traumatic events may be the weaving of these events into the life story or narrative in a way that gives them a central role, a crossroads where the path was taken to new insights about living.*[15]

The act of holding high flyers in burnout performed the role of helping them absorb the suffering, listen to the meaning they had created of the experience, and assimilate the realization that either their personal myth had stopped evolving, or that it did not exist. The very act of accepting help when offered was a difficult one for most high flyers and a lesson in humility that, of itself, produced positive change. Studies of learning from trauma have found that 'Events that lead to help being offered within a collaborative framework may produce the most growth'.[16] This was certainly the case for those who were held in burnout.

Most of the non-learners from burnout appeared to be shielded against the outer experience of burnout penetrating their inner experience of themselves. Those who did begin to question whether their story was a good one to live by, did so tentatively and without conviction. Ultimately their internal dialogue reverted to a 'What is happening to me?' conversation. It may be that those who did not learn from burnout possessed beliefs or ideologies which served to control their distress and thus weaken the blow that burnout was making:

*To the degree that a person's assumptions allow some flexibility or absorption of shock from trauma, suffering can be mitigated. In this way, traumatic events lose their sting and growth is less likely because existing schemas are unchanged...Religious schemas are included in this category. These higher-order beliefs are not open to empirical disconfirmation because they can account for virtually any event, and they allow for comprehensibility and meaning to survive the experience with trauma.*[17]

## Model of coaching practice that enables high flyers to learn from burnout

We posited a model of coaching which enabled high flyers to learn from burnout, while simultaneously ensuring they do not derail. This model focused on transformational learning – bringing about profound and lasting change at the level of personal identity – and adopted a systemic perspective, in which change at the level of the mind, body, emotions or identity effected change at every other level.

We recommended that the development of identity was best done by adopting a narrative consciousness or personal mythological approach to identity. We suggested some approaches to working in this way, using myths to help the high flyer negotiate transition, and cross the threshold from one phase of their lives to another.

Our research pointed to the absolute importance of coaches holding their clients, rather than merely trying to support them, and being at a developmental stage beyond those they are coaching. The Gestalt notion that the therapist must allow themselves to be changed by the relationship with the client is equally applicable to the coach working with those in burnout. As Tedeschi and Calhoun put it, 'If the clinician entertains any hope that the traumatized person can be positively changed by his or her struggle, the clinician must allow for a similar change in him or herself'.[18] They go on to illustrate this with the treatment of Vietnam veterans:

> *To achieve trust, listeners must respect the narrator. The advice that veterans consistently give to trauma therapists is 'Listen! Just listen'. Respect, embodied in this kind of listening, is readiness to be changed by the narrator. The change may be small or large. It may be simply learning something not previously known, feeling something, seeing something from a new perspective, or it may be as profound as redirection of the listener's way of being in the world.*[19]

## Summary

These different perspectives thrown up by our research represent a contribution to the theory of burnout, and, more importantly, offer a grounded and research-based direction for responding to burnout in organizations and among talented individuals. The next section outlines these implications for practice.

## Putting it all together – the implications for organizations, high flyers and those who work with them

The implications of these findings are far-reaching. We have chosen to focus on six which we believe are of the most immediate significance to high flyers and their organizations, as well as those who work with them. These are:

- destigmatizing and detrivializing burnout
- the nature of the psychological contract between high flyer and organization, and the organization's paradigm of leadership
- sustainable models of leadership development
- coaching high flyers in burnout
- putting the leader's story at the centre of their development
- building careers aligned with individual meaning and purpose.

We discuss each of these below.

## Destigmatizing and detrivializing burnout

On the one hand burnout represents a clear and present danger to organizations' continued existence, and on the other it offers grail-like development possibilities. The biggest threat to preventing one and enabling the other is the stigma of burnout and its trivialization – or indeed the denial of its very existence – in the hands of the ill-informed. Burnout deniers are an interesting breed. We suspect they are not unrelated to the kind of people who believe depression and other related psychological disorders are a con, dreamt up by the work-shy. Their idle rantings are interesting because they represent a strong form of the unwillingness to engage with the issue of burnout.

Stigma creates a conspiracy of silence; trivialization or denial makes burnout seem unworthy of attention. The combined weight of these negative forces has the effect of stopping organizations and high flyers doing anything about burnout. For organizations this means they do not take preventative action to avoid reputational damage to employer brand, and to retain and develop high-value employees. For high flyers it means they continue to burn out and are lost to the organization and their careers. It also means that organizations and high flyers are unwilling or unmotivated to take advantage of burnout's learning potency.

At a recent UBS Wolfsberg conference we asked participants to brainstorm ways in which leadership teams and their HR departments, high flyers at risk of burnout, and external coaches and consultants, could help to destigmatize and detrivialize burnout. Participants felt leadership teams and HR executives could be more aware of the cause and effect of burnout, could understand that mental health issues are a possible consequence of burnout, not a cause of it, and could base their management of people on a belief that high performance and high resilience were one and the same. High flyers at risk of burnout could break the taboo by accepting what was happening to them and talking to other high flyers about it. In doing this they might validate their own sensations and realize they were not the only one to whom this was happening. Coaches and consultants could help by destigmatizing the coaching given to those who might be burning out. They also needed to know when they had reached the limits of their capability and needed to stop. To continue beyond their capability would effectively trivialize the burnout experience of the high flyer.

## The nature of the psychological contract between high flyer and organization, and the organization's paradigm of leadership

The psychological contract between the organization and the individual high flyer is usually tacit and unspoken and infused with the leadership teams' experience of what it took for them to reach high office. In our experience, this lack of transparency, together with the unstated assumptions of leadership, leads to high flyer programmes that generate burnout.

We believe a thorough examination of the organization's actual as opposed to its espoused expectations of high flyers by the executive leadership team and its human resources department would be time well spent. This would inevitably lead to a discussion about how high flyers are identified and the organization's current paradigm of leadership and leadership development. What do we look for in a high flyer? Conformity with a set of competencies, or people who follow their own purpose? Are leaders born or made round here? Is our approach to developing high flyers inherently developmental or based on survival of the fittest? If the former, what kind of leaders are we seeking to develop? Are we really more interested in developing bricklayers than leaders? If the latter, what implications does this have for what we tell prospective high flyers and how we manage them? (An excellent guide to the issues involved in such a discussion is given in Burgoyne et al's *Leadership Development: Current Practice, Future Perspectives.*[20])

A survival-of-the-fittest approach involves – to use Morgan McCall's terms – the selection of those who are deemed to have the 'right stuff' of executive leadership – pre-existing qualities that need only be honed and finessed through trial by fire. This approach is not really about the development of leaders. It is about checking to see whether the right people with the right stuff were selected in the first place. It also creates a fertile climate for the fires of burnout to rage unchecked. Earlier in this book we talked about it being our experience that most organizations adopted this approach to leadership development. For example, research participants repeatedly recounted tales of being asked to make presentations to senior leadership at the last minute, even though the visit had been planned months in advance.

Making the organization's expectations of high flyers and its paradigm of leadership more visible would provide employees with information to help them make an informed choice about participating in a high-potential programme. It would also assist organization leaders and their HR departments in making clearer decisions about their continued approach to high-flyer development, and their readiness to use learning from burnout. Leadership teams can choose to either make a fundamental shift in their approach to the development of leaders, or they can choose to work within their existing paradigm. Burnout's lessons are more likely to be forthcoming in more nurturing and developmental organizational cultures with models of leadership that are vital and human.

## *Sustainable models of leadership development*

In order to get a full return on their considerable investment in high flyers, organizations need to develop a focus on sustainable approaches to their development. This includes extending their duty of care to cover high flyers' psychological as well as their physical wellbeing. Specifically this means the organization holding a model of mental health at work. It means organization leaders articulating what healthy psychological functioning looks like in practice. It means organizations accepting partial responsibility for supporting employees to form full adult identity and being appropriately and validly concerned with the individual's current stage of maturation and ways in which it might move to the next stage.

Greater emphasis will need to be given to the ability of the high flyers to understand their own limitations and fallibilities and to gain a more balanced sense of perspective, of their careers, place of work in their lives and in business decision making generally. In addition, much more attention will need to be given to the development of high flyers as reflexive practitioners. The quality of high flyer self-interaction – their ability to have conversations with themselves – to discuss, evaluate and interpret what comes towards them and act upon this interpretation, is critical to the development of their leadership identity (or indeed any identity); it allows them to take control of their lives rather than simply respond to external stimuli.

Last but by no means least, organizations will need to accept that for some high flyers, at some points in their lives, going to the edge is a relevant part of forming this identity.

## Coaching high flyers in burnout

The literature is rife with fervent exhortations to prevent, banish, avoid or otherwise cast out burnout (the biblical connotations of which we think are significant). But coaches are not there to stop people from burning out. They are not there to provide salvation. They are not there to deliver high flyers from the evil of burnout. Burnout is not, in any sense, demonic, although it does hold the potential of transformation. Coaches are there to enable the high flyer to harness the powerful learning potential of the burnout experience; and in so doing, permit them to develop a sustainable version of themselves as leaders.

Burnout is fundamentally an issue of individual identity, meaning and purpose. It is not an issue of performance, although performance is affected. Performance may be the presenting issue but it is not the cause of the problem. Using performance coaching with a client in burnout is both professionally irresponsible and ethically reprehensible. It is like treating a pregnant woman for obesity. The focus of the coaching must be transformational. It must and should focus on the development of identity above all else.

Effective coaching of high flyers in burnout requires the coach to adopt a systemic perspective. This may be a disturbing notion for some coaches, particularly those who rigidly adhere to a cognitive perspective. Western culture has lionized disconnected thinking, abstraction and fantasy: 'We foster the belief that cognition is the great experience. This is what we call "learning". Almost all of our social learning forms are based upon the assumption that experience and its communication are cognitive...the body's resonating lights up its powers of cognition. The brain is the servant of the body and not vice versa'.[21] Although we may fantasize that we experience the world through our minds, we can, in fact, only experience the reality of the world through our bodies. The competent coach has therefore to ensure they work with the interdependencies of the heart, head, body and the gut of the high flyer in burnout.

A separate but related issue concerns the development of coaches who are sufficiently skilled to use burnout as valid developmental material. Experience tells us that currently a lot of coaches either refer cases of burnout to psychotherapy or they provide inappropriate methodologies – such as performance coaching – that only serve to make matters worse. There is a need to establish some clear standards and expectations for coaches in this area. One of the aims of Edge Equilibrium – the organization we have established to work in the area of burnout in talent – is to achieve this.

## Putting the leader's story at the heart of their development

Our research has demonstrated the veracity of Bennis' notion that becoming a leader is synonymous with becoming yourself. It has shown that the path of individual maturation is also the path of becoming a fully-functioning and effective leader. It follows that organizational leadership teams and those in charge of talent management need to develop a valid interest in supporting the development of high flyers' individual identities. We have seen that this is best done by attending to their current story and building narrative consciousness. The telling and retelling of a story (of burnout or indeed of one's journey as a leader overall) to others helps high flyers make sense of its significance to their lives and the meaning it holds for them. We have seen also that individuation – particularly as the result of trauma – is a heroic quest. The hero

> is usually the founder of something…In order to found something new, one has to leave the old and go in quest of the seed idea, a germinal idea that will have the potentiality of bringing forth that new thing…You might also say that the founder of a life – your life or mine, if we live our own lives, instead of imitating everyone else's life – comes from a quest as well.[22]

Those of us who claim a role in the development of leaders have come to resemble the high flyers whose 'more of the same' pathology put them on the road to burnout. We are in danger of burning out the leaders we purport to develop, and ourselves, through the use of more of the same – albeit evermore sophisticated – solutions to the 'problem' of producing leaders. In a sense it is this rich panoply of solutions – be they competencies, assessment centres, training programmes, psychometric instruments, and so on – that have now become the problem. For they cloud our minds and make us forget that leaders cannot be produced or even developed, they emerge as the result of choices made in an individual life. It is the leader's individual story that should be at the centre of our attempts to bring them on, above all else. In her acceptance speech for the Nobel Prize for Literature, Doris Lessing addressed our species' deep need for finding ourselves in story:

> The storyteller is deep inside everyone of us. The storymaker is always with us. Let us suppose our world is attacked by war, by the horrors that we all of us easily imagine. Let us suppose floods wash through our cities, the seas rise…but the storyteller will be there, for it is our imaginations which shape us, keep us, create us – for good and for ill. It is our stories that will recreate us, when we are torn, hurt, even destroyed. It is the storyteller, the dream-maker, the mythmaker, that is our phoenix, that represents us at our best, and at our most creative.[23]

## *Building careers aligned with individual meaning and purpose*

Throughout this book we have argued vehemently for individual high flyers to find their own sense of purpose and meaning, rather than it being concocted for them by the organization. Our history as a human race is littered with attempts by those in positions of power to control the minds and behaviour of the less powerful. As a consequence we are extremely wary of organizational attempts to provide employees with meaning. And we have pointed out the dangers of high flyers finding meaning through work rather than their own, inner sense of purpose. However, we believe there are ways in which high flyers (and others!) can find a connection between their individual mission and that of the organization which does not leave them vulnerable to abuse. For example, they might respect and value the leadership of an organization, believing that they are performing a good job; they might respect the organization's record of social responsibility; their personal mission might coincide with that of the organization (for example, someone dedicated to providing clean water to people working for a water company); or they might use their position in the organization to pursue their own personal mission. The *sine qua non* in all of this, however, is that the individual must have a purpose or mission of their own. They cannot simply inherit it from the organization: their mission must come first for them. Equally, they must keep their own purpose or mission inviolate and independent from the organization's. Their own purpose may coincide with that of the organization but they must avoid the trap of thinking it will ever be identical. Our reason for saying this is that organizations are social constructs – they do not 'live' as such. To imagine that they do is to reify them and engage in 'the fallacy of misplaced concreteness'.[24] The purpose of the organization will depend on its interpretation by those currently leading it. Different leaders are likely to have different interpretations, and these interpretations are likely to change dependent on the nature of the challenges facing the organization and the individual leader. Individual and organizational purposes may, for a time, appear to be heading in the same direction, but it is an act of utter folly to surrender one's purpose to the organization, believing that it wants exactly the same thing. Leaders who are sustainable, who are in it for the long haul, keep their purposes separate from their employers.

There is a scene in the film *The Bourne Ultimatum* which illustrates this point. The vengeful hero asks the CIA's Deputy Director – who has assisted him at great risk to herself – why she has helped him. She replies, 'This isn't what I signed up for…This isn't us'. The leadership of the organization has interpreted its purpose in a way that no longer connects with her own sense of purpose; she is able to make a distinction between the two and, in so doing, go against the organization in order to serve her own conscience and sense of mission.

Burnout is significant because it opens a window through which high flyers may perceive – perhaps for the first time – their own purpose, that which, in Angeles Arien's words, 'Has heart and meaning' for them.[25] Within the personal trauma of burnout, something happens to high flyers that is in some sense connected with the ultimate meaning of their lives. Something new, unexpected and transforming shows itself. This is the remarkable meeting with oneself to which we referred earlier, and it is ultimately the reason why prevention, without fostering the learning that is about to happen, is a huge disservice.

## Creating a new paradigm of leadership learning

We believe those of us tasked with the development of executive talent have got ourselves into a bit of a bind. Our pursuit of 'more of the same' is built on the erroneous belief that leaders can be produced, or built, or even developed. We have fooled ourselves into thinking that either leaders are machine parts which can be turned out like widgets, or that we are divine and can create leaders in our own likeness. More of the same leads us to sanitize leadership and run yet more ineffectual training courses; to inculcate organizational values and norms into the heads of employees; to normalize leadership through psychological profiling, competency modelling and engagement strategies, and attempt to police conformity. More of the same is developing bricklayers and ciphers rather than leaders. We need to give up our fantasies of making leaders, and realize that ours is the more humble task of making environments and shaping experiences that make leaders, and that these experiences include the experience that others have of us. Leadership is not something that organizations bestow. It is not given by the organization. It is developed in and by the individual in the course of a human life. Leaders emerge as the result of formative experiences, particularly those that involve adversity, hardship and challenge.

A new paradigm of leadership learning would recognize that learning to lead requires leaders moving down the path of psychological integration, and that a degree of suffering is a necessary part of the journey. It would recognize that hardship experiences are essential for the development of the leaders of tomorrow, and that burnout – as a special form of personal trauma – has the power to catalyze maturation and accelerate the development of identity and self-transformation.

Burnout is something that predominantly happens to young high fly-ers. Of course there are many other types of personal trauma that can generate potent learning – anything from divorce to serious health prob-lems, near-death experiences or bereavement. What makes burnout dif-ferent is its causation in the work environment as a result of actions – or lack thereof – by both employee and organization, thus rendering it a legitimate role in leadership learning. Learning from burnout is ethically accessible and practically manageable in organizational terms. Learning from other types of trauma is quite clearly not. However, learning from hardship and trauma is a vital ingredient in the development of any leader. What should organizations do to ensure their leaders are learn-ing the lessons of hardship? Whereas they cannot pry into other forms of personal trauma they can be legitimately interested in whether their lead-ers have ever experienced them. They can also legitimately explore what learning has emerged from other kinds of hardship and failure such as career setbacks or serious business mistakes.

This new paradigm of leadership learning would be concerned that leaders learnt lessons of sustainability, and it would be as interested in the high flyer's durability as much as their performance. It would foster an attitude of 'healthy selfishness'[26] amongst leaders, encouraging them to find ways of looking after themselves and paying attention to their own needs as a prerequisite of effectiveness. It would also encourage leaders to hold the notion of 'recovery space'[27], in which they could escape from their addiction to action and regain their sense of perspective in order to make space for reflexivity and a sense of what is happening to them. This is a 'process of recovering your wits. The essence of this recovery space is the opportunity to get back in touch with your own feelings. Self-maintenance is essential, not an indulgence'.[28]

The new paradigm would also involve organizations holding a clear model of healthy psychological functioning at work which would explic-itly question prevailing norms of 'normalness'. It might, for instance, question the mental health of many of the prevailing norms of behaviour in the organization, such as working 15 hours a day for the sake of get-ting a promised promotion, ensuring that one doesn't have a successor for fear of being undermined and forced out of the organization, working subordinates like dogs so as to increase one's share of revenue, or trying to change one's personality in order to rise up the greasy pole (these are all real-world examples taken from our research interviews).

Most of all, organizational leaders would be interested in the emer-gence of leaders rather than bricklayers, and would support employees finding their own identity, meaning and purpose. In so doing they would be honouring their most important social responsibility, namely by recognizing that 'The problem is nothing if not that of rendering the modern world spiritually significant – or rather (phrasing the same principle the other way round) nothing if not that of making it possible for men and women to come to full human maturity through the conditions of contemporary life'.[29]

Finally, the leaders that such a new paradigm would be concerned with fostering would be those who have the will, the wisdom and the maturity to serve something larger than themselves, who have an in-built sense of the consequential nature of their actions and their responsibilities in the world beyond the confines of the organization's boundaries. Leaders who are, in essence, utterly committed to their own evolution, even when it is deeply painful and disturbing, and who recognize that the completion of the journey 'requires a major reorientation of one's way of life. That reorientation is predicated, in turn, on the recognition that one's life is no longer one's own, but instead must in some way serve the larger concerns of both the self and one's community'.[30]

## A call to leadership

This book has been about how leadership emerges within the conditions of contemporary organizational life. Those conditions include the ascendancy of modern organizations to become the most powerful force on the planet, together with a prevailing social paradigm in which work has become central to our lives. We have called on organizational leaders to recognize their social responsibilities extend one step beyond where they currently think they end – to the fostering of individual identity of the people who work for them. But what if they do not heed this call to leadership? Do we descend into what Madeleine Bunting calls a 'crisis of human sustainability'?. 'Just as the late 20th century grasped the fact that there was a crisis of environmental sustainability, the 21st century is beginning to grasp the dimensions of a comparable crisis, this time of human sustainability – a scarcity of conditions which nurture resilient, secure individuals, families, friendships and communities.'[31] We do not believe so. Our sense is that it was ever thus. Eliot's 'The Wasteland', written in the 1920s, describes a land 'filled with people doing what they are supposed to do instead of what their inner urgency moves them to do'.[32] The supremacy of the organization has existed but for a short while. Previously it was the state, and before that the church. There have always been powerful forces in our society wanting to control our thoughts and even our very souls. Life is about fighting for our existence as independent beings separate from others' oppressive ideologies. The task of the modern hero is to guide and save society, a society which is ruled by the organizations for which most of us work:

> *The modern hero, the modern individual who dares to heed the call and seek the mansion of that presence with whom it is our whole destiny to be atoned, cannot, indeed must not, wait for his community to cast off its slough of pride, fear, rationalized avarice, and sanctified misunderstanding. 'Live,' Nietzsche says, 'as though the day were here'. It is not society that is to guide and save the creative hero, but precisely the reverse. And so every one of us shares the supreme ordeal – carries the cross of the redeemer – not in the bright moments of his tribe's great victories, but in the silences of his personal despair.*[33]

## End notes

1  McCall, M.W., Lombardo, M.M. and Morrison, A.M. (1988). *The Lessons of Experience: How Successful Executives Develop on the Job*. New York: The Free Press

2  Weick, K.E. (1998). 'Fire-fighting as a microcosm of organizing.' University of Michigan. www.si.umich.edu/ICOS/Presentations/110698/index.html

3  Stand to Reason: www.standtoreason.org.uk

4  Babiak, P. and Hare, R.D. (2006). *Snakes in Suits: When Psychopaths Go to Work*. New York: Regan Books

5  Ruiz, A. (2002). 'Narrative in post-rationalist cognitive therapy.' Trans S. Aronsohn. www.inteco.cl/post-rac/inarrat.htm

6  Stromer, R.S. (2003). 'Faith in the journey: Personal mythology as pathway to the sacred.' Phd dissertation, Pacifica Graduate Institute

7  Tedeschi, R.G. and Calhoun, L.G. (1995). *Trauma and Transformation: Growing in the Aftermath of Suffering*. California: Sage

8  Tedeschi, R.G. and Calhoun, L.G. (1995). *Trauma and Transformation: Growing in the Aftermath of Suffering*. California: Sage

9  Tedeschi, R.G. and Calhoun, L.G. (1995). *Trauma and Transformation: Growing in the Aftermath of Suffering*. California: Sage

10  Osborne, J.W. and Baldwin, J.R. (1982). 'Psychotherapy: From one state of illusion to another?' *Psychotherapy: Theory, Research and Practice*, vol. 19, pp266–75

11  Tedeschi, R.G. and Calhoun, L.G. (1995). *Trauma and Transformation: Growing in the Aftermath of Suffering*. California: Sage

12  Tedeschi, R.G. and Calhoun, L.G. (1995). *Trauma and Transformation: Growing in the Aftermath of Suffering*. California: Sage

13  Watzlawick, P., Weakland, J. and Fisch, R. (1974). *Change: Principles of Problem Formation and Problem Resolution*. New York: Norton

14  Tedeschi, R.G. and Calhoun, L.G. (1995). *Trauma and Transformation: Growing in the Aftermath of Suffering*. California: Sage

15  Tedeschi, R.G. and Calhoun, L.G. (1995). *Trauma and Transformation: Growing in the Aftermath of Suffering*. California: Sage

16  Tedeschi, R.G. and Calhoun, L.G. (1995). *Trauma and Transformation: Growing in the Aftermath of Suffering*. California: Sage

17  Tedeschi, R.G. and Calhoun, L.G. (1995). *Trauma and Transformation: Growing in the Aftermath of Suffering*. California: Sage

18  Tedeschi, R.G. and Calhoun, L.G. (1995). *Trauma and Transformation: Growing in the Aftermath of Suffering*. California: Sage

19  Shay, J. (1994). *Achilles in Vietnam: Combat Trauma and the Undoing of Character*. New York: Simon & Schuster. Quoted in Tedeschi, R.G. and Calhoun, L.G. (1995). *Trauma and Transformation: Growing in the Aftermath of Suffering*. California: Sage

20  Burgoyne, J., Boydell, T. and Pedler, M. (2005). *Leadership development: Current practice, future perspectives*. Henley: Corporate Research Forum

21  Keleman, S. (1975). *Your Body Speaks its Mind*. Berkeley: Center Press

22  Campbell, J. with Moyers, B. (1988). *The Power of Myth*. New York: Doubleday

23  Lessing, D. (2007). 'A hunger for books.' Nobel Prize for Literature acceptance speech. Reprinted in *The Guardian*, 8 December

24  Whitehead, A.N. (1925). *Science and the Modern World*. New York: Free Press

25  Arrien, A. (2005). *The Second Half of Life: Opening the Eight Gates of Wisdom*. Louisville: Sounds True

26  Binney, G., Williams, C. and Wilke, G. (2003). 'Leaders in transition: The dramas of ordinary heroes.' Ashridge Report. Ashridge Management College

27  Binney, G., Williams, C. and Wilke, G. (2003). 'Leaders in transition: The dramas of ordinary heroes.' Ashridge Report. Ashridge Management College

28  Binney, G., Williams, C. and Wilke, G. (2003). 'Leaders in transition: The dramas of ordinary heroes.' Ashridge Report. Ashridge Management College

29  Campbell, J. (1949). *The Hero with a Thousand Faces*. London: Fontana

30  Stromer, R.S. (2003). 'Faith in the journey: Personal mythology as pathway to the sacred.' Phd dissertation, Pacifica Graduate Institute

31  Bunting, M. (2005). *Willing Slaves: How the Overwork Culture is Ruling our Lives*. London: Harper Perennial

32  Campbell, J. (2004). *Mythic Worlds, Modern Words: On the Art of James Joyce*. New York: New World Library

33  Campbell, J. (1949). *The Hero with a Thousand Faces*. London: Fontana

# Appendix 1

## The physiological basis for burnout

Individuals who have been identified as suffering from burnout can usually be found to have evidence of physiological disruption/dysfunction. Specifically, burnout is very commonly associated with impaired function of the adrenal glands – the chief organs in the body responsible for dealing with stress.

Once 'stress' is sensed in the brain, two main systems are activated:

### 1 The sympathetic nervous system

The sympathetic nervous system is part of the so-called 'autonomic' nervous system that controls unconscious processes (such as heart rate, circulation and digestion) in the body. When the sympathetic nervous system is activated, various changes occur in the body which are inherent in the stress ('fight or flight') response. For example, heart rate increases, as does blood supply to the muscles.

### 2 The hypothalamic-pituitary-adrenal (HPA) axis

The other major system responsible for the body's response to stress concerns the adrenal glands (two organs that sit on top of the kidneys). The activation of the adrenal glands starts in the brain. Stress activates a part of brain known as the 'hypothalamus', which in turn activates a small gland at the base of the brain known as the 'pituitary gland'. The pituitary in turn releases a hormone known as adrenocorticotrophic hormone (ACTH) that activates the adrenal glands.

In response to stress, the adrenal glands secrete 'stress' hormones – principally adrenaline and cortisol. Stress hormones have a variety of effects in the body which help the body cope with stressful events.

These effects include an increase in pulse rate, raised blood sugar levels, enhanced metabolism and enhanced blood supply to the muscles. These changes are viewed as the body's attempt to respond to and deal effectively with a stressful event.

While the adrenal response is an inherent to the way the body reacts to stress, these organs only have a finite capacity to secrete hormones. Long-term stress can exceed the capacity of the adrenal glands to respond appropriately. As a result, the adrenal glands can weaken. Impaired adrenal function is an extremely common finding in individuals suffering from burnout.

## Features of adrenal fatigue

Some of the features of adrenal weakness include:

- *Fatigue* This is a core feature of adrenal fatigue. It is often present on waking, even after a good night's sleep.
- *Easy fatigue* Adrenally weakened individuals often have little in the way of energy 'reserve'. Not only do they generally feel tired, but they often get tired out quite easily. For people with adrenal weakness, additional stress (of a physiological and/or emotional nature) on the body can cause a worsening of symptoms, particularly fatigue.
- *Low mood/mental energy* Adrenally compromised individuals are usually not just physically tired, but mentally fatigued too. Common symptoms include reduced capacity for mental work, impaired focus and concentration, low mood and depression.
- *Reduced capacity to cope with stress* Individuals with adrenal fatigue often confess to feeling unable to cope with stress in a way they have been used to previously.
- *Impaired immunity* Adrenal fatigue can cause lowered immune function. This can manifest as relatively frequent infections (e.g. cold and flu) that can linger and prove difficult to 'shake off'.
- *Low blood pressure* Low blood pressure (hypotension) is quite a common feature in individuals who have weak adrenal function. The normal blood pressure is usually around 120–130/70–80 mmHg. Adrenally weakened individuals often have a blood pressure of 110/70 mmHg or less. These individuals also tend to have a blood pressure which drops on standing from a seated or lying position. This condition, the medical term for which is 'postural hypotension', can cause occasional dizziness on standing.

- *Salt craving* Some individuals with adrenal weakness will crave salty foods such as salted peanuts.
- *Sugar craving* Those with adrenal compromise are often prone to fluctuations in blood sugar levels. Low blood sugar levels can trigger cravings for sweet foods such as chocolate, biscuits and confectionery.
- *The need to eat regularly* Individuals with adrenal weakness tend to need to eat regularly to keep them from feeling weak and light-headed. If the body is not being fuelled from the outside (by eating), the body needs to generate sugar from the breakdown of stored fuels in the body such as glycogen in the liver. If the adrenal glands are weakened, it is possible that the stress hormones such as cortisol are not made in sufficient quantities to enable adequate amounts of sugar to be mobilized in this way.

## Factors which may perpetuate adrenal fatigue

The symptoms of adrenal fatigue can be debilitating. Many individuals are anxious about feeling inexplicably tired or unwell. Some are aware that their professional and personal efficiency and productivity have declined. These experiences are usually stressful in themselves, and this can lead to a further load on the adrenal glands and further weaken them. Others, through effort, may manage to maintain productivity at an acceptable level, and can sometimes be 'blind' to the symptoms and signs of burnout they may be exhibiting.

In addition, adrenal function can be weakened by certain physical 'stressors' which include inadequate sleep time and/or depth, strenuous exercise, infrequent eating, excessive use of caffeine and/or other stimulants, and the eating of a diet which tends to disrupt blood sugar levels (i.e. a diet rich in refined sugar and starchy carbohydrates such as bread, potato, rice, pasta and breakfast cereals).

## Adrenal function assessment

### Conventional laboratory tests for adrenal function

The main conventional medical test used is something called the 'short ACTH stimulation test' – also known as the 'Synacthen® test'. Here a blood sample is taken, after which an injection of ACTH is given. Half an hour later a second sample of blood is taken. The cortisol levels are measured in both samples. If the first sample shows a low level of cortisol,

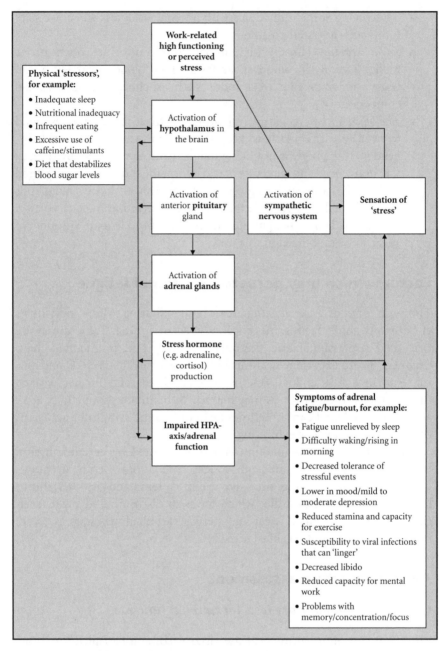

**Figure A.1** The physiological basis for burnout

and/or if there is not a sufficient rise in the cortisol level in response to ACTH, further testing is usually advised.

Conventional testing is used to confirm or dispel the diagnosis of 'Addison's disease' (also known as 'adrenal insufficiency') – a condition which is characterized by extreme compromise of adrenal function. Conventional testing may not be suitable, however, for identifying less severe and more subtle forms of adrenal weakness.

### Alternative tests for adrenal function

Adrenal hormones can also be measured using saliva samples. One of the most commonly used tests is known as the adrenal stress index (ASI) test. Here, four saliva samples taken at intervals during the day are analysed for cortisol. These tests usually include assessment of the adrenal hormone known as dehydroepiandrosterone (DHEA). DHEA is not a stress hormone as such, but levels of this hormone are generally used as a marker for adrenal function. Some tests measure DHEA at these four points too, while others just measure DHEA at just one or two points in the day.

In practice, individuals suffering from burnout are often found to have low or sub-optimal levels of cortisol and/or DHEA.

## Restoration of adrenal function

Adrenal function can almost always be restored in time. As this happens, the symptoms of adrenal fatigue (and burnout) are usually resolved. Strategies may include:

- psychological therapy and support
- work-life balance counselling
- strategies for improved sleep
- dietary approaches
- herbal medicine
- hormone therapy (in cases where adrenal hormones such as cortisol are found to be deficient/sub-optimal).

# Appendix 2

## Moment of truth conversations

Those high flyers who burn out and learn from it, experience a moment of illumination in which they confront the current version of themselves and find they are unhappy with what they see. They appear to be asking themselves 'Who is the me this is happening to?'. This leads to a dawning awareness that theirs is no longer a good story to live by. This conversation is a memorable event that occurs during the burnout experience, not after it, and kicks off a sense-making process that awakens them at an emotional and intuitive level.

The following examples of these 'moment of truth conversations' are taken from the transcripts of the high flyers we interviewed and complement that of Fiona, given in Chapter 5.

### Dimitris

*Researcher*: What was the predominant feeling that you had at this time?

*Dimitris*: What I am doing in my life? At this stage I had been working for a year and a half without a break. I had no life in Athens. I started to ask myself what I was doing there and why I was not going back home. The problem was – I didn't have any answers.

*Researcher*: What do you think made you ask those questions?

*Dimitris*: I started asking these questions because I couldn't see why I was doing what I was doing at this stage in my life. I was twenty-five or twenty-six, and I had only been working for two years. I could have gone out in Athens and enjoyed my life but I didn't do it. And I kept asking myself, why I am doing this? Why don't I leave? My original plan was to break away from my parents, go to Athens, have my own

217

flat, and have my own life. But after two years in Athens, I didn't have any life. All I was doing was working every day until midnight, and going back to an empty flat every night, to sleep. I didn't have a relationship because I was working so hard. And I realized I had a problem.

## Larissa

'People said it was like I was in a box. I didn't really see other people. Normally I smile and joke with people, but I didn't anymore. When I finally came into the office at the end of April, the manager said I had the syndrome of someone coming back from a war! I replied, "What are you talking about?! You're not doing anything here! You haven't given me enough support. You didn't review the reports I have been writing. Why didn't you stay longer, like two hours longer, and review them?!" I was so angry. I was travelling like hell around the country, and so was my team. I was writing all those reports, and he wasn't reviewing them in time. It's not my job to review them when I'm writing them! I didn't have any other interests. I didn't want to go anywhere. I didn't want to think about anything else. The only thing I could talk about was this stuff. I had 35 people on the project, and I had to analyse every draft they wrote. So every five minutes somebody would come up and ask me a question. And as a result I was getting short-tempered really quickly. After four months of working on this project, I was unable to recognize myself anymore.'

## Stratos

'I woke up one morning and didn't have the energy to pick up the glass next to my bed. I was that tired. Extremely tired. I was burnt out. I was angry and I took it out on the people who worked for me. Instead of asking them to do things, I was just telling them to do them. This is not me. Normally I am so friendly with colleagues – the feedback I get from the annual 360-degree survey proves this. I like to have fun while we're working. I like to laugh. But for a while I was angry. And, as a result, I was on my own, isolated. It was a bad experience.'

## Scott

'I had to see it for myself. I wasn't taking in the opinions, the advice, the thoughts, and the comments of those around me, who were probably trying to say to me "What's going on? You need to stop and have a look at this". I only believed myself, and there was some kind of self-destruction going on that said until you can show yourself that what you've become is not what you want to be, you aren't going to believe it. One day I stared in the mirror and I said, "Right. What you see now with your own eyes is what those around you have been telling you for a couple of years", and the penny dropped. Whether you call it a moment of clarity I don't know, but the rose-tinted spectacles came off when I took that cold, hard look in the mirror and didn't like what I saw.'

## Li-Ying

'Then slowly, by and by, I realized I was exhausted because I was holding so much within myself. I didn't talk to anybody at home. So, on the advice of my line manager I spoke to my family. It turned out they were really supportive. That was great. It was something I wasn't used to because we were brought up to be independent and to sort out our own problems. I never realized how much everyone loved me. I stopped taking medication and became less emotional. And I was able to clear my mind and step back. And that's when I recognized that I had a part in making this situation happen. So, I got myself back into my work slowly, going to the office a little bit more each day. I felt more in control and was able to decide on the course of action I would take regarding my life and career. I began to feel more positive.'

# Bibliography

American Institute of Stress website. 'Job stress.' See website http://www. stress.org/

Argyris, C. (1991). 'Teaching smart people how to learn.' *Harvard Business Review*, vol. 69, no. 3, pp99–109

Arrien, A. (2005). *The Second Half of Life: Opening the Eight Gates of Wisdom*. Louisville: Sounds True Inc.

Axelrod, E., Hadfield-Jones, H. and Welsh, T. (2001). 'War for talent (Part 2).' *McKinsey Quarterly*, no. 2

Babiak, P. and Hare, R.D. (2006). *Snakes in Suits: When Psychopaths Go To Work*. New York: Regan Books

Bains, G. et al (2007). *Meaning Inc. The Blueprint for Business Success in the 21st Century*. London: Profile Books

Barrett, A. and Beeson, J. (2002). *Developing Business Leaders for 2010*. New York: The Conference Board

Baumeister, R. (1991). *Meanings of Life*. New York: Guilford Press

Bennis, W. (1998). *On Becoming a Leader*. London: Arrow Books

Binney, G., Williams, C. and Wilke, G. (2003). 'Leaders in transition: the dramas of ordinary heroes.' Ashridge Report. Ashridge Management College

Blakeley, K. (2007). *Leadership Blind Spots and What to do About Them*. San Francisco: Jossey-Bass

Blumer, H. (1998). *Symbolic Interactionism: Perspective and Method*. Berkeley: University of California Press

Boyatzis, R. and McKee, A. (2005). *Resonant Leadership: Renewing Yourself and Connecting with Others Through Mindfulness, Hope and Compassion*. Boston: Harvard Business School Press

Boyes, R. (2007). 'Forget burnout, boreout is the new office disease.' *The Times*, 15 September

Brewer, E.W. and Shapard, L. (2004). 'Employee burnout: A meta-analysis of the relationship between age and years of experience.' *Human Resource Development Review*, vol. 3, no. 2, pp102–23

Bunting, M. (2005). *Willing Slaves: How the Overwork Culture is Ruling Our Lives*. London: Harper Perennial

Burgoyne, J., Boydell, T. and Pedler, M. (2005). *Leadership Development: Current Practice, Future Perspectives*. Henley: Corporate Research Forum, August

Campbell, J. (1949). *The Hero With a Thousand Faces*. London: Fontana

Campbell, J. (2004). *Mythic Worlds, Modern Words: On the Art of James Joyce*. New York: New World Library

Campbell, J. with Moyers, B. (1988). *The Power of Myth*. New York: Doubleday

Casey, D. (1987). 'Breaking the shell that encloses your understanding.' *Journal of Management Development*, vol. 6, no. 2, pp30–37

CHA (2008). 'Worthwhile work: A CHA report.' See CHA website www.chapr.co.uk

Chambers, E.G. et al (1998). 'The war for talent.' *McKinsey Quarterly*, vol. 35, no. 3, pp44–57

Chandola, T. et al (2008). 'Work stress and coronary heart disease: what are the mechanisms?' *European Heart Journal*, vol. 29, pp640–48

Charon, J.M. (2001). *Symbolic Interactionism: An Introduction, an Interpretation, an Integration*. New Jersey: Prentice Hall

Clarkson, P. (1989). *Gestalt Counselling in Action*. London: Sage

Clutterbuck, D. and Megginson, D. (2005). *Making Coaching Work: Creating a Coaching Culture*. London: CIPD

Conference Board Report (2007). *US Job Satisfaction Declines*. New York: The Conference Board

Cooper, C.L., Dewe, P.J. and O'Driscoll, M.P. (2001). *Organizational Stress: A Review and Critique of Theory, Research, and Applications*. London: Sage

Cordes, C.L. and Dougherty, T.W. (1993). 'A review and an integration of research on job burnout.' *Academy of Management Review*

Corporate Executive Board (2007). *Improving talent management outcomes*. Washington DC: Corporate Executive Board

Corporate Leadership Council (2000). *Challenges in Managing High-Potential Employees: Results of the Council's Membership Survey*. New York: Corporate Leadership Council

Corporate Leadership Council (2005). *Unlocking the Full Value of Rising Talent: Capturing Returns on the Identification and Development of High Potential Employees*. New York: Corporate Leadership Council

Covaleski, M.A., Dirsmith M.W., Heian J.B. and Samuel S. (1998) 'The calculated and the avowed: Techniques of discipline and struggles over identity in Big Six public accounting firms.' *Administrative Science Quarterly*, vol. 43, pp293–327

de Haan, E. (2008). *Relational Coaching: Journeys Towards Mastering One-to-One Learning*. Chichester: Wiley

Drath, W. (2001). *The Deep Blue Sea: Rethinking the Source of Leadership*. San Francisco: Jossey-Bass

Erez, M. and Earley, P.C. (1993). *Culture, Self-Identity, and Work*. Oxford: Oxford University Press

Fischer, H.J. (1983). 'A psychoanalytic view of burnout,' in B.A. Farber (ed.), *Stress and Burnout in the Human Service Professions*. New York: Pergamon

Frankl, V.E. (1946). *Man's Search for Meaning: The Classic Tribute to Hope from the Holocaust*. New York: Rider

Freudenberger, H.J. and Richelson, G. (1980). *Burn Out: The High Cost of Success and How to Cope With It*. London: Arrow Books

Gibran, K. (1926). *The Prophet*. London: Penguin

Glickhauf-Hughes, C. and Mehlman, E. (1995). 'Narcissistic issues in therapists: Diagnostic and treatment considerations.' *Psychotherapy*, no. 32, pp213–21

Glouberman, D. (2002). *The Joy of Burnout: How the End of the World can be a New Beginning*. London: Hodder and Stoughton

Goodman, A. (1990). 'Addiction: definition and implications.' *British Journal of Addiction*, vol. 85, pp1403–8

Grattan, L. and Pearson, J. (1994). 'Empowering leaders: Are they being developed?,' in C. Madley and P.A. Iles (eds), *Managing Learning*. London: Thomson Learning

Harrison, R. (1997). 'Consultant as healer in an addictive world of work: Life on earth remembering earth's wisdom.' Unpublished article

Hawkins, P. (1999). '*Organisational unlearning*.' Learning Company Conference, University of Warwick

Hawkins, P. and Smith, N. (2006). *Coaching, Mentoring and Organizational Consultancy*. Maidenhead: Open University Press

Health and Safety Executive (2007). 'Stress-related and psychological disorders.' See website www.hse.gov.uk/statistics/causdis/stress

Heron, J. (1989). *The Facilitator's Handbook*. London: Kogan Page

Hewitt Associates (2003). '*Building high potential leaders*.' Lincolnshire, Illinois: Hewitt Associates

Hong, H.V. and Hong, E.H. (eds), *The Essential Kierkegaard*. Princeton: Princeton University Press

Hudson. (2005). *Burnout Britain: Raising the Alarm for Employers*. See website www.hudson.com

Hunter, J.E., Schmidt, F.L. and Judiesch, M.K. (1990). 'Individual differences in output variability as a function of job complexity.' *Journal of Applied Psychology*, vol. 75, pp28–42

Iles, P. (1997). 'Sustainable high-potential career development: A resource-based view.' *Career Development International*, vol. 2, no. 7, pp347–53

Jamal, M. (2005). 'Burnout among Canadian and Chinese employees: A cross-cultural study.' *European Management Review*, vol. 2, pp224–30

Kaplan, R.M. (1990). 'The expansive executive.' *Human Resource Management?*

Kayes, D.C. (2006). *Destructive Goal Pursuit: The Mount Everest Disaster*. London: Palgrave Macmillan

Keleman, S. (1975). *Your Body Speaks its Mind*. Berkeley: Center Press

Keleman, S. (1979). *Somatic Reality: Bodily Experience and Emotional Truth*. Berkeley: Center Press

Keleman, S. (1987). *Embodying Experience: Forming a Personal Life*. Berkeley: Center Press

Kelly, G. (1955). *A Theory of Personality*. New York: Norton

Kline, N. (1999). *Time to Think: Listening to Ignite the Human Mind*. London: Cassell

Koukoulaki, T. (2002). 'Stress prevention in Europe: Review of trade union activities – obstacles and future strategies.' *TUTB Newsletter*, no. 19–20

Lessing, D. (2007). 'A hunger for books.' Nobel Prize for Literature acceptance speech. Reprinted in *The Guardian*, 8 December

Lindsey, E., Holmes, V. and McCall, M. (1987). 'Key events in executives' lives.' Technical Report 32, Centre for Creative Leadership

Llorens, C. (2001). 'Work-related stress and industrial relations.' *European Industrial Relations Observatory Online*. www.eurofound.europa.eu/eiro/index.htm

Macalister, T. (2007). 'Fallen titans show charisma is the most volatile stock of all.' *The Guardian*, 9 October

Management-Issues Limited (2003). 'Talent management strategies are stuck in the past.' 7 November

Maslach, C. (1982). *Burnout: The Cost of Caring*. Englewood Cliffs, NJ: Prentice-Hall

Maslach, C. (2001). 'Job burnout.' *Annual Review of Psychology*, vol. 52, pp397–422

Maslach, C. (2006). 'Understanding job burnout. In stress and quality of working life: Current perspectives in occupational health,' in A.M. Rossi, P.L. Perrewe and S.L. Sauter (eds), *Stress and Quality of Working Life: Current Perspectives in Occupational Health*, pp37–53. International Stress Management Association Information Age Publishing

Maslach, C., Jackson, S. and Leiter, M. (1996). *Maslach Burnout Inventory Manual* (3rd edn). California: Consulting Psychologists Press

Maslach, C. and Leiter, M.P. (1997). *The Truth About Burnout: How Organizations Cause Personal Stress and What to do About It*. San Francisco: Jossey-Bass

May, R. (1965). 'Intentionality, the heart of human will.' *Journal of Humanistic Psychology*, vol. 5, pp202–09

McAdams, D.P. (1993). *The Stories We Live By: Personal Myths and the Making of the Self*. New York: Guilford Press

McCall, M. (1998). *High Flyers: Developing the Next Generation of Leaders*. Boston: Harvard Business School Press

McCall, M. (2005). 'Identifying and Developing Leadership Talent Globally.' ICEDR HRD Leadership Programme. April

McCall, M.W., Lombardo, M.M. and Morrison, A.M. (1988). *The Lessons of Experience: How Successful Executives Develop on the Job*. New York: The Free Press

McCrae, R.R. and John, O.P. (1992). 'An introduction to the Five Factor Model and its applications.' *Journal of Personality*, vol. 60, pp175–215

McKinsey Quarterly Survey, March 2005

McManus, I.C., Keeling, A. and Paice, E. (2004). 'Stress, burnout and doctors' attitudes to work are determined by personality and learning style: A twelve-year longitudinal study of UK medical graduates.' *BMC Medicine*, vol. 2, no. 29

Megginson, D. and Clutterbuck, D. (2008). 'What is new in creating a coaching culture?' Presentation at the 15th European Mentoring and Coaching Council Conference, Prague, December

Megginson, D., Clutterbuck, D. and English, P. (2008). 'An own goal for coaching'. Unpublished article

Murlis, H. and Schubert, P. (2002). 'Engage employees and boost performance.' Hay Group Working Paper

Osborne, J.W. and Baldwin, J.R. (1982). 'Psychotherapy: From one state of illusion to another?' *Psychotherapy: Theory, Research and Practice*, vol. 19, pp266–75

Paoli, P. and Merllié, D. (2000). *3rd European Survey of Working Conditions*. European Foundation for the Improvement of Living and Working Conditions

Pedler, M., Burgoyne, J. and Boydell, T. (2004). *A Manager's Guide to Leadership.* Maidenhead: McGraw-Hill

Peterson, R. (2004). 'Ruthless compassion: Reflections on the treatment of an alcoholic.' *Clinical Case Studies*, vol. 3, pp234–49

Pines, A.M. (1993). 'Burnout: An existential perspective,' in W.B. Schaufelli, C. Maslach and T. Marek (eds), *Professional Burnout: Recent Developments in Theory and Research.* London: Taylor and Francis

Pines, A.M., Ben-Ari, A., Utasi, A. and Larson, D. (2002). 'A cross-cultural investigation of social support and burnout.' *European Psychologist*, vol. 7, pp256–64

Roffey Park (2007). 'Roffey Park reports on research project into enlightenment at work.' Roffey Park press release, 9 May 2007

Rosinski, P. (2003). *Coaching Across Cultures: New Tools for Leveraging National, Corporate and Professional Differences.* London: Brealey

Rothlin, P. and Werder, P.R. (2007). *Boreout!: Overcoming Workplace Demotivation.* London: Kogan Page

Ruiz, A. (2002). Narrative in post-rationalist cognitive therapy. Trans Aronsohn, S. http://www.inteco.cl/post-rac/inarrat.htm

Schaufeli, W. and Enzman, D. (1998). *The Burnout Companion to Study and Practice.* London: Taylor and Francis

Schwartz, J. (2004). 'Always on the job: Employees pay with health.' *The New York Times*, 5 September

Scott Peck, M. (1978). *The Road Less Travelled.* London: Arrow Books

Scott Peck, M. (1997). *The Road Less Travelled and Beyond: Spiritual Growth in an Age of Anxiety.* New York: Rider

Senge, P., Ross, R., Smith, B., Roberts, C. and Kleiner, A. (1994). *The Fifth Discipline Fieldbook.* London: Brealey

Senge, P., Scharmer, C.O., Jaworski, J. and Flowers, B.S. (2005). *Presence: Exploring Profound Change in People, Organizations and Society.* London: Brealey

Shaw, P. (2002). *Changing Conversations in Organisations: A Complexity Approach to Change.* London: Routledge

Shay, J. (1994). *Achilles in Vietnam: Combat Trauma and the Undoing of Character.* New York: Simon & Schuster

Shirom, A., et al (1997). 'Effects of work overload and burnout on cholesterol and triglycerides levels: The moderating effect of emotional reactivity among male and female employees.' *Journal of Occupational Health Psychology*, vol. 2, no. 4, pp275–88

Smart, B. (2005). *Topgrading: How Leading Companies Win by Hiring, Coaching and Keeping the Best People.* New York: Portfolio

Snipes, G. (2005). 'Identifying and cultivating high-potential employees.' *Chief Learning Officer*, www.clomedia.com

St John of the Cross. (2002). *Dark Night of the Soul*. New York: Dover

Stern, S. (2008). 'The meaning of life at work and other employee perks.' *Financial Times*, 11 March, p16

Stromer, R.S. (2003). 'Faith in the journey: Personal mythology as pathway to the sacred.' Phd dissertation, Pacifica Graduate Institute

Taylor, H. and Cooper, C.L. (1989). 'The stress prone personality: A review of research in the context of occupational stress.' *Stress and Medicine*, vol. 5, pp17–27

Tedeschi, R.G. and Calhoun, L.G. (1995). *Trauma and Transformation: Growing in the Aftermath of Suffering*. California: Sage

Torbert, W.R. (1973). *Learning from Experience: Toward Consciousness*. New York: Columbia University Press

Tsoukas, H. (2003). 'Commentary: Vulnerability, moral responsibility, and reflexive thinking.' *Reflections*, vol. 4, pp14–15

Vanwesenbeeck, I. (2005). 'Burnout among female indoor sex workers (psychology of prostitutes).' *Archives of Sexual Behaviour*, vol. 34, no. 6, pp621–39

Vogler, C. (1998). *The Writer's Journey: Mythic Structure for Storytellers and Screenwriters*. London: Pan Macmillan

von Schiller, F. (1982). In *On the Aesthetic Education of Man*, E.M. Wilkinson and L.A. Willoughby (eds). Oxford: Oxford University Press

Watzlawick, P., Weakland, J. and Fisch, R. (1974). *Change: Principles of Problem Formation and Problem Resolution*. New York: Norton

Weick, K.E. (1998). *Fire-fighting as a Microcosm of Organizing*. University of Michigan Press

Whitehead, A.N. (1925). *Science and the Modern World*. New York: Free Press

Wooldridge, A. (2006). 'The battle for brainpower: A survey of talent.' *The Economist*

# Index